Lenin Lives?

Lenin Lives?

CHRISTOPHER READ

Great Clarendon Street, Oxford, OX2 6DP,
United Kingdom

Oxford University Press is a department of the University of Oxford.
It furthers the University's objective of excellence in research, scholarship,
and education by publishing worldwide. Oxford is a registered trade mark of
Oxford University Press in the UK and in certain other countries

© Christopher Read 2024

The moral rights of the author have been asserted

All rights reserved. No part of this publication may be reproduced, stored in
a retrieval system, or transmitted, in any form or by any means, without the
prior permission in writing of Oxford University Press, or as expressly permitted
by law, by licence or under terms agreed with the appropriate reprographics
rights organization. Enquiries concerning reproduction outside the scope of the
above should be sent to the Rights Department, Oxford University Press, at the
address above

You must not circulate this work in any other form
and you must impose this same condition on any acquirer

Published in the United States of America by Oxford University Press
198 Madison Avenue, New York, NY 10016, United States of America

British Library Cataloguing in Publication Data
Data available

Library of Congress Control Number: 2023942430

ISBN 978-0-19-886608-4

DOI: 10.1093/oso/9780198866084.001.0001

Printed and bound in the UK by
Clays Ltd, Elcograf S.p.A.

Links to third party websites are provided by Oxford in good faith and
for information only. Oxford disclaims any responsibility for the materials
contained in any third party website referenced in this work.

Table of Contents

List of Figures	vii
Introduction	1
Part One: Lenin before Leninism	10
Who was Lenin?	10
Early Years	10
Emergence from Obscurity	15
The Birth of Lenin	18
Wartime	32
To Power and Beyond	38
i) From the Finland Station to Finnish Exile: April to July 1917	38
ii) Pause for Thought: *The State and Revolution*	42
iii) 'The Great October Socialist Revolution'	50
From Drawing Board to Battlefield: The Tribulations of Transition	57
Part Two: Lenin as Icon and Inspiration: Leninism after Lenin	78
1. The Communist Movement after Lenin	78
Foundations of Leninism	80
The Party	88
Leninism Goes Global	94
i) Comintern and the Struggle against Fascism	95
ii) The Weakest Link: Imperialism, Colonialism, and Peasant Revolution	103
iii) Endgame in Europe—1956–91	116
2. Independent Leninism in Global Thought and Politics	121
From Fellow Travellers to Liberation Theology	121
Leninism since the Fall of Soviet Communism: 1991 to the Present	134
Conclusion	151
Endnotes	165
Bibliography	177
Index	187

List of Figures

1. The Ulyanovs of Simbirsk, Lenin's conventionally middle-class family until eldest brother Alexander (top centre) was executed for participating in an assassination plot against the tsar. The young Vladimir Ulyanov (bottom right) followed his revolutionary path, becoming Lenin. His family actively supported his opposition to tsarism.   11

2. Tsarist Tyranny—The Force that Created Lenin. Exemplified here on Bloody Sunday—St Petersburg, 9 January 1905. Troops fire on unarmed civilians.   26

3. Trotsky with his wife Natalia Sedova and Frida Kahlo in Mexico.   79

4. Lenin's death becomes the moment of birth of Leninism (Stalin to the right, Molotov behind him, Zinoviev(?) and Tomsky in front of him, and Bukharin in left corner).   81

5. Lenin sweeps away the class enemies of working people. A poster from 1920 with the caption 'Lenin cleanses the world of the unclean'.   95

6. Solemn Opening of the 2nd World Congress of the Comintern in Petrograd, 19 July 1920: Lenin's speech. (Isaak Izrailevich Brodsky 1926). While the painting shows considerable ethnic diversity it reveals the strong gender bias, not only of the Congress, but of the communist movement which had relatively few powerful and influential women in its ranks.   96

7. Women of the Republican and socialist Largo Caballero Battalion in the Spanish Civil War, 1938.   100

8. Ho Chi Minh (Sung Man Cho) in a British prison. Photo: Victoria Prison, Hong Kong, 1930. (*Source*: Archives nationales d'outre-mer, HCI SPCE 364).   104

9. Zhou En Lai, Mao Zedong, and Zhu De on the Long March.   106

10. Tito (far right) and fellow partisans in the mountains, c.1944.   109

11. Fidel Castro and Camilo Cienfuegos enter Havana, 8 January 1959.   112

12. One of the last photos of Chilean president Salvador Allende, the first of an increasing number of Marxist–Leninists elected to power in a democratic parliamentary system in Latin America, as he gazes skywards at US-backed bombers attacking the Presidential Palace in Santiago to inaugurate a savage coup, 9 November 1973.   119

viii LIST OF FIGURES

13. Liberation Theology meets Marxism–Leninism. Pope Francis at a meeting with Fidel Castro in Havana, officially described as 'intimate and familial' (19 September 2015). Photograph: Cubadebate/Alex Castro/EPA. 132

14. The sculptor, Georgy Frangulyan, stands at the Wall of Grief, Moscow, a memorial to the victims of Soviet-era repression. It was inaugurated by President Putin and the Patriarch Kirill of Moscow in October 2017, around the 100th anniversary of the Bolshevik Revolution. 135

15. Communists in Kerala, south India, celebrate the election of 21-year-old student Arya Rajendran as mayor of the 2.5 million population capital city on 28 December 2021 (from Monthly Review). 149

16. From history to heritage—Marx, Lenin, and Stalin impersonators by the Kremlin Wall. 156

Introduction

One hundred years after his death, is there anything worth salvaging from Lenin's political ideas and activities in the light of, among other things, the wreckage of his main project—the Soviet Union—and the retreat of Leninist communism from its mid twentieth-century high points?

A defining difference between Lenin and liberals and social democrats who seek greater social justice in the world is the question of violence. The latter group look to and expect to achieve their objectives peacefully, by liberal democratic means. While hating violence, Lenin's view of it was more pessimistic in that, deeply entwined in Lenin's political actions, analyses, and philosophy, is the assumption that those who exercise power and own and control property, will, in many cases, not give up their privileges without violence. Therefore the party that seeks social justice, redistribution, and real equality before the law, must be prepared for violence. It should be made clear from the outset that Lenin detested violence and was deeply horrified by the mass slaughter of the First World War.[1] But he was convinced that, no matter how great the electoral majority, the rich and powerful would not hand over their privileges and property quietly. Many, though by no means all, historical situations in the modern world where the issue has arisen have shown that this was the case. Also, another century of liberal democracy, with social democratic intervals here and there, has not reduced but strengthened capitalism, inequality, and imperialism. The reflexive pursuit of economic growth, without which capitalism cannot function, has pushed the world to the brink of climate disaster. The Duke of Westminster remains one of the richest men in Britain, thanks to his massive land ownership that has resisted all efforts at redistribution. Oligarchs with 400-foot 'yachts' have emerged from the wreckage of post-Soviet Russia. American billionaires can fund private space programmes. That any process to exert social or community control, even over such blatant excesses of property, will only be accomplished by violence is a central challenge Lenin poses. This is not to say that his approach achieved its desired results. No one overthrew the tsar and Provisional Government in order to

---

Lenin Lives?. Christopher Read, Oxford University Press. © Christopher Read 2024.
DOI: 10.1093/oso/9780198866084.003.0001

2 LENIN LIVES?

build the Gulag. Nor is it to say that Lenin is the only, or even, perhaps, the most important, revolutionary of our era.

Starting from the assumption of fierce, violent opposition by the dominant social class, Lenin devised a number of institutions, ideas, and practices appropriate to the conditions as he perceived them. In the forefront was his idea of a democratic political party. Lenin did, from time to time, toy with the idea of a democratic path to revolution, which reminds us that, in analysing Lenin's ideas and practices, we are not dealing with an immobile fixed system but a dynamic set of interactions with current political conjunctures. Lenin was a brilliant analyst of successive political situations in Russia and sometimes abroad, though he was not always correct in his conclusions. No one ever is. He approached issues from different angles at different moments, but the notion that there would be a violent clash dominated his outlook in and before 1917, despite occasional nods to the possibility of peaceful transition in the newly fledged soviets of that year. Lenin would, nonetheless, be shocked to be thought of as anything other than a democrat. First and foremost, his whole activity was geared to the unarguably democratic task of liberating the exploited workers and peasants of Russia and the world. However, in Russian conditions of autocratic dictatorship, he was clear this could not be done in a parliamentary fashion. To do that one would at least need a parliament! Russia's *Duma* was far from that. But even so it was the case that, like the liberal Kadet Party, the mainly peasant-oriented Socialist Revolutionary Party and both wings of the worker-facing Social Democratic Party, including Lenin's Bolshevik supporters and the Menshevik wing, all put the convening of a Constituent Assembly to create a constitution as the first item in the party programme.

However, Lenin's major contribution to democracy, as he and his followers understood it, was to establish a very different idea of democracy. Instead of an open political organization which anyone could join, Lenin made his political name by calling for a party of 'professional revolutionaries', organized, like its populist predecessor of the 1870s, on a cell basis. This was done to protect it from deep incursions by the tsarist political police, since, at the time this model emerged in 1903, all political parties were illegal in Russia. Argument about it was an important, but not the only, cause of the party splitting into bickering Menshevik and Bolshevik wings. For better or worse, the Leninist model became very influential after 1917 and many, but not all, communist parties all over the globe adopted it irrespective of local situations. In the debates around the model, Lenin presented it as a way of progressing towards a more conventional democracy

INTRODUCTION 3

which was suitable for tsarist conditions, not as the universal model which it evolved into after 1917. In outlining his plans he makes it clear that 'Here and further on, I, of course, refer only to absolutist Russia.'[2] Trades unions should have as broad a membership as possible but 'on the other hand, the organization of the revolutionaries must consist first and foremost of people who make revolutionary activity their profession...Such an organization must perforce not be very extensive and must be as secret as possible.'[3] He reiterates the point a few pages later. The problem of a broad organization would be that, while it 'is supposedly most "accessible" to the masses...[it] is actually most accessible to the gendarmes and makes revolutionaries most accessible to the police.'[4] Despite Lenin pointing out his prescription was for tsarist Russia's specific ailments, the basic elements of Lenin's party structure became a supposed medicine for many other types of sick polity and remained a distinctive feature of Leninism.

The issues of unavoidable violence and party structure led to two other related issues. First, the question of party discipline based around the concept of democratic centralism, and second, though Lenin always denied this was what he had done, revolution from above as proposed by the nineteenth-century French socialist Louis Auguste Blanqui.

Democratic centralism had three key components. First, in theory, free discussion of political issues was permitted within the party. Second, there was a clear hierarchy stretching from local party cells, via regional and other bodies, to the party Central Committee. The highest institution in the party was the Party Congress which, before 1917, could only be held in secret, whether in the Russian Empire, like its founding conference in Minsk, or abroad. Wherever it took place, the secret police would attempt to infiltrate it. Congresses and less authoritative conferences were held in Brussels, London, Stockholm, Prague, and elsewhere. Motions for discussion could be passed up the hierarchy but once they were decided upon, at Central Committee or Congress level, the third component kicked in—all such decisions were binding on all members and dissent could lead to expulsion. In the complex situation before 1917, when many leaders were in exile abroad, in judicial exile in Siberia, or in and out of regional prisons, this model was very fluid. After 1917, and especially at the Tenth Party Congress in 1921, it was firmed up to give almost complete authority to the leadership in the name of a much more centralized conception of 'dictatorship of the proletariat' and, even more foreboding, the voluntary option of a one-party state.

The second issue, revolution from above, was a logical outcome from the other issues we have been looking at. Without going into the precise

4   LENIN LIVES?

complexities of the October Revolution at this point, suffice it to say that the outcome was a Bolshevik government led by Lenin, which was essentially in a minority, not least because Russia was a country in which over 80 per cent of the population were peasants, a class having no future in the Bolshevik scheme of things. Only by temporarily stealing the populist Socialist Revolutionary party's policy of handing land to the peasants did they get the brief support of this class in 1917. However one cuts it, when the Bolsheviks came to power, very few people—even hundreds rather than thousands— had any idea of what they ultimately stood for. Immediate policies and slogans, like land to the peasants, power to the soviets, and so on, had extensive traction, but they were not the key Bolshevik aims. Ultimately, Lenin stood for a world proletarian (working class) revolution which, as analysed by Marx, would destroy capitalism and imperialism and usher in a perfect society. Lenin's response to the task of building the socialist order was to construct it from the minority who knew what the aims were, who would pass on that awareness in a process of raising the consciousness of the workers and peasants.

The Bolsheviks, and Leninists in general, did not see their task to be the implementation of the wishes of the workers. Indeed, for Lenin this was a political heresy known as *khvostizm*, meaning 'tailism'—hanging on to the tail of the labour movement rather than leading it to emancipation. The party, comprising those with a raised consciousness, believed it was up to them to lead the workers to liberation, to have the workers fulfil the schemes of the mostly intelligentsia party leaders, not the other way round. This was a Confucian approach to revolution. The master had the authority, the pupils learned from him. Schools do not run by students voting on the subject matter they are being taught. The rules of grammar or of physics are what they are. In the Leninist schema, the role of the enlightened was to lead. Though Lenin and his followers objected strongly, it is hard not to see a form of elitism at work here. Elitism cuts across democracy. Some within the party, and many beyond in the non-Bolshevik left, argued that the contradiction could be reconciled by winning over the masses first. Lenin's practice was to win them over *after* the seizure of power, leading to a revolutionary elite trying to create the preconditions which, in a straightforward reading of Marx, were supposed to be necessary to bring them to power in the first place.

A main consequence of this 'back-to-front' approach to Marxist revolution was the rapid emergence of productionism, the effort to maximize economic output, as the central task of party and state. This happened because mass productive potential and a large working class were the foundation of any Marxist-inspired transition to socialism and communism. Lenin, needless to say, vigorously defended conducting revolution in this way. His critics argued that this process led only to 'premature revolution', that is one which arrived before the circumstances needed for its success were in place, and they predicted failure. It is worth noting that one of the most influential Marxists of the twentieth century, the Italian revolutionary and anti-fascist Antonio Gramsci, proposed that gaining intellectual hegemony, for instance by raising the workers' consciousness, should be the primary focus of revolutionary activity *before* taking power. Leninists (of whom Gramsci was essentially one in his admiration for the Russian Revolution) argued that this was naive. The ruling class held all the intellectual and cultural cards and could fatally interrupt the process of forming radical class consciousness with ruthless efficiency. From ancient tactics of 'bread and circuses'[5] or 'divide and rule',[6] through to contemporary mechanisms like control of education, the media, political systems, and the legal system, ruling classes (and one does not have to resort to notions of 'conspiracy theory' here) can ensure that their interests will prevail and the 'masses' will have the utmost difficulty in forming their own class identity. Instead, in Marxist terms, the non-ruling classes will be imbued with the supposed 'universal' values of patriotism, liberal freedom, national interest, property, and other constructs behind which lurked the values and interests, not of society as a whole, but of its dominant members.

There were many other characteristic features of Lenin's theories and practice, and particularly their legacy and impact, but perhaps three more need to be pointed out before we move into a more detailed consideration of them. They are the question of imperialism, which, perhaps surprisingly, is closely linked to the second issue of Leninism/communism becoming attractive to peasant rather than worker activists around the globe, and thirdly, Lenin's deeply entrenched hostility to all forms of religion and the metaphysical/supernatural.

Most of Lenin's writings are closely linked to the immediate circumstances of Russian radical politics. *Imperialism: The Highest Stage of Capitalism* is an example. Written in 1915 in the heat of the First World War, it was, for Lenin, a refutation of the ideas of a group called 'the Economists', and others, who argued that Russia was insufficiently capitalist to have a Marxist revolution, which, therefore, must lie long into the future. However, although it is more about monopoly capitalism and big banks and the pursuit of profit triggering the war, it became a foundation, especially in

6   LENIN LIVES?

the 1960s and 1970s, for many theories about the global reach of twentieth-century capitalism and colonialism. In a sense this was a by-product, since Lenin's main purpose was to show that, as Lenin's colleague and possible successor Bukharin had put it, borrowing a concept from the Bolshevik heretic Bogdanov, capitalism was a world system and could be broken at its weakest link. Since Russia was a weak link in the capitalist chain, it could be a catalyst to world revolution if a socialist revolution broke out there. It circumvented the argument that Russian capitalism was too underdeveloped to allow the idea of a Marxist revolution, which, according to Marx, was to be expected only when capitalism had overdeveloped itself into exhaustion. Russia was only just over the threshold of capitalism, not at the exit door, but if it set off a revolution that spread to the advanced countries, then they could help Russia advance rapidly to socialism. In a second irony, it was the notion of Soviet Russia as an anti-imperialist power that attracted colonial and Third World revolutionaries to it. Soviet Marxism, and the example it became of a country industrializing itself by a non-capitalist and non-imperialist route, attracted attention in the pre-industrial parts of the world, as well as in the advanced capitalist countries. The outcome was that no revolutions (apart from the largely fake versions exported to eastern Europe after 1945) occurred in primarily industrial countries. But they did come about in a number of peasant countries, notably China, Vietnam, and Cuba, where communism still holds sway.

Finally, it is worth recalling that Lenin was fanatically anti-religious, far more so than Marx. Lenin frequently referred to all religions as, in Marx's words 'the opium of the people', by which Lenin meant a toxic substance which poisoned humanity. He conveniently overlooked the rest of Marx's comment: 'Religion is the sigh of the oppressed creature, the heart of a heartless world, and the soul of soulless conditions. It is the *opium* of the people.'[7] Writing at a time when opium smoking was widespread and legal, Marx's words meant that opium was a comforter in the soulless and heartless world of capitalism, a much more finely nuanced concept. With his emphasis on religion and the state, Lenin had a distinct similarity to Marx's Russian rival in the 1860s, the anarchist Mikhail Bakunin, for whom the chief enemies of a free humanity were God and the state. In the conditions of Russian autocracy, where the church was deeply assimilated into the oppressive autocratic state, this was an unsurprising emphasis. However, it led Leninists head-on into unnecessary battles with the religious sensibilities of the mass of their Russian peasant citizens, and, to the outside world, often made them look like fanatics in their persecution of religion, a process

INTRODUCTION 7

which deeply antagonized the populations inside and outside Russia they were trying to win over. It may have made the activists feel good ideologically, but it was an unnecessary drag on revolutionary development.

Indeed, many of the key points of Leninist criticism of religion were shared by many believers themselves who criticized the clergies and hierarchies for corruption, self-interest, and exploitation. Lenin shared the common late nineteenth-century assumption, arising from Darwin's ideas, that science and religion (mainly Christianity was assumed at that time) were incompatible. The former would replace the latter as education became more widespread and society became more rational. Clearly, in this respect, Leninism (and Marxism) was a child of the enlightenment of the seventeenth and eighteenth centuries, which assumed that reason would capture more and more ground and religions would shrink into husks and wither away. Secularization would become universal. The resurgence of political religion, for better or worse, the continued dynamism and development of existing religions, and the self-evident fact that there are many prominent scientists who are religious suggests a more nuanced approach would enable Leninists to join more easily with believers fighting for social justice and cultural liberty. Indeed, in a letter, Marx himself said that his ideas had no impact on the fundamental questions of life, death, and meaning.

Lenin's legacy has many more features, some of which we will encounter later, but in looking for lasting influence, the challenge of violence, the nature of the party, democratic centralism, the dictatorship of the proletariat, the top-down revolution, the concept of imperialism, and anti-religious dogmatism (and wider intolerance) are all potential players. We will begin our investigation by looking at how they had emerged in Lenin's thinking and practice before moving on to look at how key aspects of Lenin's ideas developed within Russia and in the wider world, and finally weigh up if any of it still speaks to the twenty-first century situation. Perhaps the paradox of the contemporary situation is that neoliberal values and practices seem unchallenged globally in a way they have not been since before 1900, giving the contemporary centre-left a perspective of massive obstacles to the realization of their ideas comparable to that facing Lenin. At the same time, today there are critical issues pushing humanity to the brink of disaster, even extermination. Climate change is in the forefront of the global mind today, but there are also nuclear weapons, which are little considered but may pose an even more immediate threat than global warming as the tragic, absurd, and unnecessary war in Ukraine has reminded us in opening an unlikely but possible escalatory path to nuclear annihilation. But the list

8   LENIN LIVES?

does not stop there. Ever-growing national and global inequalities, expanding flows of political and economic migrants, and, finally, the environmentally driven need to move away from notions of endless expansion of material production based on assumptions of the unlimited exploitation of natural resources, constitute existential threats to modern human life. Arguably, all require 'socialist' solutions (that is collective, not individual, decision-making; planned, not market-driven, strategies; and inclusion of social justice and property rights in any initiatives to deal with them) and some form of international, global governance, or at least extensive co-operation, for their resolution. It is no coincidence that climate summits in the COP series, such as Paris, Rio, Glasgow, and Sharm el-Sheikh, are sponsored by the United Nations Organization and are the largest assemblies of national leaders that have ever taken place. Somehow the contradiction between rampant neoliberal capitalism and the very survival of the species has to be resolved. Can Lenin's ideas and political practice add anything to the pot?

In answering such wide-ranging questions, even in a relatively brief account such as this, one inevitably stands as a diminutive figure on a mountain of work produced by a myriad people. I am deeply indebted to them all and gratefully acknowledge the contributions of predecessors with a wide range of opinions often very different from my own. I cannot hope to thank them all but I happily acknowledge their great work, of which the main sources can be found in the notes and bibliography. Beyond that I have had many stimulating conversations and exchanges with friends and colleagues, the gist of some of which can be found in the later pages of the present work, though I have retained the anonymity of the particular individuals who preferred not to be named with respect to actual comments. Among those with whom I have had stimulating discussions are current and former colleagues from Warwick, notably Fred Reid, James Hinton, Robin Clifton, Robin Okey, Christoph Mick, Claire Shaw, Mark Harrison, Jonathan Davis, Mark Sandle, and Rainer Horn. A number of others were also generous enough to share their thoughts on my ideas and plans for this book. These were Lee Jones, Mike Haynes, Philip Cunliffe, Robert Service, Steve Smith, and Dan Orlovsky. There are many others whose influence, collegiality and friendship have helped me form my ideas about Lenin—Ian Thatcher, Geoff Swain, Lara Douds, Geoffrey Hosking, Brendan McGeever, Lars Lih, Chris Ward, James White, Donald Nichol, Jack Miller, John Miller, Martin Dewhirst, Leonard Schapiro, Bob Davies, and Alec Nove. Apologies to those who should also be on this list. My personal debts are enormous, none more than to my family—Françoise, Alexandra, and Natalia, who keep my feet firmly on the ground.

I am writing this during the unthinkable war between Ukraine and Russia. I dedicate the book to all those, Ukrainian, Russian, and beyond, suffering from this totally unnecessary conflict and to the hope for the most rapid possible restoration of peace between the Ukrainian and Russian people and between their governments.

Sadly, in the last days when I was completing this work, a great friend for fifty years, colleague, and discussant of the issues in this book, Dr Robin Clifton, died at his home in Mid Wales. This book is also dedicated to his memory and to Vivien Clifton-Jones who will miss him even more than the rest of us.

Part One
Lenin before Leninism

Who was Lenin?

There was nothing in Lenin's childhood and early adulthood to suggest he would become one of the most influential figures of the twentieth century; begin the political, economic, social, and cultural modernization of his country; inspire revolutions around the globe; and inspire the creation of one of the world's most powerful war machines which would, literally, stop Nazism in its tracks. Still today, Lenin is seen in China as a major source of China's own modernization. Neither he nor the Soviet system he inspired completed the building of socialism, still less communism, in Russia. It was always a work in progress. Even so, the vastness of his influence, achievements, and failures is hard to reconcile with the modesty of his beginnings.

Early Years

The family into which Vladimir was born on 23 April 1870 was that of a moderately prosperous local teacher, headmaster, and, eventually, school inspector. The family name was Ulyanov. The conspiratorial pseudonym, Nikolai Lenin, came later. Oddly, the name by which he is known today, Vladimir Lenin, was a hybrid of his real and pseudonymous names and was rarely used in his lifetime, though the familiar form Vladimir Il'ich (Il'ich is a traditional Russian patronymic derived from his father's name, Il'ya) was. He lived a comfortable middle class life, with his parents and three brothers and three sisters, in the town of Simbirsk, located on the river Volga in the deepest central provinces of European Russia. A surviving photograph shows the Ulyanovs as a typical middle-class family of the time. (Fig.1). Summers were spent on his wealthy aunt's country estate at Kokushkino. Later, he himself inherited a small estate at Alakaevka, near another Volga city, Samara. The young Vladimir Il'ich spent some time working there and, he later recalled, his mother hoped he would settle down there. How different would the world have been had he done so? We obviously cannot know,

Lenin Lives?. Christopher Read, Oxford University Press. © Christopher Read 2024.
DOI: 10.1093/oso/9780198866084.003.0002

Fig. 1 The Ulyanovs of Simbirsk, Lenin's conventionally middle-class family until eldest brother Alexander (top centre) was executed for participating in an assassination plot against the tsar. The young Vladimir Ulyanov (bottom right) followed his revolutionary path, becoming Lenin. His family actively supported his opposition to tsarism.

but meditating on it is one way of answering our central question about his enduring legacy.

There was nothing in the young Lenin's life to suggest political involvement until the family was hit by a cataclysmic blow. Vladimir's eldest

12 LENIN LIVES?

brother, Sasha (short for Alexander), a biology student at the University of St Petersburg, was arrested in 1886 for conspiring to assassinate Tsar Alexander III. Sasha had, indeed, been part of a small group of potential bomb-makers and assassins. Altruistically, he tried to protect the other members of the group and take all the blame upon himself, but the authorities wanted to make an example of them all. Only five years earlier, in 1881, the current tsar's father, Alexander II, had been assassinated. The authorities were still very nervous and not prepared to show mercy. Sasha and four other conspirators were executed on 8 May 1886. The execution of the mild-mannered and gentle eldest brother changed the family, especially the surviving brothers and sisters. They all, to one degree or another, became more radicalized, but none more so than Vladimir, who was sixteen at the time. Some have argued the trauma created some kind of psychological damage to the young Vladimir, but the most likely explanation is much more simple. He and the rest of the family were simply horrified, as Sasha had been, by the tyranny of the autocracy which intruded so cruelly into their lives. Even Vladimir's parents, who were God-fearing and conventional in many respects, were opposed to the prevailing conditions in Russia. Vladimir's father, Il'ya, used his influence as a teacher and school inspector to do his best to bring education to the most deprived, notably village peasants. As such, he was a living example of what was known as 'small deeds' liberalism—bringing betterment to the masses by immediate, practical, everyday actions rather than by devotion to the cataclysmic solution of general revolution. Vladimir's mother, Maria, was, in the gender-restrictive conventions of the time, less active outside the family, but for the rest of her life (that is until 12 July 1916) she supported Vladimir when he needed it, as he never held down a money-earning job,. The money came from the modest pension she received as a widow of a senior public servant after Il'ya died in January 1886 of a vascular brain haemorrhage, possibly exacerbated by anxiety over Sasha's imprisonment and trial.

Despite the trauma of losing his father and beloved brother within a few months, there was no reason to expect Vladimir to become the figure he later was. From scanty sources we can piece together that Vladimir's dormant political instincts were aroused by curiosity about what his brother had been secretly doing. Why did he sacrifice his life? The answer was not hard to find. At his trial Sasha spoke out against political and social repression and in support of the downtrodden peasantry. He associated himself quite clearly with the peasant-facing *Narodnik* ('populist') tendency among the revolutionary intelligentsia in Russia. The term is completely distinct

LENIN BEFORE LENINISM 13

from its predominant twenty-first century meaning of irrational, demagogic right-winger. Vladimir seems to have also been partly radicalized by starting to read political books and pamphlets from Sasha's collection. This may or may not have included the well-known novel *What is to be Done?* published in 1863 by one of the founding fathers of populist ideology, Nikolai Chernyshevsky. Central to the book's message, and to Sasha's short, heroic life, was the notion that it was the duty of the privileged intellectual to use her or his talents in the service of the oppressed. We have good evidence that Vladimir was heavily influenced by this book. He is quoted by one of his early political acquaintances as having said that reading *What is to be Done?* 'ploughed him over' and recast his mind in a new form.[1] It was in 1888 that this first encounter happened. It does imply that Vladimir's first political affiliation was as a populist. Vladimir's early political awakening and other radicalizing experiences were linked to his brother and his brother's fate, but not in a morbid or psychotic way, but out of admiration for and association with what he stood for.

His brother's shadow also loomed over the young Vladimir's position in society. Thanks, no doubt, to lobbying by his headteacher—ironically the father of Alexander Kerensky, the prime minister overthrown by Lenin in 1917—and his stellar school results (also, ironically, including top marks in religious studies), he was admitted to the local university in Kazan. However, at the first sign of student protest some months after he began his course, he was expelled. We do not know if he was involved in the protests, Lenin never claimed that he was, but legends grew. It is more likely that he was expelled as the brother of an executed terrorist. This did not completely shut off a university career and he was able to enrol as a student by correspondence to study law at the University of St Petersburg, one of the leading higher education institutions in the country. Despite the obvious drawbacks of studying alone and at a distance, he once again excelled, achieving top marks in the final exams in 1892. There can be no doubt that he was an exceptionally gifted young man.

Apart from that we know less than we would like about his life in these years. He seems to have been following up his executed brother's political interests through reading, and he lived a conventional provincial life with his mother and other family members. We do know he did not seriously practice the law for which he was so outstandingly qualified and throughout his life he only took a few cases here and there, including one in his own interest in Paris in 1909 when he was knocked off his bike on the way to the Paris air show by a wealthy car driver—a direct example of class struggle!

14 LENIN LIVES?

There is no evidence of political activity until what seem to be his first political writings emerged in 1893. Their most significant feature is that they show that the young Vladimir Il'ich, by the time he was twenty-three, was supporting the small group of Russian socialists, known as social democrats, who prioritized the working class as revolutionary actors, rather than supporting the dominant socialist tendency of the time, the populist (*Narodnik*) group to which Alexander Ulyanov had belonged. They expected the revolution to be carried out by the broad masses (the *narod*), especially the 80 per cent or more of the population who were peasants, not just the 5 per cent or less who were workers. Frustratingly, we have no insight into how the young Lenin arrived at this position. We have noted the influence of Chernyshevsky and we might assume that was early in his radical reading programme, but we do not know for sure. We do know he absorbed himself in his brother's books early on. Both of these would indicate a populist orientation and almost certainly this was Lenin's first stage in radicalization. We do know that, later in life, during what seemed endless polemics between and among populists and social democrats, Lenin insisted on the greatest respect for the founding generation of populists—Chernyshevsky, Lavrov, and others—even when he was ripping their arguments to shreds. He must have come into early contact with the leading social-democratic voice, Georgi Plekhanov, whose two path-breaking pamphlets, *Socialism and Political Struggle* (1883) and *Our Differences* (1885), laid down the distinguishing features of the new worker-oriented social democratic tendency.[2]

Visiting Plekhanov, who was in exile in western Europe, became one of Lenin's goals, but we have no record of his first intellectual encounter with him through reading. It makes sense that it was in his student years, and we might also speculate that to have already made such a commitment to a small and as yet insignificant political tendency, oriented to a very small and barely emerging proletariat (working class) in Russia, suggests a person for whom the written word, the apparent source of those commitments, was of vital importance, since there were almost no social democrats or workers in the Volga provinces where he lived for him to be in contact with. The fact that he most likely arrived at such propositions via theory rather than experience suggests something that characterizes aspects of Lenin's ideas later on. Although he developed a highly acute judgement for immediate political circumstances, there were also, as we will see later, notions, such as his analysis of social layers within the peasantry and to a lesser extent the workers, and even his expectations of world revolution, that were driven by ideology rather than observation. However, we can say few of these thing for certain. Happily, Lenin's personal and political life and intellectual evolution become increasingly easy to follow from the early 1890s.

Emergence from Obscurity

The decade from his graduation and first published writings (1892–3) to the appearance of one of his best known works, *What is to be Done?*, and the fateful Second Party Congress (1902–3) was the only period of his adult life when Vladimir Il'ich lived in obscurity as just another young radical. He was gradually establishing a personal reputation as well as continuing to undergo formative experiences, but for the time being he remained more or less unknown even in radical circles. They were years in which important things happened. He toured western Europe to meet prominent exiles; he was arrested on his return and went into Siberian exile (1897–1900); he wrote one of his most interesting but rather inaccessible books; and, in 1900, he took the decision to leave Russia and become part of the emigré community himself. He also met and married Nadezhda Krupskaya, his supportive life companion who shared his exile in Siberia and his sojourn in western Europe. She was an intelligent, sensible, and strong-minded woman who had already committed to radical action before she met Lenin. She wrote wonderful memoirs of Vladimir Il'ich which provide our best insight into his life and career from the mid-1890s.

Incidentally, it is worth noting that from 1896, Lenin was at liberty in Russia for only a few months after his Siberian release and before his voluntary departure for western European exile. Thereafter he spent very little time in Russia before his return 'to the Finland Station' in April 1917. He was in Russia only from autumn 1905 to the end of 190739, and from March to early July in 1917, remaining in safe houses in Finland until around 10 October (two weeks before taking power), but even then he remained in hiding within Petrograd until he emerged again on 24/25 October, catapulting himself and his party into power and making a decisive mark on the twentieth century and even, many would argue, beyond. His remaining years, his years in power (1917 to his death on 21 January 1924), were spent in Petrograd (the war-time name of St Petersburg, adopted because it sounded less Germanic), and then the Kremlin in Moscow from the time the capital was moved there in March 1918, plus weekends in the nearby countryside in the village of Gorky.

16 LENIN LIVES?

His emergence from the relative obscurity of the Volga provinces took place in stages. Graduation in law brought him to St Petersburg, and he spent time there in the early 1890s, beginning to write revolutionary pamphlets. We have little direct information as to his precise whereabouts as he continued to move between the capital and his home provinces. He visited his beloved younger sister, Olga, in St Petersburg when he was there to take exams. Poignantly, she wrote a reassuring letter to their mother to tell her Volodya (the family name for Vladimir Il'ich) was bearing up well under the stress. A month later she herself died at the age of nineteen, a victim of typhoid. When Lenin returned to Russia in 1917, one of the first things he did was visit her grave and that of his mother, who had died the previous July. Throughout his life Lenin enjoyed warm relations with his family. Olga's letter also points to another enduring feature of Lenin's life, which was his tendency to stress-related illness. When engaged in political argument he was, from early on, very intense, so much so that on one occasion in 1903, while out cycling in Geneva with Krupskaya, he was thinking so intently about his current polemics that he ran into the back of a tram.[3] Krupskaya was always trying to keep him away from stress. Her chief assistant in this was Lenin's love of nature, and Krupskaya made sure he always got plenty of exercise. They were both fond of mushroom gathering in autumn and of cycling, for example in the woods around Paris when they lived there. She also set up frequent holidays on the striking north Brittany coast or, Lenin's particular favourite, in the Swiss Alps, where he walked extensively, absorbing the extraordinary beauty of the landscape. Many of his political battles were followed by extensive breaks in which he repaired the nervous exhaustion he invariably underwent. This endured until the end. He spent most of his last years at the country house in Gorky, visiting the Kremlin so rarely that, on one occasion when he did visit, he was not allowed in because he had forgotten to bring his pass and the security guard did not recognize him. It was in Gorky that he died in January 1924, under the loving care of Krupskaya and one of his sisters, Maria.

In addition to these lifelong personal traits, his political foundation began to firm up. By the late 1880s he had not only read Chernyshevsky but he also embarked on reading Marx's first volume of *Capital* while in Kazan. He only escaped arrest along with the small radical political reading group he belonged to in Kazan by virtue of the family inheriting Alakaevka and moving to Samara just before the group was swept up by the tsarist police. He had also read *The Communist Manifesto* and *The Condition of the Working Class in England*, written by Marx's fellow German expatriate in

LENIN BEFORE LENINISM 17

London, close intellectual associate, sponsor, and, perhaps ironically, Manchester factory owner, Friedrich Engels (1820–95). He also, touchingly, practised singing the socialist anthem the *Internationale*, in French with Olga in Alakaevka when she was nineteen and he was twenty. By 1894, by which time he was living in St Petersburg and earning a little money from work as a clerk in a law office, Lenin was firmly supporting social democratic rather than populist positions in that a key theme of his early writings appeared around then. The young Lenin had become convinced that the populists' lean towards the peasants and hope of moving to socialism without undergoing the misery of capitalism were mistaken. Russian capitalism was in its infancy but was growing fast. The implication was that, as it grew, the working class, the proletariat, was also expanding and would become the agent of revolution as Marx had predicted. By 1895 he was becoming noticed in radical circles, and from May to September he undertook a kind of revolutionary Grand Tour of western Europe to meet the great eminences of social democracy face to face.

Vladimir Il'ich visited Switzerland (which, characteristically, included a stay in a Swiss health spa) and Paris, partly to learn more about the Paris Commune uprising of 1871, plus a month and a half in Berlin, funded by a subvention from his ever-generous mother when his funds ran out. He met Plekhanov, Marx's son-in-law Paul Lafargue, and the leading German social democrat Wilhelm Liebknecht. They inspired him, and he left his calling card with them as a fine young socialist prospect. On his return he liaised with a small social-democratic group which, as was the case until 1917 with most radical groups, focused its activities around the production of a newspaper. Lenin was connected to important newspapers from this time on and much of the many volumes of his pre-revolutionary writings were newspaper articles, so much so that after the revolution, on his Communist Party membership card, he described himself as a journalist, even though he was chair of the Council of People's Commissars, the Soviet 'cabinet', at that time. However, this early venture did not last long, and forty or so activists, including Lenin, were rounded up. In February 1897 he was sentenced to imprisonment and exile, which he served in the remote Siberian village of Shushenskoe. Krupskaya, herself sentenced for a separate political offence, and her mother eventually joined him and, to stay on the right side of the regulations so that they could not be separated, Nadezhda Krupskaya and Vladimir Il'ich were married in a local church in 1898. Far from being an ordeal, the conditions of political exile were reasonably comfortable. The couple and entourage rented a village house, made of wood like all the

18 LENIN LIVES?

others, gathered firewood, read, wrote, walked in the forest in summer heat and winter chill, did a little hunting and fishing, and even hired a young local teenager to help with housekeeping and particularly cooking, which was not Krupskaya's forte. It was even possible to hold seminars with other exiles from the regime from time to time right under the noses of the sleepy local officials. Lenin wrote and had published one of his longest, most complex, original, and least read books, *The Development of Capitalism in Russia*. In the guise of a quasi-academic economic analysis of the direction of development of the Russian economy, Lenin was also putting, as he thought, the final nails in the coffin of the populist theory of avoiding capitalism in Russia and going direct to socialism. As was the case with most of Lenin's works, there was a key dimension of current Russian left-wing polemics, sometimes artfully, concealed within.

As Krupskaya tells us in her memoirs, despite the loss of freedom, the sojourn in Siberia was good for Lenin's health. He walked regularly, was insulated from the immediate nervous pressures of bruising political encounters, immersed himself in the glories of Siberian nature, and was in vibrant good health for once in his life. It was, in many respects, a happy interlude. On his release in 1899, he evaded restrictions banning him from the metropolitan cities and travelled energetically between various political groups in Moscow and St Petersburg. However, he knew he was living on borrowed time with respect to the police and he took a decision, shared over the decades by many leading Russian radicals, and left Russia to join the emigration in western Europe, where he remained, as we have noted, for all but eighteen months, before his definitive return in 1917.[4]

The Birth of Lenin

In 1901, Vladimir Il'ich used the pseudonym N. Lenin for the first time, and though he used others, such as Il'in, Lenin became his predominant signature and that is what we will use from this point on. The 'N' was rarely specified, but occasionally it became Nikolai and he was often referred to in his lifetime as Nikolai Lenin. Lenin was born into a very unpromising world for a Marxist radical. Imperialism was rampant, having just swallowed up much of Africa. The imperialists were squabbling among themselves, especially Britain and France. Russia was considered to be a pariah state, based on medieval principles of government, which, rivals feared, harboured ambitions to continue to drive through Central Asia to threaten the British

LENIN BEFORE LENINISM   19

Raj in India. The dramatic emergence of a unified Germany in 1871 had created a powerful, rapidly industrializing state which was using its elbows to create its 'place in the sun' and to catch up on the global political looting spree that was imperialism. Germany's rise achieved the impossible, but not the one Kaiser Wilhelm II wanted. Abandoning the subtle and careful approach of Bismarck had brought the arch-enemies France, Britain, and Russia into an alliance. Revolutionary Marianne was in bed with a decaying autocracy. John Bull was appeasing the Russian Bear which threatened 'his' jewel in the crown—India. Europe split into two camps—the Central Powers, namely Germany, Austria-Hungary, and Turkey, against the peripheral powers, Russia, France, Britain. The immediate outcome was a costly arms race. In order to sell such policies to their populations the imperialists created what remains one of their trump cards. They sowed the seeds of extreme jingoism through an unscrupulous mass press which, often under the guise of apparent respectability, peddled racism, hatred of the 'enemy', lies, scandals, lurid crime stories, and titillation. Fake news was born and carried a semi-educated public along with it. From a socialist point of view, imperialism seemed impregnable. States were getting ever more powerful. Police forces, including political police and secret services, were increasingly professional. The military, the state's ultimate defence force, was expanding exponentially as the arms race blazed on. The socialist movement itself was succumbing to a fatal split as the more revolutionary wing kept closer to the ideas of Marx (who had died in 1883) in the face of the challenge of 'evolutionary' socialism propagated by Eduard Bernstein, which believed a form of socialism was evolving organically in capitalist societies. Only in Russia did there appear to beany severe economic weakness. In 1899 the first signs of economic crisis were felt. University students led protests and the university system was shut down. In the following years, the crisis affected industry and agriculture, defeat in an imperialist squabble with Japan in early 1905 undermined the prestige of the autocracy, and a full-blown revolution, the outbreak of which had little to do with the actions or ideas of revolutionaries including Lenin, shook the system to its foundations. However, apparently against all the odds, the autocracy turned the tables, survived the year, and spent the following years retracting most of the limited concessions it had been forced to make and restoring 'order' by inflicting terror on workers and peasants. By 1907, even the hope which had arisen had been ruthlessly extinguished and Russia joined the list of apparently secure and unchallengeable imperialist governments. The outlook for radicals across the continent, across the world, could barely have looked more bleak.

20 LENIN LIVES?

Lenin, however, was not deterred, and his determination and optimism about creating a better world in the face of all the odds is one of the characteristics that links him as an inspiration to the current world situation in the 2020s, where conservative, reactionary forces seem to be in control and synthetic, calculated, rabid nationalism and anti-migrant racism are on the rise. Imperialism was swallowing up the world and the bloated imperial nations were measuring up to one another in a way which led to a conflict which wrenched the self-satisfied nineteenth-century world off its axis. The idea, in 1900, of Lenin ever achieving power looked remote in the extreme. Nonetheless, he set about his task with energy and enthusiasm. The threads running through this period of his life were the relatively modest ones of constructing a revolutionary party and sustaining a party newspaper.

Lenin's first major responsibility as a national figure was his role as editor of the party newspaper *Iskra* (*The Spark*). The first issue came out in December 1900 in Leipzig. It was, said Lenin, to be the spark that would set off a prairie wildfire. It was published intermittently until 1905 from wherever Lenin was living or wherever he could find someone to print it. While in London, Lenin used a small office at 37A Clerkenwell Green, which can still be visited as it is within the Marx Memorial Library established at that address. Lenin was assisted while there by the pioneer British Marxist Harry Quelch, who oversaw the printing process for his Russian visitor who spoke only broken English (though he was fluent in German). After *Iskra* ran out of funds, Lenin edited or was closely associated with *Vpered,* (*Forward!*), *Proletarii* (*Proletarians*), and the best-known and longest-running of all, *Pravda* (*Truth*), which first appeared in 1912 under Stalin's nominal editorship within Russia, a post which brought his arrest that year and Siberian exile until the outbreak of the revolution in February 1917. The newspaper continued and was the main newspaper of the Soviet Communist Party throughout the Soviet era. It is still published today by the Communist Party of the Russian Federation, the post-1991 successor to the fallen former ruling party. Lenin also contributed many articles. The fullest edition of his collected works runs to fifty-four volumes, the majority of which are articles. He sometimes wrote almost entire issues, a fact disguised from the readers by his use of several pen names simultaneously. In the years before 1917 he spent more time on writing articles and editing than anything else. For *Iskra* he wrote thirty-two articles. His friend and ally of the moment, Iulii Martov, contributed thirty-nine and Plekhanov twenty-four; the other three editors, Zasulich, Aksel'rod, and Potresov managed only twenty between them. As the revolution rolled along in Russia in 1905, Lenin spent

LENIN BEFORE LENINISM   21

three days a week on *Vpered!* until his return in November, writing ninety articles in its twenty-six issues. Between then and its closure in December 1905, he contributed an extraordinary twenty articles to Gorky's paper *Novaia zhizn'* (*The New Life*). Lenin's articles were not subtle and were written in unadorned, direct prose. Among their chief characteristics was an often brilliant analysis of the current political situation combined with a thundering, hammering, insistent, and repetitive tone and theme. His writing was sometimes obscure but always direct and declamatory, demanding to be read at the top of one's inner voice. They were rarely witty or humorous but often dripped with heavy sarcasm.

The newspapers had a second important dimension beyond their actual content. In the context of a small group which counted supporters and members in thousands rather than tens of thousands, the newspaper was a central field of battle for control and for party construction. The newspaper was the central praxis (activity) of the party leaders and therefore it reflected the dominant group in the party. Activism for rank-and-file members was often based on smuggling and clandestinely distributing these illegal imports. In the years from 1900 to 1917, the newspaper was the party and party construction went on in parallel with it. The issue of party construction came to the fore in 1902, when Lenin published his ideas on it in his second major work, *What is to be Done?* (yes, Chernyshevsky's title but a very different content), and in 1903, when the ideas of Lenin, Plekhanov, and Lenin's close friend and close associate on *Iskra*, Martov, were aired at an increasingly bitter Second Party Congress—a congress which began its life in Belgium, but crossed the Channel in the middle of proceedings to escape the attention of the tsarist police, who had favourable backing from the Belgian government, and set up in the East End of London because the British authorities were less friendly to tsarist agents. The wranglings and divisions in the party continued even until the 1917 October Revolution that catapulted Lenin into power, and even for some time after it. It was a decade and a half of often bewildering arguments, administrative battles, cultural-philosophical disagreements, and rapidly changing alliances and political positions. We do not need to follow them in their grim detail but, to help us define Lenin's legacy, we do need to note a number of features of these tumultuous years, leaving the main discussion of the battle of ideas and revolutionary strategies to our account of Leninism in the next chapter.

Even so, we need to comment briefly on the ideas that launched this period of bitter argument. Lenin's first major intervention was to promote the concept of the need for a party and for it to be led by 'professional

22 LENIN LIVES?

revolutionaries'. Suffice it to say for the moment that Lenin had started to mine an intellectual seam which remained one of his chief characteristics, or, to be precise, two linked characteristics. The question of why the revolution had not yet happened by 1900 was puzzling Marxists. In Germany, Bernstein had proposed what became known as evolutionary socialism, arguing that revolution was occurring through 'natural' capitalist processes of, to take a crucial area, spreading wealth and ownership of land and capital and filling out a better-off middle class rather than having it dissolve in class polarization between capitalist and proletarian. All wings of Russian social democracy rejected his views. Lenin argued that revolution had not happened because the working class had not been able to evolve a revolutionary 'consciousness', that is, a realization of its true class interest. Going back to one of Plekhanov's crucial texts, *Socialism and Political Struggle*, Lenin pointed to the need for a 'conscious' leading group—a political party—to guide them beyond the struggle for simply economic gains, what Lenin slightly contemptuously called 'trade union consciousness'.[5] In a striking and controversial phrase he argued it needed 'professional revolutionaries' to form such a party. For many of the prosperous classes, the concept of a professional revolutionary sparks fantasy images of conspiratorial, bearded, male, 'anarchist' malcontents, inhabiting the shadows from which they occasionally emerge to throw a bomb, lead a riot, or enrage a crowd. Lenin proposed no such thing. Confusingly, it seems, the examples he gave of such a group of people came from the, by then, stolid and respectable ranks of German social democracy; Bebel, Liebknecht, and so on. Lenin was focusing on something different, the need to update the party, to push it from its early status as a group of what Russians called *kruzhki,* circles, and instead become a properly constituted political party, albeit one with, as we have already noted, structures appropriate to Russia's profoundly hostile and undemocratic conditions.

We will pick up the implications for the construction of 'Leninism' later, but as a guide to Lenin's personality, the main characteristic of the debate, which started in 1902 and was still raging in 1904, is that it showed that Lenin had sky-high self-confidence even at this relatively early stage of his career and that he put forward his ideas without a scintilla of doubt that he was completely correct. The argument started as a slow burner. Everyone welcomed *What is to be Done?* as a helpful and progressive text. However, as Lenin's pursuit of its implications unrolled, others began to see red lights flashing. Lenin showed increasing ruthlessness in ensuring the victory of his line. At first, he graciously accepted the support of the respected founder

LENIN BEFORE LENINISM   23

of the movement, Plekhanov. However, when Plekhanov saw Lenin using what were deemed uncomradely and even underhand tactics to get his way, he changed sides. Lenin launched bitter attacks on him. At the Second Congress, where the debates played out, Lenin was outnumbered. He lost the crucial vote on the definition of whether a party member should be all in, a 'professional', or, in Lenin's scathing comment, just be someone who devoted spare evenings and weekends to the cause. But there was still one important vote to be held, a vote for the editorial board of the party newspaper *Iskra*. Lenin started to use what his opponents considered 'dirty tricks' to weaken the opposition further. In particular, he helped organize a vote which challenged the credentials of one of the most committed and respected groups of revolutionaries at the congress, the Jewish Bund, a vote to be held before the vote on the editorial board. They were disenfranchised on the grounds they were a separate party and, in so doing, Lenin's minority position turned into a majority on the issue of the editorial board. He proposed dropping the unproductive Zasulich, Aksel'rod, and Potresov and retaining only Plekhanov, Martov, and himself. The motion was accepted. It was on this basis that Lenin's group became known as Bolsheviks—the majority people—while their opponents came to be called Mensheviks—the minority people; hardly an inspiring name. But to cement Lenin's victory, his crucial allies, Plekhanov and Martov, were so appalled at his heavy-handed and vicious pursuit of winning by administrative means (keeping his group united, disenfranchising and insulting opponents) rather than by prevailing in argument, that they refused to work with him, leaving, as Lenin had hoped, *Iskra* firmly in his hands.

A further observation to which we will return needs to be made at this point. The outcome of the Second Congress is widely seen as having 'split' the party so that the two factions were, in effect, separate parties. It is also assumed that the Mensheviks were more dogmatic in their attachment to Marxism and clung to Marx's 'theory of stages'. Mainly this referred to the transition from feudalism to capitalism and then from capitalism to socialism, which, Marx had argued about the latter, required the right conditions to have matured, notably the exhaustion of capitalism at the end of its long, exploitative life, a situation which would arise when it had so exploited society that it was no longer possible for capital to make a profit and workers would 'have nothing to lose' by revolution 'but their chains'.[6] It is usually argued that the Mensheviks wanted to 'wait' for capitalism in Russia to work for the 'bourgeois', that is, capitalist revolution as the next stage in a Russia which was still in the hands of a feudal autocracy, while the Bolsheviks

24 LENIN LIVES?

wanted to press on with socialist revolution regardless. The split was not quite so clear, nor so definitive. In terms of positions on key issues, it was not the Mensheviks who wanted to 'wait', it was the so-called Economists, a group of three main members—Akimov, Prokopovich, and Kuskova—who associated with social democracy until they were effectively forced out of the Second Congress. It was they who prioritized 'economic struggle' via trade unions, not 'political struggle' via the emerging political party.

In fact, it is difficult to define either Bolshevik or Menshevik groups consistently by their policies. Rather, they were like two squabbling spouses never quite reaching the complete dissolution of their marriage. They circled round each other and, at grass roots level, co-operated freely. They were better together in that they were a small minority facing the Socialist Revolutionary party on the left and a powerful autocracy on the right. Splitting their already weak forces would undermine them both. Until 1918, both wings retained the same party programme which began with affirming the establishment of democracy via a Constituent Assembly as the next revolutionary step. While Bolsheviks were, by and large, more actively revolutionary and more ruthless in their tactics, and Mensheviks were more democratic and aimed to bring the working class with them, on most key issues the two factions changed and interchanged positions frequently. Mensheviks were more favourable to soviets in 1905 where Lenin paid them little attention, though both supported them in 1917, despite Lenin distancing himself from them in July and August. On the issue of armed struggle as a means to take power, Lenin supported this notion in 1905 but, when it failed, abandoned it just at the moment the Mensheviks were coming to accept it. Why? Because there were constant attempts to reconcile the two wings and align their policies in 1906, 1912, and even in 1917 before Lenin's return in April when he squashed the idea as firmly as he could, as he had done on most other occasions. Even so, even he dallied with ideas of reunification and cross-party alliances before 1914, when a further cataclysm occurred in the socialist movement which is discussed later, and even in September 1917. In July 1917, Trotsky, a profound critic of Lenin's approach to revolution since 1906, associated himself with Lenin because events had made their main differences irrelevant. Ironically, Trotsky had been the one to argue that Russia could speed up the 'stages' of revolution and engage in 'permanent revolution' whereby socialist transition could precede the exhaustion of the potential of capitalism. Lenin had stuck to the theory of stages. He mentions it in his 'April Theses', his most critical strategic statement of 1917, where he says now the bourgeois revolution had been accomplished in the shape of the downfall of tsarism in the February Revolution of 1917, it was time to 'move on to the second stage',[7] proletarian socialist revolution.

Considering also Lenin's sometimes dizzying U-turns on central policies after the October Revolution—such as stepping away from spreading the revolution to Europe; soviet power; workers' control; the independence of trade unions; attitude to the peasantry, and many more—it is more accurate to say that Bolshevism was not defined by specific positions, since they changed constantly, but by personal adherence to Lenin and a willingness to follow him through a variety of hoops. Even when opposition within Bolshevism did take the form of fighting for positions against Lenin's views, those proposing them often recognized—as Alexandra Kollontai did in explaining the nature of the Workers' Opposition in 1920, which she led with others—that victory would come about because 'Il'ich [i.e. Lenin] will be with us yet'.[8] Personally changing Lenin's mind would be the surest guarantor of victory, not party opinion.

These aspects of Lenin's development and the intertwining relationship with the Mensheviks continued for more than a decade after the beginning of the party 'split'. The next test for Lenin came with the outbreak of revolution in Russia in 1905. The trigger for the revolution was the events of 'Bloody Sunday', 9 January, when tsarist troops opened fire on an unarmed crowd outside the Winter Palace in St Petersburg (Fig. 2), an event which encapsulated the tyranny of tsarism which had, in effect, created Lenin the revolutionary out of the young Vladimir Ulyanov. For reasons which have not been clarified, Lenin delayed his return to Russia until November, when the tide had already turned against the revolution. By December 1905 he had been forced into hiding, mainly in autonomous Finland, from which he emerged from time to time to make speeches in St Petersburg and Moscow, as well as for foreign travel to party congresses and conferences in Stockholm, Stuttgart, Copenhagen, and London. However, Lenin was not a public activist. He continued to work through the study, the reading room, the committee room, and the print shop rather than the street or institutional political arena. His thoughts returned in part to organization as much as action, and in the brief weeks after his return and before he went off the radar again he wrote two articles which came back to haunt the post-revolutionary communist movement. One was entitled 'Party Organisation and Party Literature', which made the not unreasonable claim that pamphlets issued in the name of the party should be approved by it in advance. It did imply a rather unrealistic element of control freakery in the fluid

Fig. 2 Tsarist Tyranny—The Force that Created Lenin. Exemplified here on Bloody Sunday—St Petersburg, 9 January 1905. Troops fire on unarmed civilians.

circumstances of the time, but that was not the problem. Later, in the 1920s, after Lenin's death, it was seized upon as a weapon in the culture wars of the decade and used by incipient 'Stalinists' as a warrant for party control of all literature, including fiction. The second was entitled 'Socialism and Religion'. In it, Lenin condemned all forms of religion and called for all believers to be excluded from the party. It set the Bolsheviks on a pointlessly anti-religious path in that, while there were many abuses associated with religion, religions, and clerical institutions, there were many believers who were happy to associate with socialism. To declare war on them was unnecessary, especially given the weakness of the left at the time. It was not an isolated attack. Provoked by allies like Gorky and Lunacharsky, who were arguing at that time for socialism as the culmination of world religious experience, Lenin took a foundation of a reasonable critique of religious abuses and shortcomings and fanned it into a passionate fire of anti-religious bigotry and superficial prejudice which has come to define many left-wing zealots ever since.[9] His approach was another example of Lenin channelling his inner Bakuninism, which was similarly deeply anti-religious, rather than the more nuanced and sensitive critique of Marx. This, too, was costly to the Bolsheviks, and the immense revival of religion in

LENIN BEFORE LENINISM   27

Russia since 1991 is an indication of what a powerful force they were wasting their energy to attack when a more subtle approach might have brought better results from the party's point of view. The debate continued fiercely within the party and for the years after the failure of the 1905 revolution, philosophical debate marched at the forefront of party squabbles. Lenin wrote the nearest thing he ever produced to a philosophical treatise in the form of his book *Materialism and Empiriocriticism* (1908), which was polemic against the ideas of Alexander Bogdanov which he feared were creeping into the party. Bogdanov, Lunacharsky, and Gorky were also the first to focus on the issue of raising class consciousness among Russian workers through the establishment of party schools, which they set up in Bologna and Capri in 1908–9, to be challenged, in 1911, by one set up by Lenin in Longjumeau in the southern suburbs of Paris.

Unlike Trotsky, who threw himself into political activism and speeches at every opportunity, even when he was in British detention in April 1917, Lenin by and large kept out of the streets in 1905, a pattern repeated in 1917. Also unlike his later ally, who briefly chaired the Petrograd Soviet, Lenin did not see any really special significance in soviets at this time. He also threw his weight behind the Moscow armed uprising of December 1905 which was viciously crushed. Nonetheless, he continued to advocate armed uprising well into 1906. He also unequivocally stated that socialist revolution was not on the immediate agenda. This led him to proclaim a need to ally with all democratic forces, including bourgeois liberals, to bring about a democratic system as a preliminary to establishing a revolutionary democratic dictatorship of workers and peasants as a transitional step to the goal of proletarian revolution. However, as 1906 continued, the revolution underwent further bloody and demoralizing defeats as the government sent death squads around the country, used army artillery to batter striking factories into submission, and strangled the limited democracy that had been forced out of the autocracy in 1905. Lenin increasingly feared being arrested. Incidentally, Lenin's main motivation in this was not fear of the authorities but fear it would prevent him from carrying out his leadership tasks. In December 1907 he decided to leave Finland and the Russian Empire and return to western Europe, where he remained until April 1917. Using the most accessible ferry port at Åbo (Turku) bore too great a risk of being intercepted by the authorities. He hired two guides, who turned out to be drunk, to lead him in a perilous journey across cracking sea-ice to a more remote ferry stop on a small island. His 1905–7 sojourn had ended in defeat and risky withdrawal.

28 LENIN LIVES?

From 1900 to 1914 Lenin had risen from promising youngster to the most controversial faction leader, from hungry acolyte of Plekhanov to the elder statesman's leading challenger. He was forty-four in 1914. He had reached maturity and become, more or less, whoever he was going to be. Politically he was, most obviously, deeply committed. He lived, breathed, and slept revolution. He embodied the ascetic Rakhmetov in Chernyshevsky's *What is to be Done?*, who did everything to harden himself so he could better serve the revolution. Rakhmetov slept on a bed of nails. Lenin's bed of nails was the opponents he wrestled with in the endless party struggles which brought on his nerve-related episodes, which Krupskaya was so concerned to shield him from.

Lenin had some features in common with the figure defined by Sergei Nechaev in his *Revolutionary Catechism*, written around 1870: 'The revolutionary is a doomed man. He has no personal interests, no business affairs, no emotions, no attachments, no property, and no name. Everything in him is wholly absorbed in the single thought and the single passion for revolution.'[10] Lenin gave no thought to his personal interests. His life decisions after his graduation in 1891 were based on pursuing political objectives, not his desires, though he was not immune from them. He mused about what his life would have been like, what difference it would have made had he remained a farmer and local landowner (and so might we!). His romantic attractions to Krupskaya, who was as much his personal assistant as wife, and to Inessa Armand, a beautiful French Bolshevik feminist with whom he may—or may not—have had an affair around 1910, were shaped by political considerations. Inessa was his representative at important socialist conferences and was an often underestimated active comrade until her death from cholera in 1920. In the words of another formidable revolutionary, Angelica Balabanoff, Lenin was 'utterly broken by her death'.[11] Here he differed from Nechaev's paradigm. He certainly had emotions and attachments—to his brother Sasha, to sister Olga, to his mother, to Krupskaya, to Inessa, and many more. But many of them had a strong political dimension. He had close friendships with Iulii Martov and his sister Lydia Dan, but when they were separated by political argument in the great explosion of 1903, all friendly relations ceased. Similarly, friendships with Bogdanov, Trotsky, and even Plekhanov flourished or withered depending on the political weather. Reconciliation, with his arch-critic Trotsky in 1917 for example, could be spectacular as well as the splits. As for other criteria, he certainly had no property; borrowing money to live on, always renting lodgings and living in state-owned properties like the Kremlin and his country house near

LENIN BEFORE LENINISM   29

Moscow when he was in power, and never taking a regular salary or accumulating savings. Nor did he have his name. Instead he had 146 pseudonyms.[12] Revolution was his 'single passion' and he suppressed his others, though not entirely, for fear they would weaken his revolutionary resolve. The classical affirmation of this comes from an often-quoted encounter recalled by Gorky at the time of Lenin's death:

> One evening, in Moscow, in a friend's flat, Lenin, listening to a Beethoven Sonata, said to me: 'I know nothing that would equal the "Appassionata". I could hear it played every day. Marvellous, supernatural music. When I hear it, I always think, maybe with naive, childish pride: What wonders human beings are capable of accomplishing!'
>
> And smiling, with half-closed eyes, he added merrily:
>
> 'But I can't listen to music too often; it gets on my nerves, rouses the desire to say charming nonsense, and stroke the heads of the people who, in spite of living in a dirty hell, are able to create such beauty. And today one can't allow oneself the luxury of stroking people on the head; they would bite your hand off. One must hit them on the heads, hit mercilessly, although, in ideal, we are against all violence over men. Hm...Hm...the job is not an easy one.'[13]

Lenin also had a broad love of life, of nature in which he absorbed himself in Siberia during his exile, and of good-humoured banter with workers, peasants, children, and other strangers. He frequently gave away whatever surplus he currently had to fund politics or to give to someone in need. He was no automaton or monster as he is sometimes depicted. The Gorky anecdote is very illustrative. He hated violence but was not so sentimental that he could ignore the fact that the point would come when it would have to be used, and used as quickly, sharply, and effectively as possible.

When political necessity called, it would be answered by whatever action Lenin considered was needed, irrespective of personal cost to himself or, when in power, of others, including innocents caught up in revolutionary war, economic collapse, and targeted terror. Lenin girded up his loins on such occasions and forced his more sentimental self into battle. No quarter was asked or given. Ruthlessness was regrettable but unavoidable. It was one of the characteristics by which Lenin and his group were best known among European, especially German, socialists. In addition to arguments about principles, Lenin and his former friends and enemies also argued about the

30 LENIN LIVES?

crucial practical issue of party finance. Lenin was prepared to take funds from wherever they could be found, including theft, deception, and soliciting donations even from capitalists. On the last point, Gorky, in addition to donating personally from his sizeable book royalties, also raised funds from industrialist acquaintances. It is hard to understand all the motives behind such a counter-intuitive act by rich capitalists, but it was not uncommon. Many such links were motivated by the idea of using the Bolsheviks and other extreme revolutionaries as a battering ram to break down a backward-looking, interfering, feudal autocracy which capitalist and socialist hated equally. One idealistic young capitalist, Nikolai Schmidt, became a Bolshevik in Moscow, died young, and left his money to the party, except there was no clear will and, by a mixture of legitimacy and deception, a fictional marriage of a Bolshevik to his sister enabled her to fulfil his bequest and hand the money over to Lenin to guarantee the future of his newspaper *Proletarii*. Numerous other dubious sources of funds are often linked to one of the party's fixers, Alexander Parvus-Helphand, who may have diverted money from arms trading and, very disputedly, from the German government, to Bolshevik funds. The biggest example of theft involved a massive bank raid in the capital of the province of Georgia, Tiflis, in which an armed raid, led by a local revolutionary named Kamo, seized 270,000 roubles, about 350,000 dollars today. Sadly for the party, the money was in large denomination notes and many party associates who tried to change them in banks outside Russia were arrested. A number of these issues turned into bitter disputes between Lenin and the 'Bolshevik Centre', which had a financing group, and Mensheviks (who claimed a share of funds as, they argued, they were part of the same party) and Bogdanov, who controlled some party funds at the time Lenin broke with him. The disputes were sometimes mediated by western socialists, including the Second International (a broad organization to which labour and socialist parties of many kinds adhered), who professed frustration at the bitterness and hostile energy shown particularly by Lenin. Russian social democracy developed a reputation among western counterparts for its rancorous disputes and tendency to split and split again.

As already noted, the strife played havoc with Lenin's health. His father had died at the age of fifty-four, and it has been suggested that the stroke-inducing cerebral-vascular degeneration was something that Lenin knew, from visits to Swiss specialists in 1916, was affecting him, leading him to believe he did not have much time ahead of him.[14] In fact, he died of a similar condition to his father at a similar age—fifty-three—after over two years

LENIN BEFORE LENINISM   31

of serious illness. Krupskaya was tireless in helping him stay healthy. Long walks, cycle rides, and numerous short breaks and longer vacations punctuated his life. Favourite places were the Alps, the French Atlantic coast including the Pink Granite Coast and the bay of Arcachon in the Landes, and parks near wherever they happened to live. Lenin was not impressed by Paris—'a rotten hole' he called it. Geneva was no better, an 'awful hole' as he said in another letter.[15] He also found London to be vile on first impression. London was, Lenin said on one of a number of upstairs bus rides across London from the West End and Bloomsbury to the East End recorded by Krupskaya, a city composed of two nations. He found English food and weather repulsive but Lenin was softened in his attitude by the Reading Room of the British Museum where he studied regularly and dreamed of having reading rooms in every town and village in Russia, an idea that came to fruition in the 1920s when a network of reading rooms and reading cabins of obviously modest means was set up. Soon, according to Krupskaya, Lenin began 'to study the living London',[16] which was, at the time, the global metropolis of capitalism and imperialism. Lenin remained fascinated with London but he also came to like Germany and Switzerland. In all his places of exile he and Krupskaya were frequent excursioners, including taking weekend strolls to the bandstand in the local park, to concerts, and to the theatre, though they often walked out before the end of the production or performance.[17] In Paris there were cycle rides to the surrounding woods, including the encounter in 1908 with an expensive car which crushed his bike but left Lenin unscathed. As the continent polarized and his options were being foreclosed by growing international tensions, in 1912 he moved, in order to be nearer to Russia, to a city he came to like—Krakow in Poland, part of Austria-Hungary at the time. It was, he said, good for his health, and enabled him to recover from the awful tensions of emigré backbiting in Paris by going cycling and walking in the forests and beside the lakes of the region. He also headed for the Tatra mountains and the resort of Zakopane. However, Krakow was 'provincial and barbarous' and, perhaps because he missed their impressive libraries, he surprisingly wrote that 'of all the places I have been in my wanderings I would select London or Geneva'.[18] He and Krupskaya were accompanied by their friends and co-workers, the Zinovievs and Kamenevs, and Inessa made lengthy sojourns, to the joy of both Krupskaya and Vladimir Lenin. However, the political storm clouds of impending war broke up the idyll. As a Russian citizen he was liable to be interned by the Austrian authorities, a fate he escaped through the intervention of leading Austrian social-democratic politicians, especially Victor

32   LENIN LIVES?

Adler, who had Lenin and Krupskaya released from detention as spies by the provincial police. On 5 September 1914 they arrived in Switzerland, living in Berne; 'a dull little town', but happily endowed with libraries—'I have missed them'.[19] Inessa moved in across the street. Ironically, Lenin was settling down to years of relatively quiet scholarship, oddly immersing himself in Hegel as the rest of Europe sung its way happily into war under the blazing sun of a hot summer. A vortex was, however, engulfing Europe and Lenin. It pulled them in, flung them around, and deposited them in unimaginable places. Just over three years later, the Russian Empire imploded. Lenin was catapulted into power. In autumn 1914, such an outcome would have been considered phantasmagoric. But history plays the wildest tricks.

Wartime

No one in the socialist movement was thinking about upward mobility as the largest armies in history, up to that date, began an unimaginably extensive clash of arms. War itself was a ruinous prospect, but there was an added dimension of tragedy for Europe's socialists. Since 1883, most of the major and many minor socialist and labour parties had been coming together within the framework of the Second International, the successor to the International Workingmen's Association of the mid-century, for which organization Engels and Marx had written *The Communist Manifesto* and which had also provided the backdrop for epic clashes between Marx and Bakunin over the priority of class struggle or of destroying the state. The fundamental assumption of the Second International was that workers did not have a country—their interests crossed national boundaries and linked up with those of workers in other countries. For workers, it was assumed, class rather than nation was their main social attachment; they were internationalist. As the frenzy of competing nationalisms built up in the late nineteenth century in the form of a wave of imperialism, which swallowed up much of Africa, and an escalating arms race producing ever more powerful weapons, the International stood to defend workers who, supposedly, had no interest in such struggles. They were the affair of national elites, capitalists pursuing their class interests, and most of the burgeoning middle classes. The workers' interest, so the socialists argued, lay in co-operation with each other to bring down their oppressors. The International denounced imperialism and the approaching war in no uncertain terms.

LENIN BEFORE LENINISM   33

However, as war broke out there was a tragically unexpected twist. The largest parties, notably the German Social Democratic Party and the British Labour Party, fell in line behind their governments in support of their national war efforts. Among Russians, Plekhanov reluctantly supported the war on the grounds that if Germany overcame tsarism, the prospects for socialism in Russia would decline because Germany would impose a more efficient and organized capitalist state on Russia.

Minorities in all countries and most parties howled their disillusion with their leaderships who had, they argued, betrayed the workers at the moment of greatest need. Workers had no interest in the inter-capitalist conflicts and critically competing imperialisms which had caused it. Worse, they would be the cannon fodder who would be sacrificed by their rulers to fight this massive war, which did inflict casualties on a hitherto unimaginable scale. One of the most determined voices reasserting internationalist and anti-war values was that of Lenin. In addition, where it was automatically assumed that war and the split in the International were catastrophes, Lenin began to sense the emergence of unprecedented opportunities. The capitalist elites were intent on weakening, even destroying, one another, and the pockets of enthusiasm for the war would be turned inside out as its grim realities bore in over the facile jingoism of the gutter press and the governments. Workers would resist their own slaughter and revolution would follow. In September 1914, within a month of war breaking out, Lenin was calling for the formation of a United States of Europe and, distinguishing him from those who opposed the war on pure pacifist principles like the British Labour leader Ramsay MacDonald, Lenin called for the transformation of the imperialist war between nations into a civil war between classes. For their own purposes the capitalists, so Lenin and the internationalists argued, were giving military training and weapons to the mass of workers. The interests of workers everywhere was in turning those weapons on their oppressors within their countries, not in using them to kill brother workers in the opposite trenches. The war had brought about political realignment. The task was to build on it.

The realignments were profound. The already confusing, ever-changing kaleidoscope of political conjunctures was effectively doubled. Where there had been a single group, party, or fraction, there were now two; those who were in favour of supporting their nation's war effort for whatever reason, who came to be known as defencists in Russia, and those who opposed the war as an imperialist settling of accounts, who came to be called internationalists. In a breathtakingly short time, party members found the old barriers between them and fellow defencists or internationalists in other parties had become of secondary importance, at least for the duration of the war. On the other hand, former party comrades were now on the other side of this infinitely damaging split, and one now had more in common with one's former opponents. In Russia, this split continued into the October 1917 revolution and beyond. The internationalist and defencist inter-party platforms became more important sources of political identity than the pre-war Socialist Revolutionary–Social Democratic Menshevik/Bolshevik divisions. The first Soviet government following the October Revolution was a coalition of internationalists from the Socialist Revolutionary and Bolshevik parties with some former Mensheviks like Trotsky, who had been brought into the Bolshevik fold in part by opposition to the war.

Because of the conditions of war, communications and international travel were immensely difficult and fraught with risks. Lenin could not cross the German or Austrian borders because he was a citizen of a state at war with them. He had already been extricated from internment at the beginning of the war. He could not cross Allied borders without risk of detention as a revolutionary intent on undermining one of the Allied powers, Russia. Trotsky, for example, was deported from France and Spain in 1916 and sent to the United States. The conditions made politics for opponents of the war very difficult indeed. Lenin's time in Switzerland, from September 1914 until his departure in March 1917 for the Finland Station in Petrograd, was focused on analysing the war and trying to convert it into a continent-wide revolution. He also had a lot of time for reading, including Aristotle, Hegel, and Feuerbach to try to better understand why Marx had rated them so highly. He also had time to pursue his passion for mountain walking, and he and Krupskaya would make excursions, picking up bars of nut chocolate and heading for a favourite secluded spot where they could read, or take vacations in the Alps. Shortage of funds meant they had to be as economical as possible, which sometimes led them to odd corners such as a hotel/health spa in Tschudiwiese which focused on a milk diet which, Krupskaya said, 'we howled against'.[20] On one occasion on their return they set out to catch the train back to Zurich but noted, as they descended to the station, that there were mushrooms in the woods. Despite pouring rain they picked as many mushrooms as they could carry, missing their train and having to wait, completely drenched, for two hours for the next. Rather as during his Siberian exile, Lenin had more time for relaxation and engaging in healthy pastimes. He was, however, deeply saddened by the death of his beloved mother in 1916 and the impossibility of attending her funeral. He also focused on his own mortality and it may have been at this time that he consulted specialists about his own health in the light of the vascular condition which had shortened his father's life. In any case, he began to fear that he would not live long enough to see the revolution he believed was coming.

Despite the relative isolation Lenin continued to work hard. Though he could not leave Switzerland, the country's neutral status meant it was the setting for two major conferences in Kienthal and Zimmerwald, at which anti-war groups tried to come up with a joint strategy to end the war. Unsurprisingly, they became cockpits for mutual recrimination between old enemies and old differences on the left. On neither occasion could Lenin, despite his best efforts and expenditure of his reserves of nervous energy, command a majority for his position of transforming the war into a civil war between the classes. Kienthal in particular exhausted him and it took several days in the mountains to restore his equilibrium.

In addition to trying to stop the war, Lenin attempted to analyse it. In one of his most influential works, *Imperialism: The Highest Stage of Capitalism* (completed 1916 but not published in full until 1921), he explained the war not as an outburst of conflicting nationalisms but as the outcome of competing national capitalisms. It was one of Lenin's most influential writings and, as such, we will evaluate it below, but there are a number of aspects to note here. In it, Lenin brought together the insights of the liberal economist J. A. Hobson, who viewed imperialism as a consequence of economic competition, and of the Austrian Marxist economist Rudolf Hilferding, who argued that capital was no longer invested by its owners directly but took the form of finance capital which was anonymously accumulated in banks and invested by financial managers who were not its owners. But Lenin was not just engaging in academic analysis here. One of the conclusions drawn was that capitalism had become a worldwide system and that its chief vulnerability was at its 'periphery', in the colonies, and not in the heartlands of the imperial 'cores' such as Germany, France, and Britain. The implication here was that capitalism could be challenged in the 'periphery' as well as the 'core'. This reflected on the debates about the possibility of Marxist revolution in a 'backward' country like Russia. Revolution could occur at the periphery and spread rapidly to the core, so it was not anomalous for the first blow to be struck in Russia.

It did mean, however, that such a revolution had to spread in order to survive and, indeed, until spring 1918, Lenin appeared to be a true internationalist, believing a Marxist revolution could not survive in Russia unless it spread. If not, the great capitalist forces of Germany, France, Britain, the United States, and Japan would strangle it. A second implication was that

36 LENIN LIVES?

imperialism was helping those core capitalisms fend off revolution by, as Lenin also mentioned in the 1921 preface to the French and German editions of the pamphlet, acquiring 'superprofits' from ravaging the colonies which could 'bribe' an advanced elite of the working class and make them reformist rather than revolutionary. It was this layer which, Lenin argued, supported the right wing of the labour movement, including the British Labour Party and figures such as Lenin's arch-enemies, the 'evolutionary socialist' Eduard Bernstein and Karl Kautsky, against whom the polemical final sections of *Imperialism* are directed. In other words, as was the case with many of Lenin's major works, there was an important dimension of direct political argument. In this case he had, to his own satisfaction at least, demolished the intellectual positions of two key groups of opponents. He had shown to the Mensheviks that Marxist revolution could take place in Russia and, indeed, might be considered more likely to since the forces of capitalism there were weak and immature compared to Britain, the United States, and so on. Second, he had explained the success of revisionism by pointing to a corrupt 'aristocracy of labour'[21] within the working class which was suffocating the efforts of more radically oriented sections of that class, thereby adding another response to the burning question for early twentieth-century Marxists of why the revolution had not taken place. Even when engaging with the vast scope of early globalization, Lenin still had his eye firmly fixed on the squabbles of the as yet still tiny Russian left.

Before leaving our consideration of how Lenin was affected by the war, we need to add one further important aspect. Lenin, quite naturally, was appalled by the horrific, unprecedented extent of its violence, swallowing the lives of millions. This gave rise in Lenin's mind to a calculus of violence according to which the sacrifices of the revolution were dwarfed by those of imperialism. If tens of thousands had to die in revolutionary struggle, though it was immensely regrettable in itself, Lenin frequently argued that it was a price worth paying to throw off the yoke of capitalism and make any future war on that scale impossible. When criticized, even by close supporters, on the grounds of excess revolutionary violence, Lenin tended to retort that such criticism was unjustified and even hypocritical in the mouths of right-wing and capitalist critics, because imperialism had imposed a much more bloody tariff. If such slaughter could only be ended by sacrifice, then so be it.

The final scene of Lenin's exile in Switzerland was one of the most controversial. Stuck in Zurich as the dramatic events of the fall of the tsar unrolled in Petrograd in February 1917, Lenin became very impatient to get back.

LENIN BEFORE LENINISM   37

Despite the scarcity of sources he was able to produce some of the most accurate analyses of the faraway events, notably that the tsar had been removed by the Allies and the rising Russian capitalist middle class in order to fight the war more effectively. He had no illusions about it having been accomplished by demonstrators in the streets. But how could he get back? The British or French would intern him for sure and he could not take a risk. They would not want to return opponents of their new 'democratic' allied Provisional Government.[22] On the other hand, it was very much in Germany's interests to help potential 'troublemakers' back to Russia to weaken it. The problem was that to return under German protection would undermine the revolutionary credibility of those who sought it. Lenin was well aware of the risks, and the negotiations conducted by a Swiss socialist intermediary were protracted. Eventually, agreement was reached that a party of thirty-two members of a variety of left-wing parties would be returned in a special railway carriage under special rules exempting them from some of the routine checks on the way. They were given a *laissez-passer* (free pass), enjoying the status of an official embassy. The group included Lenin, Nadezhda Krupskaya, the ever-attending Zinovievs, Inessa Armand, and Karl Radek among the Bolsheviks, but there were many from other parties. In the end, three shipments of revolutionaries, totalling 650 people and including eminent Mensheviks such as Pavel Aksel'rod and Iulii Martov, returned to Russia across Germany by train. Lenin's transport is widely known as 'Lenin's sealed train'. Each of these terms is essentially wrong. It was not 'Lenin's' but shared by others including non-Bolsheviks. It was not 'sealed'—they left it for a night to sleep in a hotel in Frankfurt—or 'secret' in that it was met by supporters in many places, though under the terms of the agreement the passengers could not talk to them. To be pedantic, it was not even a train, just a carriage which was attached to various regular trains. However, the biggest and most misleading consequence was that Lenin's enemies thereafter were able to call him a German agent. While Lenin and members of other radical parties clearly received help from Germany and probably laundered funds, he was in no sense an agent of German policy. He did not deviate one centimetre from his commitments under German pressure, and was not under any form of control by them. The facts were clearly laid out many years ago, but, because they suit particular discourses about Lenin, the charges have re-emerged on a large scale in post-communist Russia and elsewhere.[23]

Similar discourses have also claimed Lenin did not expect revolution at that time, but even a cursory examination of Lenin's writings and speeches

38 LENIN LIVES?

in his last weeks in Switzerland show such interpretations to lack evidence. His often-quoted comment that there was a 'grave-like stillness' across Europe is actually part of a warning by Lenin not to under-estimate the revolution, as the next sentence clearly reveals. He tells his audience not to be 'deceived by the grave-like stillness in Europe. Europe is pregnant with revolution'. The wide misquote that Lenin supposedly said in February 1917 that he would not live to see the revolution actually reads that 'we of the older generation may not live to see the decisive battles of the coming revolution', which clearly means he might not see its final stages, quite a different statement.[24]

So Lenin set out for Petrograd full of determination to guide the revolution into what he believed were the correct channels. He was impatient to return, unlike his previous visit to Russia in 1905. That, too, was brought about by revolution but ended up with Lenin fleeing, at risk of his life, across melting ice. Was that in Lenin's mind when, on leaving Switzerland, he joked to his travel companions that in three months time they would either be in power or hanged? Would his new adventure turn out more auspiciously than its predecessor?

To Power and Beyond

i) From the Finland Station to Finnish Exile: April to July 1917

Lenin's political life had been a long haul over more than twenty years of polemic, organization, congresses, resolutions, a myriad of articles, many pamphlets, two books, exile, skimping and saving, the consolatory charms of nature, warm companionship, bitter enmities, and endless self-sacrifice. He may have had an inkling his body would not support him for long into the future, but the next five years of his life were tumultuous and unpredictable even by his standards. He returned to Petrograd in April 1917. Increasingly, his old frailties brought on by stress caused him crippling insomnia and weakness, leading to debilitating strokes in May and December 1922, and a third in 1923 which heralded his death on 21 January 1924. The twists and turns of his life would have brought a snort of incredulity even from a Hollywood scriptwriter. Lenin was projected from refugee to ruler of the physically largest country in the world within six and a half months. How?

In Soviet days, propaganda portrayed a smooth transition from Lenin being welcomed by adoring crowds at the Finland Station, and steadily accruing mass support as the months went by and relentless Bolshevik

LENIN BEFORE LENINISM   39

propaganda opened people's eyes, until they swept the Bolsheviks into power on an unstoppable wave of enthusiasm. Such was the fairy story. If we only take one aspect of Lenin's life in the revolutionary months, notably his whereabouts, we have to factor the following into the equation. After his arrival on 5 April Lenin lived openly for only three months. In early July he fled Petrograd and went back underground, in Petrograd and then Finland, where his only communication with the party was through the post, telegraph, and personal envoys. He was always a day or two behind the curve on events in Petrograd. When he retreated in July he proclaimed the situation had returned to the pre-war period of repression and it was time for the party to return to the underground. This was a stunning point to make, implying major defeat, a position underlined by his abandonment of soviets as progressive institutions and considering them to be counter-revolutionary. Yet by the second week of September, still in hiding, Lenin sensed that a mighty revolutionary opportunity was brewing and he began to bombard a sceptical Central Committee in Petrograd with a series of demands for them to prepare, and here he went back to 1905 in another sense, an armed uprising. His fellow leaders were sceptical and Lenin's frustration reached such a crescendo that he left Helsinki and returned to Petrograd to personally impose his view on a reluctant party leadership, which he partly did on 10 October. He remained in hiding but in a safe house in Petrograd, only emerging late on 24 October to burst into the party and Soviet headquarters of the Smolny Institute and proclaim the overthrow of the Provisional Government and their replacement by a temporary Soviet Government. Two weeks after returning from Helsinki he was in power. The fairy-tale view said it was achieved as a result of party discipline, brilliant advanced planning, and Lenin's charismatic leadership. In reality, continuing party arguments show it was not party discipline which had brought this outcome. The endless last-minute improvisations showed that there was no prepared blueprint being applied. Lenin's absence from the immediate scene made it hard to see how he could have exerted sustained leadership. Was it following his theories which had raised him up? How did their generalizations impact on a volatile situation? It was much more a question of 'events, dear boy, events',[25] and Lenin's inspired improvisations which had brought him there, with a slice of good fortune to help him on his way.

Lenin's path from April to power was a rollercoaster. When he returned, the Bolsheviks were still a very small underground group, vastly outmatched on the left by the Socialist Revolutionary Party which was well-represented among the workers of Petrograd and Moscow in addition to the peasant

40 LENIN LIVES?

constituency which it considered to be its own. The Mensheviks were the second largest party after the Socialist Revolutionaries (the SRs) in the major factories of the capitals, and were a clear majority of the left in their Georgian stronghold in the Caucasus and south Russia. With only an estimated 10,000 members nationwide in a population of 120 million, the Bolsheviks seemed a long way from power or even influence. Lenin's first challenging act on his return was to give a brief but brilliant, penetrating, and widely misunderstood analysis of the situation. In 'The Tasks of the Proletariat in the Present Revolution', better known as 'The April Theses', he cut open the current political situation, defined where the party should stand, asserted what its priorities should be, and added a short list of tasks to tidy the situation up. All accomplished in a three-page list of ten propositions. Lenin's Ten Commandments. In essence he said that, despite the overthrow of the tsar in February, the war remained an imperialist war which should be opposed by socialists and workers. This was targeted at a new wave of 'defencists' arguing that the interest of the left was now to defend newly democratic Russia, even though it had been correct not to defend tsarist Russia. Ever keen to locate situations in broader theory, Lenin argued that the revolution was 'passing from its first stage... which placed power into the hands of the bourgeoisie' to its 'second stage which must place power into the hands of the proletariat' and the poorest peasants.[26] Lenin was arguing that whereas, before February, the focus had been on the necessary bourgeois-democratic revolution, now that had been accomplished it was necessary to focus on the next step, power passing to the propertyless working people. This was consistent with his proposals since around 1905 and shows clearly that Lenin worked to the standard Marxist 'theory of stages'. His main implication arising from this definition was that, whereas limited co-operation with bourgeois liberals and others was acceptable in the first stage of the revolution which was geared towards establishing democracy, under the conditions of the second stage of the revolution, when the aim was to move on to begin the transformation to socialism, it was vital not to get mixed up with them as that would dilute the strategy and tactics for achieving the transition to socialism. This led him to state starkly, in the third thesis, that there should be 'No support for the Provisional Government'. This was the clause which caused the most controversy and which also was, ultimately, the most instrumental in bringing the Bolsheviks to power, though it is unlikely Lenin foresaw the full implications of its effect until later. Even close party friends challenged Lenin over it. It was assumed across the whole left, and the Petrograd Soviet had

LENIN BEFORE LENINISM   41

built its tactics around it, that for the time being, when it was feared that counter-revolution might assert itself at any moment—for instance a military coup conducted by reactionary officers using selected troops from the front, or the Cossacks or Muslim troops such as the Chechen 'Wild Division', a loose equivalent of the British use of Nepalese Gurkhas for extreme tasks—it was necessary for all the pro-February forces to stand together against the threat. However, Lenin prevailed in arguments over the next fortnight. Other key statements included the apparently puzzling assertion that 'it is not our *immediate* task to *introduce* socialism' and, in conformity with the concept of 'Finance Capital', that the banks should be nationalized. This was seen as a short, sharp way to take control over investment flows and capital itself. In addition, there were a number of 'housekeeping' provisions to adjust the party to the new circumstances. These included a new name; an expressed preference for soviets over parliamentary institutions; the need for a new International purged of the 'defencist traitors' of July 1914; and some sweeping statements about 'abolition of the police, army and bureaucracy'. Derived from the practices of the short-lived Paris Commune which were admired by Marx, Lenin proposed that state officials should be elected, recallable, and paid two-thirds of a worker's wage, clauses intended to keep elected officials close to those who elected them and prevent them from becoming a self-interested superior group. It is often argued that Lenin was planting the flag of immediate transition to socialist revolution, a kind of fusion with Trotsky's concept of 'permanent revolution'. While Lenin waxed hot and cold on how far off the revolution was, the April Theses were based on the realistic assumption that there was a long way to go since the Bolsheviks were, in Lenin's words, 'in a small minority', even in the soviets, and that it would be necessary 'to present a patient, systematic and persistent explanation' of the errors of the majority in order to win them over. This implied a possibly lengthy timescale.[27]

Over the following weeks Lenin began to hope revolution might be close. In July, a force of revolutionary sailors from Kronstadt, in a still controversial incident, swept into Petrograd and could easily have overthrown the Provisional Government. They failed to do so because no party, including the Bolsheviks, was prepared to lead them to that goal. This was not only bitterly disappointing for the Kronstadters, but deeply unexpected. Only a month earlier Lenin had spoken loud and clear at the First All-Russian Congress of Soviets to proclaim that, despite being in a minority (there were 285 Socialist Revolutionaries, 248 Mensheviks, 105 Bolsheviks, 32 Menshevik Internationalists), the Bolsheviks were ready to take power immediately.

42 LENIN LIVES?

The July Day crisis showed they were not. Instead, the sailors were persuaded to return to their base.

This failure changed the whole dynamic of the revolution, halting the revolutionary momentum which had prevailed up to then and replacing it with the only serious counter-revolutionary conjuncture of the months between February and October. There are many suggestions as to why Lenin had refused to sanction a possible 'July Revolution'. The official line of later Soviet historians, echoed by many other supporters of Lenin, was that it was his tactical genius which recognized that such a seizure of power would have been unsustainable at that time. Others argue that Lenin was not in control of the movement and he distrusted it. Maybe it was just a mistake. In any case, its consequences for Lenin were clear. The tide had turned. The Provisional Government was determined to press on with the war and it saw the fallout from July as a moment it could grasp to fight against the anti-war left. Arrest warrants were made out for Lenin and other Bolshevik leaders, together with the release of forged materials purporting to show that they were working as German agents. Lenin, taking no chances, went underground, moving seventeen times between safe houses in Petrograd before leaving surreptitiously for Finland in early August with constant companion Zinoviev, finding safe haven initially just across the border in Sestroretsk—including living in a straw shelter in a field for a while when the police were close—and then Helsinki, where he remained until just over two weeks before he came to power. Initially, he occupied those weeks in writing his most important theoretical work, *The State and Revolution*, whose title itself evoked the revolutionary anarchist and socialist Mikhail Bakunin rather than Marx.

ii) Pause for Thought: *The State and Revolution*

The State and Revolution can be best understood as a meditation on the ten-point plan, the 'April Theses', which Lenin, at the moment of his return to Petrograd, put forward as the basis for the party's approach to the deepening revolutionary situation. As we will see, in keeping the party out of any entanglement with the Provisional Government, Lenin had constructed a key which unlocked the door to power (although this was probably as much by luck as by judgement). We have already noted that the April Theses derived a pattern of revolutionary government from Marx's writings on the Paris Commune of 1871. There have been suggestions that Marx misunderstood the practices of the Commune.[28] That suggestion has been highly contested, but for present purposes the point is that Lenin took Marx's

LENIN BEFORE LENINISM   43

analysis as his guide for post-revolutionary action. It is frequently and quite correctly said that neither Marx, nor Lenin, nor hardly any Marxist, had devoted much time to speculating on what to do when, and if, they came to power. Most attention was focused on overthrowing bourgeois rule. That prospect itself seemed so remote that musing on what would come after was constantly postponed. Lenin and his contemporaries were the first to conduct a revolution inspired by Marx's ideas and they had scant material to take them forward. The Paris Commune model was one of the few exceptions, and Lenin seized on it. The issue of whether the situation faced by the Bolsheviks in 1917 accurately mapped onto the realities of the Commune was not thought about. Nor was the fact that the Commune leaders were barely influenced by Marx and his ideas. They were much more indebted to Bakunin, another irony which spoke to the Bakuninist undercurrents within Lenin himself. Be that as it may, Lenin was, and of this he was fully aware, like Magellan rounding Cape Horn, the first (along with his comrades) to break through the demanding, treacherous, narrow strait of revolution and set sail on the great ocean of socialist transition. Without a serious chart. Making the breakthrough from the stage of taking power to that of building socialism was in itself an achievement. The 'April Theses' and *The State and Revolution* made up the first course to be plotted in this unknown, and not very pacific, ocean. It was extremely short-lived.

The main themes of *The State and Revolution* pick up a number of the cryptic points made in the 'April Theses'. These included the often overlooked but vital key to Lenin's governance, the statement that 'it is not our *immediate* task to *introduce* socialism'. The only apparent step towards socialism is the stipulation, derived from Hilferding's concept of 'Finance Capital', that the banks should be nationalized. In a breathtaking if ambiguous sentence Lenin called for 'abolition of the police, army and bureaucracy'.[29] At the time, this extraordinary (and very Bakuninist) notion appeared to apply not only to the collapsing post-tsarist state but as a postrevolutionary principle as well. It appeared to promote the replacement of professional police, army, and civil service with democratically accountable alternatives, notably a citizen police force, a citizen militia army, and a rotation of administrative tasks. This interpretation is borne out by the further clause that government officials should be elected, recallable, and paid twothirds of a worker's wages. There was also a clearly expressed preference for soviets as the future basis of government rather than parliamentary institutions. *The State and Revolution* set out to establish these principles and put them at the heart of the main task after the seizure of power, transition.

44 LENIN LIVES?

Marx had not made much of an issue of transition. To simplify, his essential view was that the 'emancipation of the working classes must be conquered by the working classes themselves'.[30] By following their desire to regain control over their work and share the profits of their own labour they would eventually realize they were not pursuing separate struggles against individual owners, but were conducting a struggle against the capitalist system itself. This would raise their awareness of their position and increase their class solidarity. They would then band together, united by class consciousness, and take over the ownership of the means of production—factories, land, capital—and create shared rather than private appropriation of profit created by their labour. For Marx, the very functions of capitalism—especially competition and the pursuit of profit—would create the necessary conditions for the workers to take control. By 1900 this had not happened, and Lenin had already made a controversial name for himself with his call, in *What is to be Done?*, not only for a party to push this process along but one composed of 'professional revolutionaries'. Closely associated with this was Lenin's idea of 'advanced' and 'backward' workers. The former were advanced in the sense of having a relatively highly developed class consciousness while the backward workers had a way to go. The revolutionary process, with Lenin's major tweak, was not the unaided process envisaged by Marx but one in which an elite with advanced class consciousness would develop an equivalent consciousness among their 'backward' sisters and brothers. It is hard, as we have already noted, to see how such a concept is compatible with democracy. The function of the Leninist party is not to represent the actually existing workers, but to educate them and raise their consciousness. In this respect it is a Confucian hierarchy of teacher and respectful student. In Lenin's eyes there is no way that the enlightened should give way to the unenlightened even if the former constituted a small minority. There is an element of democracy in that the goal is to win over, not only the majority, but eventually the totality of working women and men, and also that the whole enterprise is geared to their liberation. However, while the shining future might be democratic, the rocky path towards it was not. The idea of 'raising consciousness' spilled over the first step in revolution—taking power—and remained fundamental to post-revolutionary transition. It did not remain static—this is Lenin we are dealing with here—but it did remain crucial throughout most of the Soviet period of Russian history, from 1917 to at least 1964 and, some might argue, 1981. The Soviet Union is often considered to be the model of a socialist economy and society. However, for its architects and ideologists it was never more than a work in progress, a society aiming for socialism and communism but not one in which the process was complete. Stalin, Khrushchev, and Brezhnev claimed fundamental aspects of socialism had been achieved, but none of them believed it was a complete socialist society. Lenin certainly did not. The essence of the Soviet experience was a series of attempts to fulfil that transition. The 'April Theses' and *The State and Revolution* were at the heart of the short-lived first attempt.

From our viewpoint of looking at Lenin's legacy, we should note that despite the brevity of its application, barely six months, *The State and Revolution* has become enshrined for many as the main transition strategy adopted by Lenin. This is because of the prominence of *The State and Revolution* in discussion of the topic. As one of Lenin's few extended pamphlets and the fact it was written in the heat of the revolutionary battle, it has had great influence among Leninists and other revolutionaries. It became widely known and was, especially in the early years when hard information was scarce, believed to be an essential guide to Lenin's route to successfully taking power and to the consequential steps towards socialist construction. It fulfils neither of these functions. Lenin's path to power was improvised and somewhat last-minute, rather than being the result of a brilliant, pre-planned strategy, and the principles enunciated in the pamphlet were either not implemented after October 1917 or were quickly abandoned. Such actualities were barely noticed by those gathering around Lenin outside Soviet Russia. The subsequent alterations of priority, so-called war communism and the provisions of the New Economic Policy (NEP), were seen as temporary deviations from the principles of the first six months. Did Stalin, then, when he broke with NEP, revert to the original principles? We will touch on this later. But first, what was at the heart of the revolutionary transition embodied in *The State and Revolution* and the 'April Theses', and why was it modified so quickly?

As the title suggests, the question of the state is central to Lenin's thinking here. His argument sets out from Marx's comment about the Paris Commune that it had shown the way for future revolutionaries by not trying to take over the existing state but to 'smash' it completely. Lenin picked this up. He also made two important comments linked to this central insight. Marx had stipulated that it was 'continental states' that must be smashed, omitting the 'Anglo-Saxon liberty' states of the United States, and Britain, where the process might be different because they lacked military cliques and bureaucracy. Lenin argued that the growth of imperialism and monopoly capitalism had slammed the door shut on any parliamentary or

46   LENIN LIVES?

traditionally 'democratic' path to revolution.[31] Second, Lenin was aware
that this did not abolish bureaucracy itself: 'abolishing bureaucracy' is 'a
utopia' but 'to smash the old bureaucratic state machine' is not.[32] At risk of
over-interpreting, we might note that this rows back slightly from the April
Theses which mentioned abolition of bureaucracy without any such condition. Even so, Lenin is clear. The state must be uprooted and replaced. The
problem then loomed—how would it be replaced?

Again picking up from Marx, Lenin said the first phase of political
transition would be 'the dictatorship of the proletariat'.[33] Use of this phrase
has always been a 'gotcha' moment for anti-Leninists. It proves, they said,
that Lenin had dictatorial rather than democratic instincts. Some of his
defenders have argued that the term did not have such deeply authoritarian
dimensions as it does in the post Hitler-Stalin-Mussolini era. This is
misleading. Lenin himself, in spring 1918, described the term 'dictatorship'
as 'a big word, and big words should not be thrown about carelessly.
Dictatorship is iron rule'.[34] It implied, as Lenin says, 'coercion'. Future
communist society would run without coercion, achieve real democracy for
the first time in human history, and even go beyond that democracy which
will 'wither away'. In Lenin's words:

> Only in communist society, when the resistance of the capitalists has dis-
> appeared, when there are no classes (i.e., when there is no distinction
> between the members of society as regards their relation to the social
> means of production), only then 'the state...ceases to exist', and 'it
> becomes possible to speak of freedom'. Only then will a truly complete
> democracy become possible and be realized, a democracy without any
> exceptions whatever. And only then will democracy begin to wither
> away, owing to the simple fact that, freed from capitalist slavery, from
> the untold horrors, savagery, absurdities, and infamies of capitalist
> exploitation, people will gradually become accustomed to observing the
> elementary rules of social intercourse that have been known for centuries
> and repeated for thousands of years in all copy-book maxims. They will
> become accustomed to observing them without force, without coercion,
> without subordination, without the special apparatus for coercion
> called the state.

He defines it further: 'the dictatorship of the proletariat imposes a series of
restrictions on the freedom of the oppressors, the exploiters, the capitalists.
We must suppress them in order to free humanity from wage slavery, their

LENIN BEFORE LENINISM 47

resistance must be crushed by force.' However, at this point, Lenin minimizes the problems and suggests that crushing opponents by force might be less harsh than it sounds:

> during the transition from capitalism to communism suppression is still necessary, but it is now the suppression of the exploiting minority by the exploited majority. A special apparatus, a special machine for suppression, the 'state', is still necessary, but this is now a transitional state. It is no longer a state in the proper sense of the word; for the suppression of the minority of exploiters by the majority of the wage slaves of yesterday is comparatively so easy, simple and natural a task that it will entail far less bloodshed than the suppression of the risings of slaves, serfs or wage-laborers, and it will cost mankind far less. And it is compatible with the extension of democracy to such an overwhelming majority of the population that the need for a special machine of suppression will begin to disappear. Naturally, the exploiters are unable to suppress the people without a highly complex machine for performing this task, but the people can suppress the exploiters even with a very simple 'machine', almost without a 'machine', without a special apparatus, by the simple organization of the armed people (such as the Soviets of Workers' and Soldiers' Deputies, we would remark, running ahead).[35]

Further aspects of the transitional 'dictatorship' also give an optimistic gloss on the degree of coercion which will be needed. The specific features of the state are already sketched in the April Theses and centre on the election of all state officials, who would be recallable by a petition from their electors, and limiting their salaries to two-thirds of the wage of the average skilled worker. These provisions were intended to prevent 'careerism' whereby bureaucrats looked to climb the greasy pole of promotion by seeking favour with their superiors rather than their client masses. There would also be a rotation by which all citizens would spend a limited amount of time in the state administration. A standing professional army would be replaced by 'the armed people'.[36] The point here was that it would deprive a potential oppressor of the means to oppress because, Lenin assumed, the people would not be stupid enough to oppress themselves.[37] All citizens would be trained to bear arms and serve a term in the people's militia. The police would be organized on similar lines. The outcome, Lenin proclaimed in a ringing phrase, would be that 'under socialism all will govern in turn and will soon become accustomed to no one governing'.[38]

48 LENIN LIVES?

He went even further. Following Hilferding's views on the latest form which capital had taken, finance capital, and the fact that investment decisions were taken by managers of other people's money—banks and the like—it was now the case, Lenin concluded, that the flow of capital could be controlled by revolutionaries simply by nationalizing banks and supervising their operations. Capital could be directed according to social and government priorities, not private pursuit and appropriation of profit. It was, Lenin startlingly concluded, within the competence of anyone who knew basic arithmetic and literacy. The complexities of the modern economy could be reduced to routine operations and the social economy could be run along the lines of, Lenin said, the German post office. 'The accounting and control necessary for this have been *simplified* by capitalism to the utmost and reduced to the extraordinarily simple operations—which any literate person can perform—of supervising and recording, knowledge of the four rules of arithmetic, and issuing appropriate receipts.'[39] In Lenin's words:

> Given these economic preconditions, it is quite possible, after the overthrow of the capitalists and the bureaucrats, to proceed immediately, overnight, to replace them in the control over production and distribution, in the work of keeping account of labour and products, by the armed workers, by the whole of the armed population.[40]

Immediately! Overnight!

Lenin was quick to distinguish the administrators from the skilled technocracy needed to run a modern society. He emphasized that

> The question of control and accounting should not be confused with the question of the scientifically trained staff of engineers, agronomists, and so on. These gentlemen are working today in obedience to the wishes of the capitalists and will work even better tomorrow in obedience to the wishes of the armed workers.

This last sentence encapsulated the kind of supervision and coercion the dictatorship of the proletariat required in general. In 'April Theses' he had put it thus: 'It is not our *immediate* task to *introduce* socialism but only soviet supervision of production and distribution.'[41] The relationship implies the continuation, during a transitional period of undefined length, of capitalists, private ownership, and market relations. Later in 1917, the

LENIN BEFORE LENINISM   49

idea of nationalization was extended to include the main 'trusts' and 'monopolies' producing steel, coal, and other essential products in order to extend leverage over the remaining capitalists. In an unspecified amount of time the private sector would decline and disappear and the public sector would grow and take over the economy. It was also Bolshevik policy that land should be nationalized.

Unfortunately, we do not have the final sections of the pamphlet because Lenin turned to making revolution, not writing about it. In the completed sections he hardly referred to soviets but used Marx's term 'communes', in honour of the Paris Commune, as their nearest equivalent. They were to be, Lenin insisted, different from most parliamentary bodies in combining executive and legislative functions. The result, together with the other elements mentioned, would produce an 'active' democracy of permanent participation by all citizens. Parliamentary democracy involved only intermittent mass involvement, in periodic elections which might only be once in five years or more, in which, as Marx had commented as paraphrased by Lenin, 'the oppressed are allowed once every few years to decide which particular representatives of the oppressing class shall represent and repress them in parliament.'[42]

In *The State and Revolution* Lenin had outlined his plan for transition. The bourgeois state would be smashed and the dictatorship of the proletariat would be much less oppressive than its predecessor and would wither away as it achieved greater control, as its fundamental aims quickly became universally accepted and therefore the element of coercion would no longer be necessary. *The State and Revolution* is the most influential of Lenin's writings. It stands out above the two other major items from which, altogether, most of the key ideas associated with Lenin have sprung, namely *What is to be Done?* and *Imperialism*. Critics point out, with some justification, that much of what Lenin proposes in *The State and Revolution* is naive. The pamphlet is also repetitive and sometimes rather obscure. Nonetheless, it is one of the greatest sources of inspiration for Leninists and formed a basic model for many communists and communist parties, and even for more independent-minded leftists. This is hard to equate with the fact that the ideas outlined in it had very little relation to the historical experience of the Russian Revolution. Lenin's actual path to power was very different from anything one could derive from *The State and Revolution* or, indeed, any of Lenin's or anyone else's theoretical writings. It is also the case that the model derived from the 'April Theses' and *The State and Revolution* lasted barely six months beyond October before being fundamentally

50   LENIN LIVES?

revised. So what did propel Lenin from his Finnish hiding place to heading Russia's government within four months?

iii) 'The Great October Socialist Revolution'

In August 1917, Lenin was hiding in a Finnish haystack. The thought that power was three months away seemed improbable in the extreme. Lenin himself wrote that the Bolsheviks were back to pretty much square one. The situation was comparable to the moment of reverting to the underground in the face of repression in 1907–8. Power seemed further away than ever, not least because, as Lenin also insisted, the soviets were in the counter-revolutionary hands of defencists who were nothing more than a fig leaf concealing the actual imperialist interests which were dominating the Provisional Government. In such circumstances, the slogan 'All Power to the Soviets' was no longer valid. The Bolsheviks were deprived of liberty (not only was Lenin holed up in Helsinki, but Trotsky had surrendered himself to the authorities as a challenge and he and others were in government prisons) and of any immediate strategy. It looked more like the end of their hopes, not the immediate prelude to their realization. However, it was one event which, once more, turned the tide completely and, through exercise of Lenin's brilliant analysis of the prevailing political conjuncture and the unforeseen critical outcome of a key provision of the April Theses, Lenin and his party were actually about to be catapulted into a power they could barely have dreamed of. Another wild historical trick was about to be played.

In the July Days the left had overplayed its hand and opened up the only significant wave of resistance to the ongoing revolution which had been instrumental in creating a diversity of power through a multitude of self-assertive soviets, military committees in the army and navy, factory committees, village and *volost'* (parish committees) in the countryside, trade unions, and political parties across the spectrum, making Russia in 1917 arguably the most democratic large country the world has ever seen. From the political sphere the social movement, especially the over 80per cent of the country which was peasant, was moving rapidly towards a democratic division of property, especially land.

The moment of respite, for the displaced elites trying to control this revolutionary wave, was fleeting. They, too, undermined themselves by overplaying their hand. In this case it was the actions of the Supreme Commander of the Army, General Lavr Kornilov which rebounded spectacularly. Under the influence of many members of the elite begging him to take action to prevent the further disintegration, as they saw it, of traditional Russia, and fearing that the only beneficiaries of the situation would be the German invaders, Kornilov made a move in the last week of September, the precise objectives of which are unclear to the present day but the consequences of which are crystal clear. Kornilov ordered a hand-picked squad of Chechens and other tribal non-Russian troops to advance on Petrograd. Was Kornilov trying to support the Provisional Government, as he and his supporters claimed, by carrying out the orders of Prime Minister Kerensky, or was he also planning to displace the Provisional Government or at least put himself at the head of it as a military dictator? Whatever it was, it failed. Kerensky came to believe Kornilov wanted to overthrow him, ordered his arrest, and made a deal with the Petrograd Soviet to release its imprisoned members, such as Trotsky, and to give it weapons to repel Kornilov's force.

In fact, the weapons were not needed. Railwaymen held up Kornilov's progress by train and Chechen-speaking propagandists were sent out by the Petrograd Soviet, who explained to Kornilov's troops that they were being used to suppress democracy and the revolution. They quickly refused to obey orders and Kornilov's coup, which is what it most likely was, failed ignominiously. But that was not the most serious consequence. It had two absolutely corrosive effects, eating away the supports on which the Provisional Government had claimed to stand. First, although he eventually sided with the Petrograd Soviet, Kerensky was widely believed to have helped instigate the coup in the first place and his prestige and that of the government imploded like a burst balloon. Central power had practically disappeared. There was a dangerous vacuum at the level of national government. Second, Kornilov's actions galvanized the left. It was a clear warning that the revolution was not yet won. Workers, peasants, soldiers, sailors, and their representatives in soviets and committees started a new revolutionary wave to, in the phrase of the period, 'defend the gains of the February Revolution'. There was also rampant inflation taking essential goods, especially foodstuffs, out of the purchasing range of increasing parts of the urban working population. Peasants increasingly felt that they must seize their opportunity to make what they considered a more just distribution of land and, from September, a wave of land seizures swept the country for the next six months. Like those who had forced the abdication of the tsar in March, Kornilov and his plotters had planned to stop the revolution in its tracks. Instead they had fuelled a new, more violent, wave of radicalization.

The Bolsheviks had played no significant part in these events. Lenin and Zinoviev were still in hiding, Trotsky was only released as the coup

52   LENIN LIVES?

collapsed. Stalin led the party in the semi-underground conditions imposed after July. However, even in July, Lenin had argued that, in the event of a new revolutionary upsurge, the tactic of armed uprising and the objective of soviet power might, once more, be realizable. Lenin became very excited by the post-Kornilov conjuncture and quickly grasped its implications. He began to write a series of letters to the Central Committee and other party bodies calling for armed uprising and a soviet takeover of power. His fellow leaders in Petrograd simply thought he was out of touch. Their inactivity even led Lenin to make the extraordinary threat that he would resign from the leadership and return to the party rank and file to fight for his idea. His writings were volatile and urgent. At times, maybe simply for propaganda purposes, maybe not, he dreamed of a situation where, after taking power, it could pass between one soviet party and another in a peaceful and orderly fashion. Musings of this kind soon gave way to the more familiar insistence that the party should take power itself. He suggested, at different moments during his energetic campaign, that the uprising might begin in Moscow, Petrograd, Helsinki, or in the fleet at Reval/Tallinn. No one seemed to agree, and the wild changes of scenario seemed to support the view that Lenin was out of touch. It certainly shows there was no blueprint being realized in these weeks. It was only his return on 10 October which began to bring the Central Committee round to his way of thinking, once again showing that the key feature of Bolshevism was following Lenin, not any particular doctrine or strategy. Even so, it took a second meeting on 16 October to hammer the message home. The complexity of those final days is beyond our current remit, but we should note that the initial moves of the final drama came from the Provisional Government. Realizing the threat of an attempt to seize power focused on the upcoming Second Congress of Soviets, the Provisional Government sent out troops to guard strategic points in Petrograd, with a view to controlling the city and preventing the Congress from convening. The Petrograd Soviet countered by sending its forces—Red Guards, civilians, sympathetic military units—to persuade the government troops to return to base, which they did. In this way the Military Revolutionary Committee of the Petrograd Soviet found itself in charge of the capital. On the night of 24/25 October Lenin broke cover and joined the activities at the Soviet headquarters at the Smolny Institute. Lenin drafted a proclamation of soviet power and the overthrow of the Provisional Government. The ministers were arrested, although the prime minister, Kerensky, had slipped out of the city to raise troops to reassert control. Despite putting a raggle-taggle force of Red Guards to flight in a skirmish at

LENIN BEFORE LENINISM 53

Gatchina in the suburbs, Kerensky's attempt failed when, like Kornilov's force, propagandists talked the rank and file out of doing the officers' dirty work for them.[43]

As one acute observer put it at the time, the Bolsheviks had not seized power, they had found it lying in the streets and picked it up. Lenin's draft decrees were accepted by the majority of delegates at the Second Congress, which had succeeded in convening only to provide convenient cover for what quickly became a Bolshevik, not Soviet, seizure of power. The first key difference between the two was that Lenin aspired to full control of government by the Bolsheviks alone, while most supporters of soviet power wanted governmental responsibilities to be shared by a coalition of all soviet-based political parties. Within days Lenin had prevailed, although, for the first six months, he was forced to accept a small number of Left Socialist Revolutionary ministers in the new government.

Lenin was not propelled into power by a great mass of workers in the streets chanting his name and acclaiming his genius, as portrayed in later propaganda. It is unlikely most workers even knew his name at this moment. They certainly had no idea what Bolshevism stood for. Its long term goals encompassed world revolution and the transformation of humanity. Why was it that, of all the left-wing forces of the moment, it was Lenin and the Bolsheviks who came to power? Whatever it was, did it reflect on Lenin's theory, practice, or ideas? There are two main considerations we need to look at.

First, the way Lenin came to power had little to do with his theories. It was not the outcome of a decisive plan implemented by a vast and organized party. There were probably some 250,000 members, most of whom had joined since the spring and had hardly had time to understand the deeper policies of the party, still less to become disciplined. Politics at the time was volatile. Most of those who came over to the Bolsheviks seem to have come from the Mensheviks. But it was here that Lenin had made his impact, not as a theoretical genius but as a brilliant tactician and improviser who probably enjoyed, as is widely the case for the successful, an often unacknowledged element of luck. Two features brought the masses over to support the Bolsheviks at this crucial moment. First, while many had changed allegiance from one party to another, they had remained loyal to their programme. They wanted the war to end, economic improvement, land redistribution, and, more strongly than before, a transfer of power to the soviets. The slogans Peace, Bread, Land, and All Power to the Soviets had appeared early in the revolution. They were initially anarchist and SR slogans as much as

54 LENIN LIVES?

Bolshevik ones but in the heat of October they were strongly associated with the Bolsheviks. There is no mystery as to why this was happening. The majority of the leaderships of the other major parties of the left—the Mensheviks and the Socialist Revolutionaries—had been sucked into support of the Provisional Government in line with their defencist principles of 1914, heightened by the additional argument for 'revolutionary defencism' since February. Their aim in supporting the Provisional Government was to save Russia from collapse and defeat in the war which would not only wreck the country but destroy the revolution itself. The problem for them was that their supporters did not go along with them. The street protestors certainly did not want Russia to be defeated but they did want a negotiated end to the war plus land redistribution and an end to inflation and economic crisis. That is what their slogans meant. Land redistribution had been the keynote policy of the Socialist Revolutionaries from their earliest origins. However, the SRs in power were reluctant to press for it as it would, they believed, antagonize their middle-class and landowner allies in the nation-saving coalition. It had to be postponed until after the war. The peasants and workers were in no mood for delay, especially after the Kornilov affair. Even before it they had begun to turn against their former allegiance and begin to vote for Bolsheviks, seeking, as it were, better Mensheviks.

So why did the Bolsheviks appear to be the 'better Mensheviks' the masses were looking for? First and foremost, perhaps with a great slice of good fortune thrown in, Lenin's demand in the April Theses that the Bolsheviks should give no support to the Provisional Government turned out to be the vital ingredient. It paid a vast and unforeseen dividend. By staying out of the Provisional Government, the Bolsheviks, unlike the Menshevik and SR leaders who eventually came to dominate it, were not weighed down by its failure. Quite the reverse. As the prestige of Kerensky and the Provisional Government imploded, so Bolshevik stock rose rapidly as the disillusioned Menshevik and SR masses had nowhere to go but the Bolsheviks as the only force of any size on the left remaining untainted by association with Provisional Government failure and reluctance to implement the masses' revolutionary programme.

As the most brilliant observer of day-to-day politics in Petrograd, N. N. Sukhanov—a Menshevik Internationalist associate of the novelist Maxim Gorky, a long-time Lenin supporter and fundraiser; and of Iulii Martov, Lenin's former friend and close associate from before 1903; and very close to Lenin in principle—reflected that the Menshevik and SR leadership remained divided from the Bolsheviks for two reasons.[44]

LENIN BEFORE LENINISM   55

The Bolsheviks were closer to the masses and the rest of the left-wing leaders did not trust the uneducated worker and peasant masses—sometimes referred to as the dark people—and did not believe them to be capable of taking over the revolution. For his admirers, Lenin's apparent confidence in the people was a very positive feature. For his critics, including—very vociferously—his friend, ally, and party donor Maxim Gorky, it was a desperate gamble on the violent, the uneducated, and the uncivilised masses, especially the peasants.

Sukhanov's second, equally perceptive point, was that he did not believe the sincerity of the Bolsheviks in proclaiming Peace, Bread, Land, and All Power to the Soviets. Or to be precise, he saw those terms having one meaning for the masses—essentially their everyday meaning—but having alternative meanings for Lenin and Trotsky, notably civil war, state control of land, and Bolshevik not soviet power. It was here that Lenin's policies and actions had been able to make a major impact, not so much through application of theory as through brilliant improvisation, which his enemies often saw, and continue to do, as manipulation and deception.

The Bolsheviks came to power on a policy of Peace, Bread and Land, and All Power to the Soviets. However, as Lenin stated several times in 1917, a soviet revolution would not bring peace but civil war, a contingency he had been planning for since early in the war. Nonetheless, a Decree on Peace was drawn up, broadcast to the world via the radio network which hardly anyone listened to, and immediately became irrelevant to international relations. It did, however, retain significant propaganda value for the Bolsheviks, for the moment at least. It made them appear to be champions of peace even as they engaged in civil war. Additionally, a new round of revolution would not heal the economy and provide 'Bread', that is, improved living standards. Lenin did argue a soviet takeover was the only thing that could be done to avoid economic collapse, but common sense and post-October reality show there was no substance to this claim. October accelerated economic collapse. It did nothing to avert it. Similarly, on the question of 'Land', Bolshevik policy was that it should be nationalized. They did not want to see it parcelled up in private plots by what they considered a petit-bourgeois peasantry which was market-oriented and lacked socialist sympathies, a point they, and notably Lenin, had forcefully argued since their origin in the 1890s, against the SR/populist view of peasants as naturally socialist. However, in October Lenin had the Second Congress of Soviets agree to a Decree on Land based almost completely on SR policy. Like the Decree on Peace, it had little practical effect in that it merely sanctioned the land seizures on which the peasants were already actively engaged, without the impact of any paper decree from anyone. In 1919, the Bolsheviks nationalized the land, but that change remained nominal until 1929–30 when the original Bolshevik policy began to be implemented in the countryside through a bitterly contested forced collectivization. Finally, far from transferring power to soviets, October was the first step in the decline of the soviets, the independence of which had been severely undermined. In reality, power had passed to the Bolsheviks, not the soviets. By the end of 1918, the Bolsheviks had implemented a one-party state, which had never been suggested openly as a policy before October, although those who, like Sukhanov, observed Lenin closely and knew him well were sceptical that he would ever be prepared to share power with opponents, still less allow any system of democratic decision-making to take it away from him. Lenin's supporters praised him for being bold enough to throw in his lot with the worker and peasant movement when other party leaders were fearful of doing so. His critics saw, and see, it as a masterful exercise in deception. Whatever it was, by 27 October Lenin led the government of the largest country by area on the planet.

The ease with which the Bolsheviks were propelled into power has, of course, a corresponding implication. It was much harder to retain it than take it in the first place. It is not at the forefront of our current focus to go deep into how they did so, but we do have to make a number of observations as the October 'model' was part of Lenin's legacy in the eyes of supporters and numerous opponents. Nonetheless, our main focus remains on Lenin and what being in power added to his appeal in the eyes of Leninists in later years down to the present. This is most efficiently done by considering a number of propositions about Lenin and his role in the last four and a half fully active years of his life.

Given the situation of October 1917 it is quite likely that Soviet power would have been declared with or without Lenin and his associates. Even before it assembled, the Second All-Russian Congress of Soviets, the body which endorsed the takeover, was overwhelmingly committed to replacing the authority of the Provisional Government with its own. The majority of delegates had been mandated to support such a move before they left their home constituencies. Officially, when they assembled on 25 October 1917, a count gave the Bolsheviks a majority, so one might say the Bolsheviks were decisive, but it is not quite that straightforward. Soviet politics was very volatile and, as with the rest of the popular movement, commitment to policies—notably Peace, Bread, Land, All Power to the Soviets—was stronger than commitment to party. Since the Bolsheviks were the only party to support the takeover and the majority of leaders of the SRs and Mensheviks withdrew from the Congress as a protest, it followed that being a 'Bolshevik' meant, first and foremost, supporting soviet power and land distribution. Beyond that level it is unlikely that the delegates, or even the majority of Bolshevik Party members and voters, had much of an idea of the vast, visionary dimension of Bolshevism, its aim to promote world revolution and the transformation of humanity, issues to which we will return.

Finally, looking at the October events in this way also bears out the notion that it was based on an upsurge of popular revolution expressed in growing numbers of land seizures in the rural areas, amounting to an ongoing liquidation of the landowning class. In industry, more and larger strikes and the establishment of worker control in many industrial enterprises fuelled the radical political wave behind the election of the Second Congress itself. The situation had already been smouldering in August but, inadvertently and, from his and his supporters' point of view, disastrously, it was Kornilov who had fanned the flames, not Lenin. Writing in the 1870s, one of the most radical of the early populist figures, Tkachev, had said that revolutionaries do not cause revolutions, failing social elites are responsible for that. What revolutionaries do is to 'make' the revolution. What he meant by that was that though the revolutionary situation was not of their doing, revolutionaries would seize it and shape it. That is exactly what Lenin did. The tsar, the landowners, the failing Provisional Government, Kornilov and his supporters in the High Command were the unwilling architects of the October Revolution, but it very quickly came to bear a Leninist imprint.

From Drawing Board to Battlefield: The Tribulations of Transition

Constructing a 'Leninist' 'model' of revolution, or a consistent, structured theoretical/philosophical system of 'Leninism' are practices which can only begin from an unstable foundation. Lenin was not in the business of devising either a model or a systematic philosophy. His business was preparing and conducting a revolution. To achieve this, as we have noted several times already, consistency was sacrificed to expediency. Lenin stood for whatever he thought suited the ever-shifting situation of the moment. Like an ancient navigator, he followed a guiding star but he needed to tack back and forth with the changing wind and take appropriate action to deal with extremes

58 LENIN LIVES?

of weather. In that sense we can perhaps identify the star, but that will be something so general it hardly helps. For example, we can say that his goal was consistently for 'proletarian revolution', though even here there were lapses into something nearer to populism. For instance, perhaps the most important practical piece of writing he ever accomplished, the decree establishing Soviet power on 26 October 1917, does not single out the workers but claims power has been seized by Petrograd 'workers and the garrison' and by a coalition of 'workers, peasants and soldiers'.[45] This is clearly a populist rather than purely Marxist formulation and is an accurate description of what happened in October. Setting aside that later historiography down to the present has not brought out to the full Lenin's undoubtedly correct—even obvious—perception about the role of soldiers, who were the main revolutionary force from October to the end of the main civil war in late 1920, there is clearly an instinctive populist within Lenin, as was the case with many other Marxists such as Mao Zedong who was dismissed in Moscow and the Chinese Communist Party HQ in Shanghai in the 1920s precisely for being more populist and peasant-oriented than Marxist and proletarian. In the same way, there is also an instinctive Bakuninist within the brilliant fluidity of Lenin's political assessments of whatever conjuncture of events he was dealing with at any given time. Obviously Lenin was deeply immersed in Marxism as his primary intellectual source of inspiration, but he also clearly had populist and Bakuninist tones which made his views distinctive. Nowhere is his similarity to Bakunin more obvious than in his main theoretical meditation on revolution, his pamphlet, *The State and Revolution*. Writing it was Lenin's main preoccupation during the enforced lull in his activities in 1917 between July and early September, but Lenin was, as he wrote at the very end of the pamphlet, 'interrupted':

> This pamphlet was written in August and September 1917. I had already drawn up the plan for the next, the seventh chapter, 'The Experience of the Russian Revolutions of 1905 and 1917'. Apart from the title, however, I had no time to write a single line of the chapter; I was 'interrupted' by a political crisis—the eve of the October revolution of 1917. Such an 'interruption' can only be welcomed; but the writing of the second part of this pamphlet ('The Experience of the Russian Revolutions of 1905 and 1917') will probably have to be put off for a long time. It is more pleasant and useful to go through the 'experience of revolution' than to write about it.[46]

The final sentence encapsulates the whole difficulty of systematizing 'Leninism'. Theory and practice marched together but practice, not logic,

LENIN BEFORE LENINISM 59

was the proof of theory. The remainder of this chapter will look at the underlying principles and policies behind Lenin's strategy rather than a blow-by-blow account of events. Up to spring 1921 there were two intertwined imperatives behind Lenin's activities. The first was to stay in power at all costs, the second to engage in the process of transition to socialism. By 1921, the party was unchallenged internally and the former task was modified to, ironically, building a powerful party state, a process central to the work of Lenin's successor, Stalin. The new state retained mobilizing, consciousness-raising characteristics which had helped it in the civil war but which were now focused on the ultimate battle—the transition to socialism and, ultimately, communism.

Why was Lenin having to change strategy so soon and so drastically? Once again it is a question of 'events, dear boy, events'. Key assumptions proved to be wrong and predicted situations did not happen. In his intense correspondence to the Central Committee preceding the taking of power, Lenin argued a soviet/Bolshevik revolution would reduce tension and disorder in the country because it would immediately garner the support of the overwhelming majority of the population in the face of which the elite would have no option but to sue for mercy and comply with the new order. Transition, Lenin claimed, would be 'gradual, peaceful and smooth'.[47] Did Lenin believe this to be so? If not, was he being deceptive for propaganda purposes or, once again, naive in his expectations? In any case it was only hours into the revolution that such facile and optimistic expectations began to rapidly unravel.

The first crucial issue was the selection of a new government. All the evidence suggests that when the delegates to the Second Congress of Soviets called for 'All Power to the Soviets' they understood that all soviet parties would be in the new coalition. However, within days of the revolution they were confronted with, in essence, a Bolshevik government. In part, senior members of the non-Bolshevik left, notably Plekhanov and others from the Menshevik and SR parties like Chernov and Tsereteli, who had been in government, contributed to the outcome by walking out of the Second Congress in protest, expecting the congress to collapse as a result. In their eyes the only beneficiary of the new turmoil would be the kaiser and his allies. It was not just defencists who left. Martov and the tiny group of Menshevik Internationalists also left the congress to Trotsky's derisive, but sadly accurate, jibe that they were walking into the 'rubbish bin of history'.[48] Instead of putting a spanner in the works, as is often the risk with boycotts they had made themselves irrelevant and left the field to their enemy, in this case a ruthless one brimming with self-confidence. Only a small group of SR

60 LENIN LIVES?

Internationalists remained to support the Bolshevik initiative. Many figures on the left, including Plekhanov, objected. Threateningly, the Railwaymen's Union (*Vikzhel*) said they would strike, bringing instant chaos to economy, society, and war effort, thereby critically undermining the new government. Bank officials and state bureaucrats refused to recognize the incoming government and obstructed it wherever they could. Opposition to a one-party government extended to the highest reaches of the Bolshevik Party itself and, within two weeks of October, a group including Lenin's closest associates Kamenev and Zinoviev denounced the turn of events and resigned from their posts. They produced a letter with ominous words that ring through the history of Soviet Russia and pose one of the central problems in the Lenin debate. 'It is our view that a socialist government must be formed from all parties in the soviet.... We believe that, apart from this, there is only one other path: the retention of a purely Bolshevik government by means of political terror.'[49] Lenin did not flinch but gambled on an aggressive response. He threatened to dissolve *Vikzhel* and replace it with a more compliant one. He denounced and dismissed recalcitrant bureaucrats, which certainly added to economic and social disruption and undermined living standards. Inflation spiralled upwards even faster. A 'coalition' government emerged with a small number of Left-SR ministers to ineffectively conceal the reality of a one-party Bolshevik government. October had been a revolution, the first days and weeks of the Soviet era had seen Lenin pull off a Bolshevik coup. Lenin had established himself as head of government in one of the world's largest countries. No one expected him to stay there for long. Lenin himself made no assumptions. On the day they exceeded the number of days the Paris Commune had been in power Lenin was so exuberant that he went out into the snow and danced a jig. However, the problems continued to accumulate.

The first six months of Bolshevik rule were characterized by continuing chaos. Inflation rates rose rapidly, damaging living standards even further. Peasants withheld grain from their newly acquired lands in the hope of higher prices later and a lack of products to buy with any profits they might make. The first, classic, form of socialist transition had collapsed. No upsurge of conscious support had emerged to prop up Bolshevik power. The optimistic picture of soviets supervising capitalists without major short-term disruption had disappeared in a welter of capitalist elements escaping from Soviet Russia and either joining the armed resistance or simply emigrating. Many of them took resources with them, thereby effectively sabotaging the economy they left behind, which, far from recovering from crisis

LENIN BEFORE LENINISM 61

as Lenin had promised, fell deeper into the whirlpool of bankruptcy, breakdown, and devastating inflation. In particular, the vital railway network declined rapidly as political disruption and the isolation of Soviet Russia from former allies who began to blockade it made it impossible to acquire spare parts for overworked locomotives, rolling stock and infrastructure as they wore out, and supplies of coal and wood which fell below the level needed to fuel the locomotives. Civil war raged in the south and separatist movements took Finland, Poland, Armenia, Georgia, Azerbaijan, and fluctuating parts of Central Asia out of the control of the new capital, Moscow, to which city the government had moved in February. In March, a draconian treaty dictated by Germany at the frontier town of Brest-Litovsk gave away vast grain-producing territories in south Russia and Ukraine to Germany and its allies. The treaty resonates today as it literally put Ukraine on the map as an independent country for the first time in its history. On the plus side, the Bolsheviks had surprised and delighted even themselves by surviving and building an army capable of holding power. Armed squads had ensured Bolshevik victory in most cities of European Russia (and much of Ukraine before it was lost by the treaty), and they held Siberia. Brest-Litovsk had disappointed much of the party left and also fatally undermined the fig-leaf 'coalition' with the Left SRs who quit the government in protest and even engaged in a half-baked anti-Bolshevik coup four months later.

The party left was disillusioned because they had sincerely bought into Lenin and Trotsky's line on the necessity—necessity not just desirability—of international revolution. They wanted to throw everything into a gamble to spread the revolution into the heartland of Europe and end the war along the lines Lenin had argued for since 1914—turning the German, French, and British armed masses against their rulers who were presiding over their mutual slaughter. Once again, Lenin had engaged in a rapid and unforeseen U-turn, which even Trotsky was reluctant to follow and Stalin had not expected. Lenin prevailed. As he had over armed uprising in October. As he always did on key questions. That was what Bolshevism had been and continued to be, a party which followed Lenin. Conventional Leninists will argue that the treaty was only intended for the short term. Lenin had got his way in the discussion by arguing forcefully that its provisions would be short-lived as Germany would collapse by the end of the year, which it did. Lenin's foresight, or possibly just his luck, had been proven correct once again, though, with the partial exception of the 1920 war with Poland, the left never got its military incursion into Europe to spread revolution. All of these factors—economic collapse; social disruption; an end to the war; the

62   LENIN LIVES?

initial implantation of Soviet/Bolshevik power; a one-party government—required new policies and a new direction. There was one more decisive development, in Lenin's mind at least. The civil war, he said, was more or less over. 'In the main...the task of suppressing the resistance of the exploiters was fulfilled.'[50] The first phase of revolution—overthrowing the old elite, or smashing the pre-revolutionary state to use the language of *The State and Revolution*—was now over. For the first time in history, Lenin exulted, a revolutionary government had the pleasure of moving to the second stage of administering the new system. It was not a result of chaos and collapse caused by the failure of transition one, it was because a successful pitch had brought the revolution to a higher camp on the Everest of socialist construction.

> Thanks to the peace which has been achieved—despite its extremely onerous character and extreme instability—the Russian Soviet Republic has gained an opportunity to concentrate its efforts for a while on the most important and most difficult aspect of the socialist revolution, namely, the task of organisation.[51]

He did not mention, probably didn't even think about, his pre-October assurance that transition would be 'gradual, peaceful and smooth'. This was now replaced with the more realistic but much less palatable concepts that

> capitalism cannot be defeated and eradicated without the ruthless suppression of the resistance of the exploiters, who cannot at once be deprived of their wealth, of their advantages of organisation and knowledge, and consequently for a fairly long period will inevitably try to overthrow the hated rule of the poor; secondly, every great revolution, and a socialist revolution in particular, even if there is no external war, is inconceivable without internal war, i.e. civil war, which is even more devastating than external war, and involves thousands and millions of cases of wavering and desertion from one side to another, implies a state of extreme indefiniteness, lack of equilibrium and chaos.[52]

So much for Peace! The comprehensive change of direction was stridently announced on 28 April 1918 by the simultaneous publication of an article entitled 'On the Immediate Tasks of the Soviet Government' in both the party and government newspapers *Pravda* and *Izvestiia*. In it Lenin outlined the reasons for the change and the architecture of the new transition. Lenin

LENIN BEFORE LENINISM   63

being Lenin presented the change as a positive achievement. It was a step forward. The first two stages of socialist revolution had been accomplished.

> The first task of every party of the future is to convince the majority of the people that its programme and tactics are correct.... This task has now been fulfilled in the main,... but of course, it is far from being completely fulfilled (and it can never be completely fulfilled). The second task that confronted our Party was to capture political power and to suppress the resistance of the exploiters. This task has not been completely fulfilled either... In the main, however, the task of suppressing the resistance of the exploiters was fulfilled in the period from October 25, 1917, to (approximately) February 1918.[53]

This had opened the way to the new challenge of administering society. Despite the 'extreme instability' of the peace, 'no sane politician' would contemplate a resumption of hostilities with the defeated exploiters and the imperialist threat was, for the moment at least, mitigated by divisions between the imperialist powers,[54] a change of position from Lenin's assertion in 1914 that the warring powers would quickly come to an accommodation in the face of the emergence of revolution and ally to suppress it.[55] But it is clear Lenin was envisaging a period—'for a while', no more specific than that—for moving forward with transition.

> For the first time in human history a socialist party has managed to complete in the main the conquest of power and the suppression of the exploiters, and has managed to *approach directly* the task of *administration*. We must prove worthy executors of this most difficult (and most gratifying) task of the socialist revolution. We must *fully realise* that in order to administer successfully, *besides* being able to convince people, besides being able to win a civil war, we must be able to do *practical organisational work*. This is the most difficult task, because it is a matter of organising in a new way the most deep-rooted, the economic, foundations of life of scores of millions of people. And it is the most gratifying task, because only *after* it has been fulfilled (in the principal and main outlines) will it be possible to say that Russia *has become* not only a Soviet, but also a socialist, republic.[56]

The new transition brought new principles and policies to the fore. At the time Lenin used the terms 'iron proletarian discipline' and 'proletarian dictatorship' and a number of variants.

64 LENIN LIVES?

Dictatorship, however, is a big word, and big words should not be thrown about carelessly. Dictatorship is iron rule, government that is revolutionarily bold, swift and ruthless in suppressing both exploiters and hooligans. But our government is excessively mild, very often it resembles jelly more than iron. The fight cannot be waged solely with the aid of propaganda and agitation...The struggle must also be waged by means of coercion.[57]

Other features included 'accounting and control', raising the productivity of labour, setting up a socialist form of economic competition, harmony and dictatorship, and the ultimate goal, organization.

It was largely the means to achieve these goals which caused controversy at the time. Lenin advocated extending the policy of employing 'specialists' from the former bourgeoisie to help cover the critical skills gap which was crippling the economy and the military efforts of the new government. The recruitment, at much higher wages than those of the workers, of former managers, engineers, and military officers caused much resentment in the rank and file of party and working class. The slogans of the new administrative phase were much less dramatic and resonant among young militants than the heroic call to civil war. Now they were told 'keep regular and honest accounts of money, manage economically, do not be lazy, do not steal, observe the strictest labour discipline—it is these slogans...that are now...becoming the immediate and the principal slogans of the moment'.[58] As for the dream of international revolution, it would be best served by fulfilling the task of administration: 'we shall be able to render effective assistance to the socialist revolution in the West which has been delayed for a number of reasons, only to the extent that we are able to fulfil the task of organisation confronting us.'[59] Lenin had already justified the Brest-Litovsk peace by downgrading the priority of carrying the revolutionary war to the west in favour of consolidating the Soviet government first as its most important service to world revolution. He used the word retreat many times in his writings of the first half of 1918 and even stated that, if necessary, 'we must retreat (before Western and Eastern imperialism) even as far as the Urals, for in this lies the *only* chance of playing for time while the revolution in the West matures'.[60]

Lenin stated clearly that this stage of transition was preparation for moving to socialism. It was necessary, in Marxist terms, to put every effort into developing an economy of abundance before socialism could be realized. Lenin was advocating 'productionism' to overcome Russia's social and cultural 'backwardness'. Maximizing economic, especially industrial, output

LENIN BEFORE LENINISM   65

was the first step towards socialism but was not, itself, socialism. This is the situation in which Soviet Russia found itself through its whole existence. 'Productionism', and its chief promoter, Stalin, dominated the Soviet experience. It was another consequence of conducting a revolution in a country where, in Marxist terms, the preconditions were absent, thereby creating a 'premature' revolution which found itself in the ironic position of having to create the conditions needed for them to come to power in the first place according to their theory. They were also conscious of the Menshevik jibes that, as predicted by the Mensheviks, the revolution was stalling because Russia was not sufficiently developed for it to succeed.

Lenin returned to this notion later, but before we turn to that we need to note that in *Immediate Tasks* and associated writings, Lenin was proposing a policy of transition based on country-wide accounting and control; an unspecified notion of planning; an assumption of revolutionary isolation; and international, imperialist hostility in the indeterminate future which required priority military production, a need to render service to the world revolution by preserving the Soviet revolution at all costs, a need for iron proletarian discipline to overcome the crisis of collapse and chaos, and for new people formed by increasing class-consciousness to take the leading role in socialist construction. Lenin's formula here is not so much a type of 'war communism', rather it is akin to 'socialism in one country'. While this is not to agree with those who see little or no distinction between Lenin and Stalin, in that Stalin adds his own imprint to the basic model, it is incontrovertible that what emerges from this unprepossessing text is certainly not a 'democratic' Lenin but rather a very 'Stalinist' one. Clearly, there was a great deal more water to flow under the bridge, more experiences to be undergone by the as yet only six-month-old revolution, but there is sufficient here to conclude that Lenin himself originated the theory and practice of socialism in one country based on planning, discipline, and productionism.

It is also important to note that Lenin turned to these 'dictatorial' principles when it was thought the civil war was *over*, not as response to it. By and large, the real significance of this new direction has been submerged in a discourse of something called 'war communism', that is, a temporary deviation from fundamental principles brought about by the need to adapt to the realities of civil war. It was exactly the opposite. For Lenin, it was a genuine and correct form of transition. The term 'war communism' was only applied when it too had collapsed and a third transition model emerged.

Lenin had been right, and is often widely credited with 20:20 foresight, for basing policy between April and October 1917 on 'no support for the

66 LENIN LIVES?

Provisional Government', the policy element which more than any other brought them to power, and also for accepting the Brest-Litovsk Treaty on the assumption that the German Kaiserreich would soon collapse. Whether he was correct by luck or judgement, his basic assumption about transition two was spectacularly incorrect. April did not mark the last writhings of White counter-revolution. An inept response to the desire of the Czech Legion, which had fought on the now collapsed Eastern Front and wanted to get to the west to continue the fight, not only enabled the civil war to flare up again, it resulted in Moscow losing control of most of Siberia, which became a safe space for counter-revolution. Further disasters followed. During the weak attempted coup launched by Left SR elements in July 1918, one of them shot Lenin in August, wounding him and, tragically, setting off a panic in the Soviet government which resulted in the secret police, the Cheka, almost spontaneously instigating the first Red Terror. By 1919, Soviet Russia controlled only 10 per cent of the territory of the former tsarist state, though that area did include more than 50 per cent of the population. Red heroism and White ineptitude, in competing with each other almost more than with the Bolsheviks, which led the three main White leaders to fail to co-ordinate their separate attacks on Moscow, allowed the tide to turn by the end of 1919. Further adaptations were made to the system announced in spring 1918. Almost all of them, like 'Immediate Tasks' itself, were U-turns compared to the promises of 1917. Economic output, especially of industry devastated by disruption of supply chains and markets plus hyperinflation, fell to 'medieval levels' according to the best analysis.[61] Markets were replaced by naive attempts at direct allocation, as previewed in 'Immediate Tasks', and central control and vestigial planning through the *Vesenkha* (Supreme Council of the National Economy), but this was necessitated by their collapse rather than the pursuit of ideological goals. However, it was argued that this was standard transition, not deviation caused by the ever-troublesome intrusion of 'events' on the purity of theory. Other key policies were abandoned. The Red Army followed traditional structures, not those of a citizen militia. Even worse, former officers and political commissars became a part of it. Trades unions were converted from organizations of worker self-expression and protection into 'schools of communism' as defined at the Ninth Party Congress, effectively become managerial transmission belts of orders from above.[62] A harsher form of 'democratic centralism', backed up by (non-violent) purges of party members deemed not to be up to their high calling, was enforced by Control Commissions and, for state employees, by the Worker Peasant Inspectorate.

LENIN BEFORE LENINISM 67

The temporary secret police, the Cheka, grew rather than declined in power and scope. From early 1918 there was a one-party state. The sacred cause of 'All Power to the Soviets' had turned into their rapid decline and incorporation as organs of central administration, not the independent democratic voice of the people. These drastic changes were considered part of a transition, not concessions to the war situation, which, in effect, was only a heightened form of the chaos Lenin was referring to when he thought the worst of the civil war was over.

Needless to say, such an apparent betrayal of the 1917 promises of soviet democracy, worker self-government, peaceful economic development, and so on aroused massive resentment but, for the time being, the civil war blocked open expression because the threat of counter-revolution inhibited those who wanted to protest. Growing harsh repression also made its mark. But as the civil war wound down and the White threat was dispersed, so protest emerged which necessitated the adoption of a third transition strategy. But one of the main drivers towards this came from a quarter we have not mentioned but briefly need to locate in Lenin's scheme of things, the post-revolutionary peasantry.

Despite having been brought up in the small minority of around 10 per cent of the tsar's subjects who were urban, Lenin would undoubtedly have encountered peasants from an early age, not only in produce markets and the like but on the modest family estates where he spent his childhood summers and where he confronted his momentous, from the point of view of Russian and world history, decision not to devote his life to farming. As far as we know there were no special interactions at that point. By his early twenties Lenin had come on board with the social democratic discourse of Plekhanov that the workers were the future, the peasants the past. There is no direct evidence but it is reasonable to assume this was an intellectual discourse stimulated by reading Plekhanov and other critiques of populism. While living among peasants, with whom he had friendly interactions, during his Siberian exile, he wrote his massive study of *The Development of Capitalism in Russia*. Its main thrust, as we noted, was to prove that capitalism could not be sidestepped in Russia because it already had a deep hold on industrial and rural economies. One consequence would be the conversion of the landowner–peasant society left over from feudalism into a capitalist farmer–agrarian labourer relationship. The ownership of almost all land would, as in Britain or the United States, be seized by capitalist owners who would accumulate vast farms and peasants would lose their ties to land and be downgraded to the level of rural proletarians dependent on wages.

68 LENIN LIVES?

In brief, peasants would disappear as a class and, as such, Lenin did not spend much time considering them beyond the bedrock anti-populist propositions of any social democrat. For Lenin, peasants were not embryonic socialists working through the traditional commune and redistributed rather than personally owned land. They were narrow-minded, superstitious, counter-revolutionary, petit-bourgeois who aspired to personal enrichment through the market. Marx had called them 'the class that represents barbarism within civilisation',[63] an outlook shared by Lenin, perhaps prompted by his friend Gorky who had lived close to peasants and was fearful they would destroy any initiatives to build socialism and would support tsar and church instead. Not surprisingly, party policy on land was that it should be nationalized and turned into state farms with peasants becoming wage-earning state employees. No peasants supported any such programme, which was a mirror image of the capitalist rural model. Peasant policy and rural policy in general remained a discourse, a set of theories, rather than a result of empirical observation of the facts.

Lenin's view of peasants also had a second associated discourse which had baleful consequences. Marxism had a class-based view of human society. However, the peasantry, for Lenin, was not a unified class but one made up of divisions which almost formed separate classes. These were *kulaks*, *seredniaks* (middle peasants) and *bedniaks* (poor peasants). *Kulaks* are often considered to be 'rich' peasants, though the term is misleading. No peasant was actually rich, but some were, indeed, better off than others. Precise divisions and distinctions here are very complex and controversial, but for our purpose of deriving a Leninist model we need to observe two things. First, the term '*kulak*' was in frequent use but meant much more than a better-off peasant. The term is derived from the Russian for 'fist' and was associated with the grasping fist of those to whom peasants had to pay money they considered exorbitant for buying supplies, or those from whom they received sums they deemed inadequate from selling their surplus. Thus the term referred to those whom the peasants considered to be their exploiters— first and foremost moneylenders, whom they hated, then grain merchants and their agents, shopkeepers, owners of dairies, wood-yards, brickmakers, smithies, and so on, the myriad traders and merchants of rural life. Some peasants were disliked for being wealthy enough to hire sufficient labour to work on their land, a group that expanded widely between 1907 and 1916 when the government tried to sponsor peasants to leave the commune and consolidate their land into private holdings. Such peasants were known as separators and were considered traitors to the community by the commune peasants. In other words, *kulaks* were not really peasants at all, but traders and others outside the commune. Some were undoubtedly ex-peasants, exemplified in the former serf, now wealthy entrepreneur, Lopakhin, who tries to buy the cherry orchard on a declining landowner estate to build weekend retreats for the urban rich in Chekhov's play of that name.

Why did Lenin feel the need to lay the ill-fitting grid of class over the peasantry? As with other of Lenin's theoretical excursions, this one was closely related to immediate political dilemmas. In particular, Lenin and his fellow social democrats had to face the intractable fact that even the most generous definition of an industrial worker could only embrace a maximum of 10 per cent of the population. They were a very small minority and, as such, proletarian revolution was not realistic. However, if one could establish comparable class divisions in the peasantry—*kulaks* as allies of the middle-class bourgeoisie; poor peasants, largely landless peasants, as wage-dependent proletarians; and middle peasants hovering between the two—it was possible to imagine a stronger revolutionary coalition. By adding the 20 per cent or so of poor peasants and as many as possible of the 70 per cent or so who were middle peasants in a campaign against the proto-bourgeois *kulak* exploiters, one could come closer to a theoretical revolutionary majority. Peasant radicalism and refusal to support the autocracy in 1905 had strengthened Lenin's hopes.

Such were Lenin's assumptions about peasants in early 1917. They were encapsulated in the party policy of nationalizing land. Lenin feared that handing land over for redistribution among peasant households—that is, land to the peasants as enshrined in SR policy—threatened the surplus which fed the cities, which came from the estates not the peasants, and was likely to create a class of rural, market-oriented, private trading small capitalists. In the 'April Theses' he was careful to call for separate soviets for poor peasants and agricultural labourers. Lenin continued to envisage the lowest stratum of peasants as the Trojan horse by which the social democrats could penetrate the countryside and exert pressure to win over the majority of middle peasants. However, while the minority of landless peasants might welcome nationalization of land and state farms to restore their access to land, it was a hard row to hoe to get middle, subsistence peasants on board as they would lose control over their land. In any case, the period from April to October 1917 was too short and Bolshevik penetration of the countryside was practically nil. Crucial Bolshevik influence in October was in the large cities and among the armed forces. However, once they had taken power the peasant issue had to be addressed. Once again, Lenin's deeply

70 LENIN LIVES?

held and long-constructed theoretical positions collapsed, almost overnight in some places, and Lenin's genius for improvisation to the point of complete policy reversal (or 'deception' in the eyes of opponents and critics) came rapidly to the fore.

Lenin's biggest U-turn in this area is his best known, so we do not need to dwell on it. The policy implemented in the famous Decree on Land was taken, pretty much lock, stock, and barrel, from the SRs. When confronted by a heckler at the Second Congress who asserted this, Lenin's witty and effective response was to say what kind of party is it that cannot implement its own policies? Actually, according to the terms of the decree, land did not go directly to peasant households but to an intermediary, the local soviet of agricultural labourers or equivalent, and there was an injunction that landowner estates should be left intact as state farms, which would become models of socialist agriculture, towards which peasants would turn in self-interest because the state farms would, Lenin assumed, be more productive and wealthier than private plots as they would enjoy better access to machinery, fertilizers, and the like, and efficient up-to-date methods. In practice these niceties were only partially observed and the land was, by March 1918, swallowed up into communal and family plots. Despite having taken up diametrically opposing principles, the original policies were not forgotten, and in 1919 land was officially nationalized, though that had little impact on the realities of the situation.

One of the first policy initiatives driven by the Bolsheviks' own principles, and fully in the spirit of the second transition model, was the setting up of committees of poor peasants (*Kombedy*) in June 1918. The idea was to curry support in the countryside among those most likely to support the Bolsheviks and to thereby drive a wedge into the rural hostility they expected once the euphoria of land seizure had worn off. Hostility was vastly increased by a second, more desperate measure introduced in May of the same year and extended to January 1919—armed requisitioning of food by expropriation squads. This too was, in theory, a rural equivalent of the direct allocation of resources via rationing rather than the market which was being implemented in the cities as a, theoretically, integral part of the current transition model, though its implementation was forced by the collapse of the economy and conducted in an arbitrary, improvised, and cruel fashion. While peasant levies had been part of tsarist and Provisional Government activity, largely to take supplies for the army, the peasants had recognized them as a form of taxation needed for patriotic reasons. However, the Bolshevik squads were more ruthless, took whatever they

LENIN BEFORE LENINISM 71

could see, often returned several times to the same spots within range of hungry cities, and offered nothing in return. Peasants believed they were doing nothing more than feeding lazy, non-working urban workers, not their sons in the army. Though much more complex than outlined here, the net result was a massive rise in peasant resentment towards the authorities. The change of party name in the interim led some peasants to campaign for the defeat of the communists and the return of the Bolsheviks. Like other protests, they were held in check by the civil war, because, despite their hatred of requisitioning which deprived many peasant families of the seed corn for the next harvest and brought rural starvation, they did not want to see the return of the Whites who were themselves ruthless requisitioners. However, by 1919 Lenin realized the market nexus between food supply and demand would not be fulfilled by arbitrary and sometimes riotous armed squads, and he began what is sometimes termed the turn towards the middle peasant. He called for a new direction, one which would find a new separation line between sympathetic peasants and hostile ones by winning over 'waverers' among the middle peasants and distinguishing 'the peasant huckster' from 'the peasant worker', those who were deemed to be profiteers from those who were mainly subsistence farmers. Lenin considered it crucial to do this because, he said, 'in this demarcation lies the *whole essence* of socialism'.[64]

The more successful peasants were likely to be some of the most hostile to the requisitioners, not least because the *kombedy* in many villages had become an information source for malcontent peasants to spite their better-off neighbours. By backing them they had taken the opposite line from the tsarist rural reformer Stolypin who had urged support for the 'sober and the strong'.[65] By attaching their flag to the poor peasants, the Bolsheviks had found themselves in alliance with some peasants who needed support but also with many who were simply the poorest farmers because they were feckless, lazy, and drunk. Supporting such misfits alienated the majority of hard-working village dwellers. As the civil war and its White threat wound down, areas badly affected by expropriations rose up in revolt, especially in West Siberia and Tambov. A series of strikes expressed worker grievances, including food shortages exacerbated by the negative consequences of expropriation. Even the sailors of the naval base in Kronstadt, when they rebelled in March 1921, called for the abolition of armed requisitioning squads. Through 1920 parts of the country were teetering on the brink of ungovernability. Once again, to cut a long story short, Lenin's second transition had run up against the rock of peasant resistance. Very reasonably, the

72   LENIN LIVES?

peasants affected had done everything they could to prevent this theft of their produce. They had, catastrophically, produced less, on the grounds that there was no point slaving to produce a surplus which would simply be stolen from them, thereby stoking the fires of famine. Unthinkably, the peasants had defeated the party and state. There was no alternative but to turn to a third transition model normally known as the New Economic Policy (NEP).

The central feature of the new direction was announced by Lenin at the Tenth Party Congress in March 1921 under the technical-sounding title of replacing requisitioning by a tax-in-kind, that is, a fixed percentage of peasant produce. The ideologically unpopular corollary of this was that peasants would be left to dispose of the non-tax element of their surplus however they wanted, which meant via the market. The party left had another policy to rail at. Restoration of the market was, in their eyes, going too far on the dangerous path of restoring capitalism. Lenin was all too aware that by strengthening a potentially capitalist feature of the economic infrastructure he was creating space for the creation of capitalists and the reversion to capitalist values, which, for most of the population, had never gone away. To choke off these possibilities, a series of highly restrictive, even repressive, measures were adopted in the period from 1921–3. The political police force ceased to be temporary and was consolidated into the state structure. Remaining independent sectors of civil society, notably universities, had their autonomy ended. Censorship extended across all publications, performances (including music), exhibitions, and films. Party control of intellectual and political expression deepened as the decade progressed. The first political show trial, of leading SRs, was held in 1922, though the harsh sentences were not carried out.

Developments within the party followed the same path. Organized oppositions were banned. The Workers' Opposition, which called for a stronger worker element in the party and less bureaucracy, was broken up. The struggle against the twin evils of bureaucratization and careerism (meaning that party and state officials tended to look to their own interests rather than those of their clients at the expense of democratic decision-making) had become endemic in the party. Lenin had complained the revolution was drowning in red tape and Trotsky frequently fulminated against it, later associating it with Stalin's victory over him in the party struggle. What neither Lenin nor Trotsky would admit was that their model of revolution, with a 'conscious' elite leading the 'unconscious' masses who needed to be politically educated, set up a Confucian tutelary relationship of teacher and

LENIN BEFORE LENINISM 73

pupil which was profoundly undemocratic. The remedies proposed in *The State and Revolution* and the 'April Theses'—elected, recallable officials whose salary was capped at two-thirds that of a skilled worker—had gone out of the window within months of October when Lenin turned to highly paid *spetsy* (specialists) to fulfil crucial roles.

The degree to which the revolution had turned its back on key principles of 1917 was poignantly and tragically highlighted by the rebellion of workers and sailors in Kronstadt which took place at the same time as the Tenth Congress. At its heart was a demand for free soviets in which the Bolsheviks would not have an institutionalized majority. They would be open equally to all left-wing parties, but not to bourgeois remnants. Every day at midday an open meeting of the Kronstadt Soviet took place in Anchor Square. It was the essence of what soviet supporters thought they were installing in 1917. In many cases the leaders in Kronstadt were the same who had been there in the July Days and October 1917.[66] With a heavy heart but ruthless energy, Lenin and Trotsky, the latter leading the assault, smashed the rebellion. No clearer symbol could encapsulate the agonizing clash between the ideals of 1917 and what the revolution had become by 1921. If Lenin challenges liberals over the issue of violence ultimately being necessary to achieve social justice and democratic control over property, Kronstadt challenges the Leninist conscience about whether the path of authoritarian centralization and a one-party state was desirable, inevitable, or even temporarily expedient. Kronstadt presented an alternative. Lenin and Trotsky crushed it.

The Tenth Congress was Lenin's last great political initiative. He suffered the first of a series of strokes in May 1922, from which he partially recovered, followed by a totally debilitating third stroke in March 1923. During this time he wrote a number of items which, together, complement his secret political testament which evaluated all his possible successors, painting all of them in a somewhat negative light. In his main comments about possible successors, written in a series of notes in late December 1922, he warned of Trotsky's 'arrogance' and 'preoccupation with the administrative side of affairs' and of Bukharin's failure to understand dialectical materialism, an obscure but damning comment equivalent to saying a papal candidate did not understand the Nicene Creed. He said that Kamenev and Zinoviev's opposition to the October uprising should not be held against them, thereby putting exactly that behaviour under the spotlight. Stalin was 'too vulgar' for a post like that of General Secretary which, Lenin implied, called for tact and good humour. Lenin suggested removing Stalin from that role (but not from the party, the Central Committee, or the Politburo, that is the main

74 LENIN LIVES?

governing executive committee). He heightened his criticism a few days later, on 4 January 1923, after Stalin had had a bitter argument with Nadezhda Krupskaya, but Stalin quickly backed down and apologized. Lenin did not open the way to any of them to be his successor, a very unfortunate error on his part.[67]

Since October 1917, Lenin's life had been limited to a narrow space. He made a last convalescent trip to Finland over the New Year holiday in January 1918, but his preoccupation with problems meant, according to Krupskaya, that he had little sleep and little benefit from the break. Worse, his car had been shot at by thieves and his friend who had brokered his return from Switzerland, Fritz Platten, had been slightly injured. Shortly after, he moved into an apartment in the Kremlin in March 1918 when Moscow became the capital once again. From then on his horizons were bounded by the ancient fortress and a modest country house outside the city, near today's Domodedovo airport, where he was able to make recuperative contact with nature and where he passed the last years of his life after his strokes. He passed his leisure time in the *dacha* garden and surrounding countryside, immersed in nature and enjoying occasional hunting, fishing, and mushrooming excursions to which he was able to contribute less and less. In a plangent episode in October 1923 he arranged to be taken to his Kremlin office for what turned out to be the last time. The guards would not let him in because his pass was out of date and he was unrecognizable after the ravages of the strokes. He needed the verification of comrades to access his former control room of revolution.[68]

The increasing level of spatial separation from early 1922 as he retreated to the *dacha*, and his waning intellectual and physical powers, meant he withdrew from the day-to-day hurly-burly of political life. He did, however, against doctors' advice, attempt to keep in touch with the overall direction which events were taking. In fact, it was because she was helping her husband evade medical restrictions that Stalin had had the row and sworn at Krupskaya. The outcome of Lenin's final musings was a series of brief overviews of the development of the revolution. Overall, they expressed satisfaction with what had been achieved, proposed some minor adjustments of course, and praised the third transition which, he admitted, they had stumbled on by accident. He also emphasized that the party should never again confront the peasantry directly and face another defeat. Instead, he called for an alliance (*smychka*) between workers (i.e. the party) and the peasantry. In a brief article entitled 'On Co-operation', of January 1923,

LENIN BEFORE LENINISM   75

Lenin waxed lyrical about NEP and suggested that, if the principles of co-operation were cultivated in the peasants by means of a cultural revolution that would mean that

> All we actually need under NEP is to organize the population of Russia in cooperative societies on a sufficiently large scale, for we have now found the degree of combination of private interest, of private commercial interest, with state supervision and control of this interest, that degree of its subordination to the common interests which was formerly the stumbling block for very many socialists. Indeed, the power of the state over all large-scale means of production, political power in the hands of the proletariat, the alliance of this proletariat with the many millions of small and very small peasants, the assured proletarian leadership of the peasantry, etc.— is this not all that is necessary to build a complete socialist society out of cooperatives?[69]

In order to achieve this happy outcome

> Two main tasks confront us, which constitute the epoch—to reorganize our machinery of state, which is utterly useless, which we took over in its entirety from the preceding epoch; during the past five years of struggle we did not, and could not, drastically reorganize it. Our second task is educational work among the peasants. And the economic object of this educational work among the peasants is to organize the latter in cooperative societies. If the whole of the peasantry had been organized in cooperatives, we would by now have been standing with both feet on the soil of socialism. But the organization of the entire peasantry in cooperative societies presupposes a standard of culture among the peasants (precisely among the peasants as the overwhelming mass) that cannot, in fact, be achieved without a cultural revolution.[70]

Lenin was only too well aware that this sounded somewhat 'Menshevik' in implying the peasants were backward and needed a cultural revolution to catch up. He went on to defend himself against such criticism.

> Our opponents told us repeatedly that we were rash in undertaking to implant socialism in an insufficiently cultured country. But they were misled by our having started from the opposite end to that prescribed by

76 LENIN LIVES?

theory (the theory of pedants of all kinds), because in our country the political and social revolution preceded the cultural revolution, that very cultural revolution which nevertheless now confronts us.[71]

Productionism was not being abandoned because Lenin also noted that 'to be cultured we must achieve a certain development of the material means of production, we must have a certain material base'.[72] But his message was clear. Who said it was not possible to start with the most important 'prerequisite' for revolution—a workers' state—and then proceed to acquire the rest:

> You say that civilization is necessary for the building of socialism. Very good. But why could we not first create such prerequisites of civilization in our country by the expulsion of the landowners and the Russian capitalists, and then start moving toward socialism? Where, in what books, have you read that such variations of the customary historical sequence of events are impermissible or impossible?[73]

He returned to the extraordinary, and incorrect, concept that 'the machinery of state' is 'utterly useless', and had been taken over 'in its entirety from the preceding epoch' and that 'during the past five years of struggle we did not, and could not, drastically reorganize it'.[74] From a man who emphasized 'abolition of police, army and bureaucracy' and that the bourgeois state must be 'smashed' from the start, not taken over, this is astonishing. It shows how remote his theoretical writings were from his actual practices. Once again, reality had trumped theory. Theory was not forgotten. It was always there as the course which was always being altered, but such were the alterations that pursuing theory was almost continually and comprehensively postponed. It was also very odd to say that the state machinery was unaltered from pre-soviet times. The main institutions—party control; a state of soviets; the Red Army; a socialist judicial apparatus—all had revolutionary characteristics.

His response, outlining how to rectify the shortcomings of the state machine (and that of the party since the two were ever moving towards becoming a single entity by then), was the subject of his final, and, it has to be said, somewhat rambling, repetitive, and even contradictory final article, 'Better Fewer but Better'. As the title suggests, Lenin said it was better to stand back and produce quality state officials 'in two or three years' rather than scramble to plug gaps with half-baked candidates immediately.[75] This was, of course, easier said than done. The Bolsheviks aspired to control military, medical, educational, cultural, industrial, agrarian, international trade, transport, and political propaganda areas, so how could the myriad tasks which needed to be done in the state bureaucracy be done without high-quality officials and managers? In essence, though he did not come close to admitting it, Lenin was complaining about the most damaging shortage his revolution had faced from the beginning—the shortage of Bolsheviks. Even at this late stage in 1923, Lenin was trying to fast-track 'enlightened' candidates into crucial posts. Slightly slowing the process made little difference and was not practically possible. The revolution had sprouted institutions which substituted for widespread consciousness by concentrating the small number of key enlightened, loyal individuals as supervisors of the rest. These institutions included the party itself, especially the propaganda apparatus, and the political police, that is the Cheka, and so on. But even these needed more refined controllers of the controllers in the form of party Control Commissions at all levels and the Worker Peasant Inspectorate to supervise state bureaucrats at all levels. Their aim was to eliminate corruption and malpractice and ensure decisions were taken appropriate to socialist consciousness.[76] Lenin's last big idea to cope with this mess was to make another push to raise the quality of officials and, rather underwhelmingly, to merge the party Control Commissions with the Worker Peasant Inspectorate. Lenin was continuing to pull his revolution out of a swamp of its own making, a situation no Soviet leader admitted, by its bootstraps. The problems arose from Bolshevik elitism, determination not to share power, and the unshakeable belief in the correctness of their principles and objectives. Rearranging the organizational flow chart would make little difference.

Immediately after he wrote 'Better Fewer but Better' Vladimir Il'ich suffered his third stroke. He never recovered sufficiently to resume work. After returning from the Kremlin hospital he spent most of his time at the *dacha*, walking with a stick and speaking haltingly to his friends and relatives who surrounded him. On 24 January 1924, in the presence of Nadezhda Krupskaya, his sister Maria, and Bukharin who was visiting at the time, Lenin died. Even as he was dying, Leninism was being born.

Part Two
Lenin as Icon and Inspiration: Leninism after Lenin

1. The Communist Movement after Lenin

While Lenin was busy promoting revolution in 1917, the leader of one of the next, and still-existing, revolutions he inspired was travelling round the world, taking on menial employment as a sailor, ship's cook, and *plongeur* (dishwasher) in hotels in Paris and London. His name was Nguyễn Sinh Cung, a young man aged 28, born in Annam (Nghệ An, Vietnam), part of the French colony they called Indochine.[1] He had, like Lenin himself, many names, an incredible 200 according to some sources, and the one by which the world knows him, Ho Chi Minh, was not the one he was born with. By 1946 he headed a communist-dominated liberation army and clandestine government, fighting against the efforts of France to restore its power in its former colony. France had been forced out by the Japanese in their wartime imperial drive. Ho and his communists and allies had filled the vacuum after the surrender of Japan in 1945.

Lenin would no doubt have been disappointed that, apart from a somewhat similar situation in Yugoslavia where Tito and his partisans, after a bitter struggle, took over from the collapsed German occupation of their country, no Marxist revolution had taken place in any capitalist heartland by this time. The capitalist enemy had proved itself to be adaptable (even to fascism), resourceful, ruthless, and as productive as it continued to be exploitative. Nonetheless, communism came to have a strong presence in Germany, France, Italy, Spain, and many smaller countries of Europe. Britain and the United States had small communist parties which punched above their weight, partly because of the dread they caused in their opponents but also because they attracted some of the best minds. Many leading intellectuals—Picasso, Pablo Neruda, George Bernard Shaw, Jessica Mitford, Christopher Caudwell, André Gide, Jean-Paul Sartre, John Dos Passos, John Steinbeck, Doris Lessing, Diego Rivera, Frida Kahlo, Ernest Hemingway,

Lenin Lives?. Christopher Read, Oxford University Press. © Christopher Read 2024.
DOI: 10.1093/oso/9780198866084.003.0003

Fig. 3 Trotsky with his wife Natalia Sedova and Frida Kahlo in Mexico.
Source: Isaak Brodsky/State Historical Museum.

Aimée Césaire, Gabriel Garcia Marquez, Christa Wolf, Salvatore Quasimodo, Iannis Ritsos, Georges Lefebvre, Albert Soboul, E.P.Thompson, John Berger, China Miéville, the list is virtually endless—were, for at least a significant part of their lives, deeply influenced by communism. Some turned into fierce opponents, but its cultural influence was undoubtedly vast. Communism integrated into many African struggles for national liberation. The Indian state of Kerala, which has a reputation for being one of the best-run in the country, with much-admired healthcare, educational, and social policies, has been run by democratically elected, tolerant communists in various shifting alliances for much of the time since its formation in 1957. Today, the world's largest country and most rapidly expanding economy, China, has been in the hands of the Chinese Communist Party since 1949. The communist world is large and diverse. It is not our task to account for its successes and failures but to focus more narrowly, where possible, on what part Lenin's practice and ideas played in them.

One preliminary note: alongside the term 'Leninism', the word communism will also be used from now on. It is, however, a portmanteau term with many variants—Marxism-Leninism; Marxism-Leninism-Stalinism;

80 LENIN LIVES?

Marxism-Leninism-Stalinism-Maoism, and others. Usually the constituent elements are bound so closely together that it is hard to distinguish them, but the core includes Leninism in all cases. To winkle out Lenin's impact we will look at the impact of his signature ideas and practices within, and occasionally beyond, communism in its broad sense, that is, not limited to the activities of communist parties but to all areas in which Lenin had influence. To pursue this aim we will look at questions of the party; imperialism, colonialism, and the peasantry; consciousness, culture, philosophy, and religion; and some Leninist revolutions. We will begin by looking at the early transition from the living Lenin to the codification of his ideas and practices as Leninism.

Foundations of Leninism

For a new religion, a new liturgy. In a speech published in *Pravda* six days after Lenin's death, Stalin, perhaps harking back to his seminary days, invoked Lenin's name and memory in the form of a litany. The speech was punctuated by vows:

> DEPARTING FROM US, COMRADE LENIN ENJOINED US TO HOLD HIGH AND GUARD THE PURITY OF THE GREAT TITLE OF MEMBER OF THE PARTY, WE VOW TO YOU, COMRADE LENIN, WE SHALL FULFIL YOUR BEHEST WITH HONOUR!...
>
> DEPARTING FROM US, COMRADE LENIN ENJOINED US TO GUARD THE UNITY OF OUR PARTY AS THE APPLE OF OUR EYE, WE VOW TO YOU, COMRADE LENIN, THAT THIS BEHEST, TOO, WE SHALL FULFIL WITH HONOUR!

Further vows were made, in the same formulaic manner, 'to guard and strengthen the dictatorship of the proletariat...to strengthen with all our might the alliance of the workers and peasants...to strengthen and extend the union of republics.' Stalin concluded with a ringing commitment to world revolution:

> DEPARTING FROM US, COMRADE LENIN ENJOINED US TO REMAIN FAITHFUL TO THE PRINCIPLES OF THE COMMUNIST INTERNATIONAL. WE VOW TO YOU, COMRADE LENIN, THAT WE SHALL NOT SPARE OUR LIVES TO STRENGTHEN AND EXTEND THE UNION OF THE WORKING PEOPLE OF THE WHOLE WORLD— THE COMMUNIST INTERNATIONAL![2]

Fig. 4 Lenin's death becomes the moment of birth of Leninism (Stalin to the right, Molotov behind him, Zinoviev(?) and Tomsky in front of him, and Bukharin in left corner).

The hallmarks of Leninism identified by Stalin put the honour of being a party member first, then party unity, referring in its subtext to the current struggles between factions and oppositions within. Third, the dictatorship of the proletariat (linking back to the Lenin of March and April 1918 and 'On the Immediate Tasks of the Soviet Government'), and fourth the *smychka*, the alliance of worker and peasant enjoined in Lenin's yet unpublished testament, a commitment sounding particularly ironic coming from the mouth of the man who destroyed it five years later. Fifth, the union of republics (USSR), which had been formed a year earlier, and, finally, what many might consider surprising, the principles of Comintern and its road to world revolution. These were among the first tentative steps to codify Leninism. The term itself had not been used while Lenin was active. There was no need to turn his writings into hallowed texts containing first principles because Lenin was there to give guidance personally. As illness caused him to withdraw from frontline politics, so the term Leninism emerged and was still something of a neologism when Stalin launched it into the stratosphere and became defender of the faith, in his own view, for the rest of his life. A second, fuller, and equally revealing initiative quickly followed in April 1924. Stalin published lectures he gave at the Sverdlov Party School

82   LENIN LIVES?

under the title *The Foundations of Leninism*. He spent 150 pages expounding them, and this item also contains a number of surprises.

Stalin's apologia began with three background chapters on the historical roots, theory, and method of Leninism, before devoting a chapter to each of its six components. In order of presentation they were: the dictatorship of the proletariat; the peasant question; the national question; strategy and tactics; the party; and finally what he termed 'style in work'. In a brief introduction he laid out the essence of Leninism as the 'Marxism of the era of imperialism and proletarian revolution'.[3] Though seemingly bland, these words tag two key 'Stalinist' themes—the international dimension of the revolution (which is one of the first surprises for many later readers) and the absolute importance of the proletariat. In a style he often fell into, Stalin presented his views as a series of binaries. Marxism had been divided by some analysts into an early revolutionary phase and a later, more moderate phase. Lenin's achievement was to restore its revolutionary energy. Who had caused it to lose that energy? The compromisers of the Second International, the defencists who betrayed the cause in 1914 when they supported their nation states when they went to war. The second binary was that Lenin was thought to have created a Marxism appropriate to Russian conditions. Stalin admitted there was a grain of truth in this but it was, nonetheless, an error in that

> if Leninism were only the application of Marxism to the conditions that are peculiar to Russia it would be a purely national and only a national, a purely Russian and only a Russian, phenomenon. We know, however, that Leninism is not merely a Russian, but an international phenomenon rooted in the whole of international development.[4]

Again, an emphasis on international revolution which goes against many stereotypes of Stalin, many of which are based on Trotsky's important but not infallible interpretation. This is underpinned by a very strong emphasis on the mistakes of the 'opportunists' (the word appears no less than three times in the final two sentences), with the result that, 'The whole truth about Leninism is that Leninism not only restored Marxism, but also took a step forward, developing Marxism further under the new conditions of capitalism and of the class struggle of the proletariat.' Stalin was setting Leninism in a fully international context and his achievement was for Marxism in general, not just in Russia.[5]

LENIN AS ICON AND INSPIRATION: LENINISM AFTER LENIN 83

In the body of the text the binaries continue to flow. The fundamental elements of Leninist Marxism comprise three contradictions, obviously those between labour and capital and between capitalist formations themselves as a result of competition, but the third repeats, with vehemence, the somewhat unexpected element:

> The *third contradiction* is the contradiction between the handful of ruling, 'civilised' nations and the hundreds of millions of the colonial and dependent peoples of the world. Imperialism is the most barefaced exploitation and the most inhumane oppression of hundreds of millions of people inhabiting vast colonies and dependent countries. The purpose of this exploitation and of this oppression is to squeeze out super-profits. But in exploiting these countries imperialism is compelled to build these railways, factories and mills, industrial and commercial centers. The appearance of a class of proletarians, the emergence of a native intelligentsia, the awakening of national consciousness, the growth of the liberation movement—such are the inevitable results of this 'policy'. The growth of the revolutionary movement in all colonies and dependent countries without exception clearly testifies to this fact. This circumstance is of importance for the proletariat inasmuch as *it saps radically the position of capitalism by converting the colonies and dependent countries from reserves of imperialism into reserves of the proletarian revolution.*[6] [Emphasis added.]

Stalin is locating the epicentre of revolution at least as much in the colonies as in the ruling powers. The most ardent internationalist, like Trotsky, would have been proud of the final sentence in the quote. The passage reminds us that, of all the leaders of the revolution, Stalin had been formed in the colonial environment of South Russia, Azerbaijan, and Georgia, where British commercial imperialism ruled with the aid of tsarist enforcement, resulting in the subjugation of the local nations and ethnicities. Indeed, he went on, the revolution occurred in Russia precisely because it was in Russia that the worldwide contradictions of imperialism were entwined. 'Tsarist Russia was the home of every kind of oppression—capitalist, colonial and militarist—in its most inhuman and barbarous form.' It was 'a major reserve of western imperialism', and its 'watchdog' and 'faithful ally', particularly in the partition of Persia, Turkey, and China.[7] Stalin leaves no doubts about the internationalism of the revolution, including a quote from Lenin

84 LENIN LIVES?

(a practice which was then in its infancy) to underline that a successful Russian revolution would entail 'the destruction of the most powerful bulwark, not only of European, but also (it may now be said) of Asiatic reaction, [and] would make the Russian proletariat the vanguard of the international revolutionary proletariat'.[8] Surprisingly, Stalin has taken this quote not from one of Lenin's wartime writings or his *Imperialism* but from *What is to be Done?*, written way back in 1902 and usually seen as the source for what many western Marxists consider Lenin's greatest personal contribution in the form of a new kind of revolutionary party. But the internationalist theme is what Stalin sees and concludes: 'that the revolution in Russia...could not but assume an international character, and that, therefore, it could not but shake the very foundations of world imperialism.'[9] The idea is ringingly endorsed throughout the lectures. Lecture three contains the following:

> Formerly the proletarian revolution was regarded exclusively as the result of the internal development of a given country. Now, this point of view is no longer adequate. Now the proletarian revolution must be regarded primarily as the result of the development of the contradictions within the world system of imperialism...Where will the revolution begin?...The front of capital will be pierced where the chain of imperialism is weakest;...and it may turn out that the country which has started the revolution, which has made a breach in the front of capital, is less developed in a capitalist sense than other, more developed, countries, which have, however, remained within the framework of capitalism.[10]

On the key issues of the dictatorship of the proletariat and that of the future of the peasantry, Stalin presented a tissue of quotations from Lenin. Indeed, his command of Lenin's writings (assuming he wrote the lectures without assistance[11]) was formidable. He reminded his listeners and readers that Lenin had stressed the importance of a hard-hitting, though short-lived, dictatorship of the proletariat which, continuing the binaries, 'is a stubborn struggle—bloody and bloodless, violent and peaceful, military and economic, educational and administrative—against the forces and traditions of the old society'.[12] On the peasantry he defined the Leninist path as one of recognizing the revolutionary potential in the Russian peasantry under the leadership of the party and workers and to win over the peasants to co-operatives as the next step:

LENIN AS ICON AND INSPIRATION: LENINISM AFTER LENIN   85

Lenin rightly pointed out in his articles on co-operation that the development of agriculture in our country must proceed along a new path, along the path of drawing the majority of the peasants into socialist construction through the co-operatives, along the path of gradually introducing into agriculture the principles of collectivism.[13]

Perhaps the most striking word in that quote is 'gradually', underlining that at this point Stalin was a firm believer in NEP. On nationalities Stalin largely expounded his own ideas since, with his experience of the Caucasus region, one of Russia's internal colonies, he had become the party's specialist, not least because the other leading figures had little interest in nationalism.

Certain leaders of the Second International even went so far as to turn the right to self-determination into the right to cultural autonomy, i.e., the right of oppressed nations to have their own cultural institutions, leaving all political power in the hands of the ruling nation. As a consequence, the idea of self-determination stood in danger of being transformed from an instrument for combating annexations into an instrument for justifying them. Now we can say that this confusion has been cleared up. Leninism broadened the conception of self-determinism, interpreting it as the right of the oppressed peoples of the dependent countries and colonies to complete secession, as the right of nations to independent existence as states.[14]

He overlooked the similarity of the autonomy approach to what he had himself said in his pre-war writings, where he argued precisely that if nations had full autonomy of culture (he includes religion and language) they would not want independence, a policy which closely resembles the path actually followed by the newly formed USSR—Union of Soviet Socialist Republics. The remaining sections were about the need for subtlety and flexibility in strategy and tactics rather than a dogmatic approach; the nature of the party as the gathering together of the best, most advanced, elements of the proletariat; and the dangers of heavy-handedness and arrogance rather than the humility and sensitivity called for in undertaking party tasks. Such were the characteristics of Stalin's Leninism.

It may be that Stalin thought he was expressing a consensus on behalf of a party newly bereft of its great leader. If so he could not have been more mistaken. Lenin's death had exacerbated the jostling for position between the candidates to succeed him and it turned into an all-out struggle. Zinoviev and Trotsky denounced Stalin's version of Leninism, the latter describing it

86 LENIN LIVES?

as 'rubbish' and an 'anthology of banalities'.[15] Stalin's work had become the opening salvo in a new phase of bitter conflict at the highest levels of the party. So stinging was the criticism that Stalin revised the whole book and republished it as *Problems of Leninism*. The main difference was that the sections on colonialism and the impact of imperialism—'world revolution' in a sense—were omitted or ruthlessly pruned. Instead, he built on the assertion that Soviet Russia had 'all that was necessary to build socialism',[16] if one added cultural revolution (Stalin quoted these words from Lenin's *On Co-operation*) and emphasized the importance of defending the revolution within Russia at all costs. He was underlining the basics of 'socialism in one country'. It is argued that he did this because he was in the course of moving to a clearer 'socialism in one country' position and putting clear blue water between himself and the opposing factions who stood for 'world revolution'. Precise pursuit of these considerations of intra-party argument is beyond our current scope. However, we must note a factor complicating all our attempts to systematize Leninism. For individuals and groups, even entire parties, 'Leninism' was not a glacier, a frozen dogma which changed slowly if at all, but a river, at times descending quickly through rapids and even tumbling over waterfalls, at other times meandering slowly through broad, flat plains. In many ways we are attempting the impossible task of stopping the flood in its tracks. There are, however, a number of enduring points to make in connection with our investigation of what attracted people to Leninism.

First of all, there was no single model of Leninist theory and, even more important, practice. Three models were emerging. Trotsky and the Left Opposition looked to the Lenin of 1917—author of *The State and Revolution*, producer of *The April Theses*, unstoppable proponent of armed uprising in September and October—not least on the grounds that it would be a detonator of world revolution. Then there was the Lenin of NEP, championed by Bukharin and the Right Opposition, a model according to which, having captured state power, the next step was to gradually win over the peasantry to co-operation as well as to raise the consciousness of workers. Then there was the Lenin of spring 1918, the Lenin of revolutionary survival at all costs, of productionism based on the iron proletarian discipline of the dictatorship of the proletariat, a model which inspired 'socialism in one country' increasingly defended by Stalin. The 'Stalinist' model had a further major step to completion—the turn away from NEP towards forced collectivization of agriculture (a descendant of civil war grain requisitioning on steroids) and industrialization. Both would be contained within the framework of a central plan, a concept which was also a descendant of civil war practices taken to the extreme. Both of these developments, however, fit within the productionist and even state capitalist mould.[17]

Second, the war in the party over these conflicting models was increasingly conducted by the scholastic exchange of Lenin quotations. This practice had not been widespread, but Lenin's works, and those of Marx and Engels, perhaps at the cost of their inspirational and guiding value, were becoming a repository of potential weapons. Each participant reached in to produce a quote/cudgel to smash around their opponent's head, a characteristic which has taken deep roots in the Marxist-Leninist ideology-based movement (and many others) where a shared spirit, a shared inspiration, and shared values were increasingly sacrificed to polemic and personal vendettas. One consequence of this is that, with Lenin being such a flexible thinker and practitioner, an even wider variety of 'Leninisms' was being constructed. The conflict took over from and developed the earliest attempts to define party practice embodied in sometimes overlooked sources. In particular, the 1918 'Declaration of the Rights of Working People', the 1918 constitution, and the 1919 party programme, plus the associated explanation of it in the *ABC of Communism,* brought radical ideas to the fore. In particular, they underlined the class nature of the new order and also these items were produced to reference the great bourgeois declarations like the *Rights of Man* from the French Revolution and the US Declaration of Independence and Constitution. They aimed to show the superiority of socialist principles by asserting the rights of the lower classes above those of the exploiting elites, spreading liberal principles into the realm of property in the face of liberalism's unqualified support of the endless accumulation of private property, and the provision not only of 'passive' rights but also of providing the means for all to be able to exercise those rights. For example, it was all very well to have freedom of the press, but without access to it, which was governed by ownership in liberal society, it was an empty value for the vast majority. For a liberal the right to work meant having the possibility of getting a job. The Soviet constitution committed to the actual provision of jobs, and therefore incomes, for all, and so on. While these promises were way beyond the political, cultural, and economic capacity of the early Soviet state to implement, they did add substantially to the model, helped define socialism from liberalism, and declared the arrival of the world's first, in the best sense, welfare state. From this point on, however, Lenin was increasingly going global.

88 LENIN LIVES?

The Party

The first thing that often comes to mind when asking what the fundamental feature of Leninism is, the characteristic which distinguishes it from its Marxist parent and its liberal democratic rivals, is usually Lenin's conception of the party. Leninists, although they defined it differently at different times, are united by what they consider to be seminal aspects of the party, notably its role in the process of revolution, its composition, its organizational features, and its expectations of its members.

'The emancipation of the working class will be conquered by the workers themselves', asserted Marx in 1864.[18] This concept effectively excludes Marx himself and a multitude of others from the process of emancipation since they were bourgeois intellectuals. Marx did not mean that, but nor did he dwell on the contradiction. It has, however, run through the Marxist movement. As discussed later, a certain subsection of the non-proletarian intelligentsia was strongly drawn to the labour movement and in many cases dominated national leaderships. For the moment let's consider an even more fundamental aspect of what Marx proposed. The workers did not need outside tutelage from anyone and would recognize the need for expropriating their employers, for revolution in other words, through reflection on their daily experiences as a class. Local conflicts with employers for better wages and conditions might produce temporary ameliorations but, Marx argued, the process would eventually lead to exploited workers realizing the issue was not just harsh, grasping employers, but the system of ownership itself. Solidarity across the class would grow as this recognition sank in and workers of all kinds realized they shared this crucial interest with each other. Their class and revolutionary consciousness, their awareness, would grow, and as the overwhelming majority, they would unite and take control of their lives, their factories, their economic system, and their society and operate in the mutual interest of everyone. Profits would no longer go straight into private pockets but belong to the community as a whole. This would parallel developments within capitalism itself which polarized ownership with more and more capital being owned by fewer and fewer capitalists. Those who failed in the competition for profits would be eliminated from the capitalist class—'one capitalist always kills many' Marx wrote—and the losers would sink into the lower classes.[19] Capitalist societies would polarize more widely into rich owners and poor workers, the latter realizing their recourse was to act so that 'the expropriators are expropriated'

LENIN AS ICON AND INSPIRATION: LENINISM AFTER LENIN 89

and take over factories, land, capital, and so on and divert them to communal not private goals.[20] At times Marx modified this scenario, but nowhere did he prioritize a party, nor did he associate with one in any depth. In reality, Marxists, with Germany in the forefront, did found parties to engage in parliamentary struggle. However, there was, by 1900, a question haunting Marxists—why had the expected revolution not occurred? Many responses were suggested but only one is germane to our present inquiry—the one developed by Lenin.

In 1900, it was impossible for any Russian party to follow the parliamentary route because Russia lacked even a limited parliament like the German Reichstag. A small group, the Economists, admired Bernstein but Lenin saw a different priority. While Russian Social Democracy as a whole, including Mensheviks, moved to the creation of a party, Lenin provided a particular spin on the idea which has characterized Leninism ever since. He proposed an 'active' definition of party and membership. It would not mirror the parliamentary model of being open to anyone who chose to belong and accept its rules and policies, but would be an organization of those who were further ahead in the process of developing class and revolutionary consciousness. It would gather together the 'advanced' workers and their allies. The main priority of this 'vanguard' party, as it was later termed, would be to nurture advanced consciousness in the rest of the class. Where a conventional party tended to represent the actually existing views of its members, though sometimes trying to lead them onto new ground, Lenin's party existed to educate and enlighten the rest of the class, not follow its current interests. As we noted, Lenin despised 'khvostizm' ('tailism'), that is hanging on to the tail of the workers' movement. The place of the revolutionary party was unequivocally at its head. In Lenin's astonishing and spectacular rise to power, not only did this vision of the party prevail, he also adapted the whole Soviet state to doing the same thing, to conducting cultural revolution, raising consciousness, to mobilizing the class around its best interests, without being ashamed to upbraid the majority of the class for not knowing its own interests, interests which were understood in the party of advanced workers but were sometimes not yet developed in the wider class itself. As a result, party, and state where they had control, were geared to prodding history along its hoped-for channels. They attempted to speed up the otherwise slow-moving development of socialist consciousness. They maybe even implied an admission of a failure of vision by Marx for not seeing the need for such a party to realize the potential for class and revolutionary struggle.

90 LENIN LIVES?

Not all Marxists were so emphatic about the vanguard party, but all communist parties came to embody this characteristic and it was clearly defined by Lenin and his party on a multitude of occasions.

In the light of this, the importance of the apparently trivial differences of wording in 1903, at the Second Party Congress, between Martov's definition of party membership as '*regular personal association under the direction of* one of the party organisations', and Lenin, who proposed a party member should be someone 'Who recognizes the party's program and supports it by material means and by *personal participation in* one of the party organisations', take on a deeper significance.[21] Even though Lenin lost the vote his definition remained in force, in theory at least, among Leninists. It also explains one of the most important reasons Lenin had for making a newspaper the centrepiece of party activity, and for journalism to be his main day-to-day activity. The newspaper, whether it be *Iskra, Proletarii, Pravda*, or any other, was the medium through which consciousness could be raised. Reflections of this foundation fact about the party can be found in many documents, party statutes, and accounts by party members. For example, in 1919 the first post-revolutionary party programme, the fullest self-definition of the party in terms of its aspirations and ideals, stated that:

> the international Communist Party, [is] the conscious exponent of, the class movement...Setting itself the task of making the proletariat capable of performing its great historic mission, the international Communist Party organizes it into an independent political party,...reveals to it the irreconcilable opposition between the interests of the exploiters and those of the exploited masses, and explains to the proletariat the historical importance and the necessary prerequisites of the coming social revolution. At the same time it reveals to all the other toiling and exploited masses the hopelessness of its position in capitalist society and the necessity of a social revolution for the purpose of liberating itself from the yoke of capital.[22]

'Making the proletariat capable of performing its great historic mission...reveals...explains' all imply a top-down relationship. In the explanatory pamphlet produced to help explain the programme, the authors, Nikolai Bukharin and Evgenii Preobrazhensky, put it even more directly: 'the party,...is composed of the best and most energetic members of the class; thus those who enter the party lead the rest', though it does claim this is a characteristic of all political parties.[23]

LENIN AS ICON AND INSPIRATION: LENINISM AFTER LENIN   91

This was rather disingenuous as the party was already adopting practical measures to ensure the quality, commitment, and orthodoxy of party members. In 1920–1 the first 'purge' (*chistka* in Russian), itself a telling medical metaphor referring to expelling toxic elements from the body, was conducted in the form of a review of every party member's performance, as a result of which around 177,000, representing about a quarter of the members, were expelled, suspended, or downgraded. In 1920, Party Control Commissions were set up to regularize the process. In the highest tier, the central commission, only long-standing members could be appointed, a way of trying to ensure only the most committed could take part since they would be the ones who would have joined earliest, when being a member required major commitment. Descending through the tiers to regional and local commissions, the requirements for length of party membership became shorter. It was an ingenious, but fallible, way to objectivize the level of consciousness of individuals. A proliferation of special organs of 'political cultural enlightenment' began, including Proletkul't (founded 1917, reformed 1920), the Sverdlov party school (founded 1919), the Agitation and Propaganda Department of the Central Committee (1922), the Institute of Red Professors (1923, a kind of party equivalent of the Academy of Sciences), which all bore witness to the effort to build consciousness from above. Developments within the party—whereby a series of 'oppositions' lobbying for influence within the party, such as the 'Left Opposition' and 'The Workers' Opposition', were either disbanded or emasculated—came to a head at the Tenth Party Congress in 1921 when a resolution drafted by Lenin to ban 'factions' in the party was passed. The momentum was all towards more and more central control. From that time on the emphasis was on obedience over discussion, and though the latter never fully died out, under Stalin, it could become very risky, even fatal to those who tried to engage in it. Slowly but surely the 'leading role' of the party in society and its 'infallibility', in that it primarily taught its truths embodied in the programme rather than discussed their formulation, were emerging as implications of the Leninist approach to revolution.

Such developments were clear to members within and beyond Russia. Another full definition of the party was incorporated, implicitly and explicitly, in the '21 Conditions of Admission' adopted by the Second Congress of the Communist International (better known as Comintern), held in Moscow in 1920. The emphasis on centralization was very strong and the old 'populist' style of cell structure was included, the duty of cells being

92 LENIN LIVES?

defined, for example, in condition 9: 'Communist cells should be formed in the trades unions, and, by their sustained and unflagging work, win the unions over to the communist cause...The cells must be completely subordinate to the party as a whole.'[24] Conditions 13 and 14 were very explicit:

> 13. Parties belonging to the Communist International must be organised on the principle of democratic centralism. In this period of acute civil war, the Communist parties can perform their duty only if they are organised in a most centralised manner, are marked by an iron discipline bordering on military discipline, and have strong and authoritative party centres invested with wide powers and enjoying the unanimous confidence of the membership.
>
> 14. Communist parties in countries where Communists can conduct their work legally must carry out periodic membership purges (re-registrations) with the aim of systematically ridding the party of petty-bourgeois elements that inevitably percolate into them.[25]

This last point, about purges, was also deeply embodied, appearing directly or indirectly in fourteen of the conditions which called upon parties to split from all other tendencies and to expel any waverers within. The hardening of these definitions, leading to 'iron discipline bordering on military discipline', invalidated any lingering similarity between communist 'democratic centralism' and the practice of typical bourgeois-liberal and parliamentary social-democratic parties. The Leninist party had assumed the role of social and revolutionary leadership and was wrapping the cloak of infallibility around itself.

Members were well aware of this. Writing after he had broken with the movement, though not in the acrimonious spirit of many others who had done the same, the German communist and Comintern official Franz Borkenau wrote that:

> The organisation of professional revolutionaries, directly selected, bound to absolute obedience towards the superiors of the organisation, ready for any sacrifice, severed with every link from the outside world, classless in the most emphatic sense of the term, knowing neither satisfaction nor moral obligation outside the good of their organisation, is a specific creation of the Russian soil...Lenin transferred this organisation, with its

LENIN AS ICON AND INSPIRATION: LENINISM AFTER LENIN 93

peculiar methods of selection and work, its peculiar religious enthusiasm and its equally peculiar indifference to ordinary moral standards, into the Russian labour movement. Having conquered Russia with his organisation of professional revolutionaries, he attempted to transfer the same methods to the West... [where] the whole conception was foreign to even the most revolutionary socialists.[26]

While this was clearly an exaggeration of the realities, it was an example of the model as it had evolved after 1917. But his notion of Lenin's 'real genius'[27] being that 'whatever his *ideas* may contain of contradictions and inconsistencies, he founded the *organisation* able to dictate, his party, the Bolshevik party.'[28] Borkenau was also adamant that, by introducing such a structured party, Lenin implied 'no less than a wholesale rejection of the basic contention of Marxism' since Marx had argued that the proletariat 'by the natural course of industrial progress and the increase of destitution and exploitation which he supposed went with it, became more revolutionary every day... This Lenin emphatically denied. The proletariat by itself never becomes revolutionary, he contended.'[29]

In practice, Borkenau's view is heavily influenced by Nechaev and reflects the latter's prescription for the life of a revolutionary and the nature of a revolutionary party. It is also the case that Borkenau's experience of the party came in the era of Stalinization when the process of iron party discipline had greatly developed. In Lenin's lifetime the party was still relatively disorganized and more conventional in structure, though his aspiration was certainly to make it, and the society it dominated, increasingly centralized. Nonetheless, by the 1930s his presentation of the party was shared by many communists and non-communists. The party leaders wanted people to carry out their orders, not argue or act spontaneously. Obedience was one of the most important characteristics looked for in a party member. In addition, they were also supposed to be ambassadors of revolution, winning waverers to the cause by their honesty, integrity, courage, commitment, and self-sacrifice. They were expected to be saints of the new religion. Some were, most were not. The dominant position of the party in society opened up all kinds of opportunities for careerist self-advancement and acquisition of privilege. Lenin himself denounced 'communist arrogance' and warned that:

[t]he Communist who has failed to prove his ability to bring together and guide the work of specialists in a spirit of modesty, going to the heart of

94 LENIN LIVES?

the matter and studying it in detail, is a potential menace. We have many such Communists among us, and I would gladly swap dozens of them for one conscientious qualified bourgeois specialist.[30]

It was to weed such people out that the purge tradition began before taking its deadly turn in the mid-1930s. However, to be a Leninist was to be a devoted servant of the party and the party was the centrepiece of the ongoing process of revolutionary transformation and consciousness-raising. Leninism was, and remains, centrally focused on the party.

Leninism Goes Global

'World revolution' was deeply priced in to the Leninist concept of revolution. Capitalism knew no national boundaries and was indivisible. The revolution had to be the same. As we have seen, Lenin and Trotsky, in the heat of the October Revolution, both referred to the essential link between the Russian and international revolutions. However, within months, the expectation of world revolution and its nature underwent extensive and surprising mutations. By spring 1918, the reality of isolation and the need to accept, hopefully for a short time though actually for an unknown and undefinable period, the inevitability of a form of 'socialism in one country' had been instrumental in inducing Lenin to abandon his first revolutionary model and adopt his second. Ironically, however, it was during this first period of 'socialism in one country' that the revolution began to think on an international scale. In 1919, Comintern (officially the Third (Communist) International) held its first congress in Moscow. In 1920, a Congress of Peoples of the East was held in Baku, on the shore of the Caspian Sea and an old haunt of Stalin from his days as an organizer of oil workers employed by BP among other companies. Both, especially Comintern at this point, were intimately linked to the top priority of the Communist Party, the survival of the revolution through victory in the civil war. Here, as was the case under Stalin, the isolationist and internationalist perspectives underwent an unforeseen fusion. The best way to promote world revolution was by defending and constructing a strong Soviet state as a solid platform from which capitalism could be subverted. Each of these two civil war era conferences had this in mind, but out of them flowed two quite different revolutionary strategies. The Baku Congress was chaotic and had no formal successor but the cause was integrated, for better or worse, within the framework of Comintern.

i) Comintern and the Struggle against Fascism

The first Comintern congress was portentious but unimpressive. In the conditions of 1919 it was almost impossible to cross civil war front lines, negotiate western embargoes and sanctions, or defy the wrath of capitalist governments to make the journey to Moscow. The result was that most delegates were already in Moscow and had only tenuous links to their home countries. The timing also had a major impact on content. The main resolutions exhorted European and American labour movements to undermine efforts by their national governments to intervene in the civil war. In Britain this had the effect of encouraging a 'Hands off Russia' campaign, conducted notably by dock workers, to stop armaments, troops, and military supplies from being sent to the White forces in the Russian Civil War, a perfect example of international efforts supporting the Russian Revolution rather than, for the time being, the other way around. Those promoting the expansion of the revolution by means of revolutionary war, the Left Communists, the first significant post-1917 opposition within Lenin's own party, were dismayed. In 1920, their hopes rose as a war, begun by a Polish invasion to

Fig. 5 Lenin sweeps away the class enemies of working people. A poster from 1920 with the caption 'Lenin cleanses the world of the unclean'.

take advantage of Russian weakness and seize territory in the Carpathians and western Ukraine, actually turned in Russia's favour. The Polish attack was reversed and the Red Army closed in on Warsaw; and heady expectations of victory, establishment of a Polish Communist government, and continuing the triumphal progress of the troops to Berlin, temporarily rose in many minds, only to be dashed by defeat at the gates of Warsaw, followed by retreat and an eventual settlement for the status quo before the war. Though short and sharp, the campaign was an indicator of things to come in at least two key respects. First, in its actually rather desultory efforts to set up an embryonic communist provisional government for Poland, Soviet political strategists barely considered local conditions and attempted to install a government which was a clone of Russian precedents. Second, the substantial Polish working class showed little sympathy for the incoming Red Army, which, to most of them, represented a new form of Russian aggression. Poland had only escaped tsarist domination two years earlier and its population was determined not to go back under the Russian thumb, be it Red or White. For the first time since the revolution, the optimistic assumptions about international proletarian solidarity had been put to the test and had failed. They foundered on the rock of nationalism. These two

Fig. 6 Solemn Opening of the 2nd World Congress of the Comintern in Petrograd, 19 July 1920: Lenin's speech. (Isaak Izrailevich Brodsky 1926). While the painting shows considerable ethnic diversity it reveals the strong gender bias, not only of the Congress, but of the communist movement which had relatively few powerful and influential women in its ranks.

LENIN AS ICON AND INSPIRATION: LENINISM AFTER LENIN 97

difficulties, imposition of the Russian model and nationalism, beset international communism throughout its existence.

It was only in 1920 that international communism began in earnest. The second Comintern congress had wider representation than the first. There were over 200 delegates including thirty or more from Asia.

Given that blockades still existed and only one month's notice was given this is a remarkable number. The main business was to elect a Central Executive to run the organization on a day-to-day basis, and the drawing up of the Twenty-one Conditions of Admission. The main assignment for the delegates as they left the Congress was to go home and split the socialist and labour parties to form the first communist parties. The iconic Tours Congress of the French socialist movement, held in late December 1920, duly resulted in the splitting of the French Socialist Party into two main factions, the nascent Communist Party (Parti Communiste Francais CPF) which accepted most but not all of the Twenty-one Conditions, and a minority which rejected them entirely. Most delegates supported the former and they took the party newspaper, *L'Humanité* with it to become one of the most long-lived communist newspapers of the era. However, the minority of delegates who continued to identify with the already existing Socialist Party, included most of its senior figures and its elected leaders in the French parliament. One of the most passionate advocates of adherence to Comintern was the young Ho Chi Minh. The German Communist Party (KPD), which soon overtook the French (PCF) to become the most influential outside Russia, emerged from the turmoil of the collapse of the German state as the war ended. It emerged, via the Spartacists who attempted to lead a revolution in Germany in 1918, from within the German Social Democratic Party (SPD), the dominant Marxist (but obviously not Leninist) party of the late nineteenth and early twentieth centuries. By and large, it was drawn from those who had opposed the acceptance of the war and had split from the Second International in 1914 rather than vote for or support war credits. It was founded in late 1918, before Comintern itself. Despite the continuingly catastrophic tendency of the left to split and split again, a Comintern-oriented KPD stood as a serious left-wing rival to the SPD until the suppression of democracy by the Nazis in 1933. Many more communist parties, mostly small and with varying influence, were quickly emerging. By the end of 1921 they were present in China, Argentina, Spain, South Africa, the United States of America, Bulgaria, Czechoslovakia, Greece, Hungary, Mongolia, Romania, Yugoslavia, Austria, and Great Britain, where it was formed by a merger of smaller pre-existing groups rather than the splitting of a larger one.

98 LENIN LIVES?

Far from being monolithic, disciplined entities, these groups were very diverse within individual parties and as a whole. They attracted an extraordinarily diverse range of people including the Catholic radical Pierre Pascal and Ho Chi Minh in France; Rosa Luxemburg (murdered in prison in Berlin in 1919), her partner Leo Jogiches (who was assassinated as he investigated her murder), and Paul Levi, the first long-term leader in Germany; hard-nosed trade unionists like Willie Gallacher, feminist fighter and suffragist Sylvia Pankhurst, and sitting MP Lieutenant-Colonel Cecil L'Estrange Malone, an anti-communist hardliner who, after a clandestine visit to Russia in 1919, where he met Trotsky, foreign minister Litvinov and Chicherin from the foreign ministry, and other dignitaries (Rykov, Tsiurupa, and Lunacharsky), and toured factories and villages, became a supporter of the Soviet cause and admirer of their efforts to build a new society. The list could go on and the history of the groups and individuals involved goes way beyond our brief. However, closer to our theme, we might note the kaleidoscopic diversity of people involved by personality, occupation, ethnicity, and even class, many of them being middle class and even aristocrats. More of a problem for us would be to judge how 'Leninist' they were; how much had they been influenced by Leninism? Again there would be a diversity of answers. They all illustrate one abiding feature, which is that they were radicals and revolutionary sympathizers before they were Leninists. Given they were mostly active before 1917 this is almost unavoidable for their generation as Lenin was little known in those days, but it was equally true for all later generations. It was a rare individual who was converted by reading Lenin as a first step. Rather, committed radicals turned to Lenin to order and develop their thoughts and impulses in a particular, often more systematic, direction.

Of course, communism provoked deep opposition as well as sympathy and profoundly anti-communist movements emerged. Unsurprisingly, the propertied classes and the elites associated with them looked on the emergence of Bolshevism, if not in fear and trembling, then certainly with a very wary and apprehensive hostility since they were the revolution's designated prey. More surprising, violent opposition arose from very similar soil to Bolshevism itself. Fascist movements began to form from disaffected soldiers, as mass Bolshevism had done in Russia, and also from hard-pressed peasants and workers. They, unlike communists, rallied to the cause of right-wing nationalism and saw communist internationalism as a comprehensive threat to national culture, including the national state, religion, ownership even of personal property, and sexual convention. From the outset, communism in Europe was embroiled in and extensively defined by its bitter clash with fascism. In the United States, European fascism was never very influential

LENIN AS ICON AND INSPIRATION: LENINISM AFTER LENIN 99

but its own indigenous form, based on pervasive racism, aggressive white nationalism, antisemitism, anti-Catholicism, homophobia and so on, exemplified in their most extreme forms in the renascent Ku Klux Klan, was significantly powerful. Fascism and communism were the complete antithesis of each other. The former dreamed of racial and imperial domination, the latter of social and cultural liberation. They were precise opposites. Where early fascism appeared to have points in common with socialism and communism—notably in its avowed hostility to capitalism and bourgeois values—it quickly compromised and came to prominence, first in Italy, as the hired thugs of the upper and middle class elites. They were the extra-parliamentary enforcers used to batter the left whenever it appeared to be a threat to property and established social and power structures. Where the two movements were in conflict across the European continent they eventually, literally, battered each other to death. In the 1930s and the early years of the war fascism wiped out communism and socialism almost everywhere except France, Britain, and Soviet Russia. However, hubris was at hand and by 1945 fascism had crashed and burned across most of Europe, though it still dominated the Iberian Peninsula and parts of the Spanish Americas. Throughout the conflict, communists were in most cases fascism's most determined opponents. They fought it in the streets of Milan, Berlin, Munich, London, Paris, and many other places. Communist support in a popular front helped the Spanish Republic survive for three years in the civil war, but not to win. Similarly, the French Popular Front of 1936–8 fended off the internal fascist threat. During the war, communists were the backbone of the main resistance movements in France and Italy and communism emerged in 1945 with its prestige at an unprecedented high. Claims that communism and fascism were essential allies in their illiberalism are shallow. Collaborations did happen, in some strikes in Germany around 1930 and in a cynical alliance between Nazi Germany and the Soviet Union in 1939, but none of the parties to such agreements believed they were anything but temporarily convenient and transient truces before renewing the battle. In a sense, this was also true at the state level. In order to defeat Hitler even the liberal democracies of Britain and the United States were forced into a temporary alliance with the USSR, which provided 80 percent of the European war effort that overcame Hitler. At this level, too, communism was the most resolute and self-sacrificing force in the anti-fascist alliance.

Anti-fascism became the chief recruiter for international communism in the 1920s and 1930s. Communists from the beginning believed they had a special insight into the nature of fascism. It was not, they argued, a particularly new phenomenon. Rather it was, to develop Lenin's phrase, that if imperialism was the highest stage of capitalism, then fascism was the highest stage of imperialism. It was the violent, desperate, and, for some, dying thrashings of the capitalist beast. It was an extension of pre-war imperialism as interpreted by Lenin, a violent, racist, dominating, colonializing form of exploitative corporate capitalism. Fascism simply took these characteristics to new depths. The analysis appealed to many on the left and gave hope to many, though by no means all, opponents of fascism. However, many of those opponents went silent once they were personally threatened, from members of Hitler's high command to rural schoolteachers in Italy. Bourgeois industrialists and their associates went along with the new order, even finding it profitable at times. Workers and peasants also succumbed to crumbs of comfort—holidays, leisure activities, a few consumer goods—and for many, apart from the antisemites and racists who became enthusiasts for the regime, their opposition became silent, inactive indifference to what was going on around them. Communists, however, resisted to the end. Many volunteered for the International Brigades aiding the Republic in the Spanish Civil War. Many young middle-class women and men became communist to participate in the struggle.

Fig. 7 Women of the Republican and socialist Largo Caballero Battalion in the Spanish Civil War, 1938.

LENIN AS ICON AND INSPIRATION: LENINISM AFTER LENIN   101

For our purposes it is hard to distinguish what in this phenomenon was specifically Leninist. Lenin's idea of a determined professional revolutionary core to the movement certainly helped it to mobilize the most determined and the most committed, but the inspiration of many communists was to associate themselves with a more determined form of resistance to fascism than was provided by socialist and liberal movements. Liberalism in particular showed a tendency to compromise with fascism because they saw communism as a deeper threat to their property and privileges. Liberal acquiescence smoothed the paths to power of both Mussolini and Hitler.

For the most resolute fighters against fascism, there was hardly anywhere to go but to fight alongside the communists, whether they were the Moscow-supporting majority or the small but locally significant Trotskyite minority. It was not straightforward. At crucial moments communist policy split the resistance just when it needed to be united. The main example of this came in Germany during the rise of Hitler. Comintern was closely linked to the policy of the soviet party. When the party line in the USSR changed, the Comintern line changed in sync with it. It meant that what may have been the appropriate party line in the USSR was deemed to be valid for the rest of the world, no matter what the local conditions. This was idiotic. Whichever line was being pursued in Moscow, so the Comintern did the same, so infallible was the Soviet party considered to be. In the 1920s a degree of class collaboration, with peasants and non-party specialists for example, was the selected strategy in the USSR. As such, Comintern followed the party line. Profound consequences of this were felt in China. Forcing the Chinese Communist Party into an unwanted alliance with the nationalists brought disaster. When the NEP era in Soviet Russia (1921–8) brought class collaboration rather than confrontation, so the Chinese Communist Party was ordered, against the better judgement of many leaders, to ally with the nationalist Kuomintang. The outcome, in 1927, was the massacre of the former by the latter. This precipitated, perhaps fortunately for the movement, a radical change in Chinese communism. Having to flee the cities, the surviving leaders had little choice but to seek the protection of a controversial party figure, Mao Zedong. Mao had argued that, in China, the revolution needed a base in the overwhelmingly vast peasantry, not just the urban worker enclaves. He had been dismissed in Moscow, not without reason, as a 'populist', echoing the ideas of Lenin's peasant-oriented opponents in the Socialist Revolutionary Party.

102 LENIN LIVES?

Meanwhile, in Moscow, NEP collapsed in 1928 and the line turned from class collaboration to renewed 'class struggle' in the form of collectivization and industrialization. Like a slow-turning supership the world communist movement had to follow suit. Communist parties were told to break off all alliances and fight equally against all opponents. In many places this made no sense at all.

It was most damaging in Germany. As the Comintern followed the new line it abandoned alliances with other groups, notably the anti-fascist German SPD, thereby dividing the anti-Hitler forces at the crucial moments of 1929–33. Just as Hitler's movement was beginning to gain votes, the German Communist Party was ordered to treat the German Socialist Party, not to mention other less committed opponents of the Nazis like the Centre Party and some Nationalist Party members, as being as hostile as the Nazis. The opposition was fatally split and, although there is no guarantee it would have succeeded, alliance across party lines was off the agenda for the Communist Party just when it might have mattered most. Instead of fighting Nazism alongside the socialists, the socialists were deemed to be 'social fascists' themselves. The practice of following Moscow regardless was insane. By the time the party line returned to collaborations through 'popular fronts' in 1934–6 it was too late to stop the Nazis.

The return of the party line towards social toleration and class collaboration in 1934 enabled the formation of the French and Spanish Popular Front alliances with other socialists and leftists (including an uneasy alliance with Trotskyites in Spain which was partly instrumental in exporting the Moscow purges to Spain, where they severely weakened the resistance to Franco). However, that line was changed again in August 1939 when the Nazi-Soviet Treaty was signed. It came as a shock and for the next twenty-one months before the German invasion of Russia, communists and Nazis were supposed to become friends and allies. Many party members, notably in France, refused, as it would have meant welcoming the German invaders in 1940, something which no amount of party discipline could induce. In many ways the strangest aspect is that so many members remained in the party even when it made such disastrous and obvious errors. More than anything, in the dark pre-war years, it was a sign there was nowhere else to go for many radicals. A minority turned to Trotsky, who had been expelled from the party in 1927 and from the USSR in 1929. He claimed to represent a purer strain of Leninism than Stalin, who had come to power by manipulating what Trotsky saw as a

LENIN AS ICON AND INSPIRATION: LENINISM AFTER LENIN   103

degenerate bureaucracy which was stifling true worker consciousness in a morass of administrative procedures and red tape. But even Trotsky himself enjoined support for the USSR as the war began. Even as a 'degenerate' worker state it was superior to Nazism. In 1940, an agent of that state, sent by Stalin, silenced Trotsky for ever.

ii) The Weakest Link: Imperialism, Colonialism, and Peasant Revolution

If the prestige and focus of communism in the West was anti-fascism, in Asia it pivoted in a different but related direction. It has often been commented that the Baku Conference of 1920 brought together a very diverse range of people, which is certainly true, and also that that is why it failed, which is more debateable. However, the diversity of participants is revealing. Among the nearly 2,000 delegates, representing thirty ethnicities, were Ibn Saud, soon to become founder of the current royal ruling house of Saudi Arabia. The attendance of the Turkish leader, Enver Pasha, offended Armenian delegates who held him responsible for the Armenian genocide of 1915–16 and those who supported his radical opponent in Turkish politics, Kemal Ataturk. John Reed, the American journalist and admirer of the revolution, Bela Kun, the defeated leader of the brief Hungarian Soviet revolution of 1919, and other European communists addressed the delegates. Comintern head Grigorii Zinoviev described the gathering as 'motley', but they did have one thing in common. It was not communism. Many communists were present but there were many who were not. The common theme was anti-colonialism. Even some of the communist delegates had been drawn to the movement through their anti-colonialism, none more so than Ho Chi Minh.

In an article written for a Soviet journal on the occasion of the ninetieth anniversary of Lenin's birth in 1960, and in the full heat of Vietnam's war of liberation, Ho made a number of startling assertions. 'At that time [immediately after the end of the First World War] I supported the October revolution only instinctively', by which he appears to mean it was the symbolic aspect of the October Revolution, a revolution which had overthrown capitalism and established a government of workers and peasants, that had attracted him. He says he had 'not yet grasp[ed] its full importance'. Even more interestingly he writes that 'I loved and admired Lenin because he was a great patriot', a description Lenin might have found odd despite it being correct in many ways. Lenin had 'liberated his compatriots'. 'Until that time',

Fig. 8 Ho Chi Minh (Sung Man Cho) in a British prison. Photo: Victoria Prison, Hong Kong, 1930.
(*Source*: Archives nationales d'outre-mer, HCI SPCE 364).

that is after becoming an admirer of Lenin, 'I had read none of his writings'.[31] This is, at first sight, extraordinary and a great illustration of the difficulty of knowing what we mean by 'Lenin's' influence and legacy. Ho was an admirer of a revolution he saw as one of national liberation for its ordinary people. This drew him into socialist and communist circles in France where, at around the age of thirty, he made a striking intervention at the Tours Congress, speaking up for the workers and peasants of Indochina and implying that even the socialist right was indifferent to that struggle. From his writings of that era it is clear he was motivated by fighting against imperialism. A graphic story he recounted in 1922 depicts the sadistic evisceration by drunken French colonizers of a mother, the rape of her eight-year-old daughter, and the roasting of an old man on a spit.[32] Whether true or symbolic, the story exemplifies the passions that brought him to revolution. They led him to Comintern ultimately because, at first, French socialists 'had shown their sympathy to me, towards the struggle of the oppressed peoples' even though 'I understood neither what was a party, a trade union, nor what was Socialism and Communism. It was one of these ' "ladies and gentlemen"—as I called my comrades at that time' who suggested he read an article of Lenin's published in *L'Humanité* entitled 'Theses on the National and Colonial Question'. He spoke for many when he said:

LENIN AS ICON AND INSPIRATION: LENINISM AFTER LENIN   105

There were terms difficult to understand...but by dint of reading it again and again, finally, I could grasp the main part of it. What emotion, enthusiasm, clear-sightedness, and confidence it instilled into me! I was overjoyed to tears...After then I had entire confidence in Lenin, in the Third International.[33]

Suitable thoughts for an anniversary, but Ho also mentioned on several occasions his indebtedness to other philosophical and religious influences. 'When I was young I studied Buddhism, Confucianism, Christianity as well as Marxism. There is something good in each doctrine.'[34] His moral compass was based on 'Diligence, frugality, justice and integrity',[35] a quartet rooted in the philosophical-religious codes rather than standard Marxism. Unsurprisingly, Ho has often been interpreted as a nationalist first and a Marxist-Leninist second. One of his close comrades puts the issue thus:

How many times in my life have I been asked: you who know Ho Chi Minh so well, can you say whether he is a nationalist or a communist? The answer is simple: Ho Chi Minh is both. For him, nationalism and communism, the end and the means, complement one another; or rather, they merge inextricably.[36]

Marxism as the means, nationalism in the form of national liberation as the end. Such a formulation would be incomprehensible to many Marxist-Leninists in the European tradition, for whom nationalism was the essence of false consciousness, a distraction promoted by the elite to paper over the cracks of class struggle. But it is profoundly revelatory of the appeal of communism in the colonial and postcolonial world.

Ho Chi Minh proclaimed the independence of Vietnam on 1 September 1945, and although, probably for tactical reasons, the declaration opened with the words of the American equivalent of 1776 and referenced the French Declaration of the Rights of Man and there is no mention of Marxism or Leninism, he went on to set up the second Marxist-Leninist state. The Leninist elements strengthened over time as the new state was embroiled in a bitter thirty-year war of national liberation. The attempt by France to reimpose colonialism was fought off by 1954 and the United States picked up the baton until the last remnants of its rule scrambled for the last helicopter out of Saigon on 30 April 1975. Anti-colonialism remained the backbone of Vietnamese resistance. Leninism, the means. Liberation, the end. Setting aside the ersatz revolutions in Soviet-controlled areas of Europe, the next two independent Marxist-Leninist revolutions embodied each of our paradigms. Tito rose to power in Yugoslavia on a communist revolution powered by anti-fascism and dogged resistance to Nazi occupation. The Federal Republic of Yugoslavia was proclaimed on 29 November 1945. Lenin was having a good war. In passing we might note that the savagely independent revolution in Albania was also built on anti-fascism but also pivoted to anti-colonialism and later sided with the Chinese communists rather than Moscow. The Chinese revolution, which brought Mao Zedong and the Chinese Communist Party to power, where it remains to this day, was, like its little Vietnamese sister, nurtured in anti-colonialism as the end, Marxism-Leninism as the means.

Before analysing the Chinese communists' origin and path to power, we should recall that, for this generation, Marxism-Leninism incorporated what was later identified as Stalinism. Marxism-Leninism-Stalinism was the standard version for the overwhelming majority of communists until Khrushchev's bombshell revelations of 1956 which began a process of de-Stalinization. Before then, Trotskyites were few and far between and the Fourth International, founded by Trotsky in 1938 while he was living in France, remained small. Even worse, it was riven by factions, splits, and schisms which reduced its effectiveness even further, and it

Fig. 9 Zhou En Lai, Mao Zedong, and Zhu De on the Long March.

LENIN AS ICON AND INSPIRATION: LENINISM AFTER LENIN 107

rarely rose beyond being an intellectual curiosity. No Trotsky-inspired revolutions have occurred.

Chinese communism was born from similar roots. In particular, it emerged from the May Fourth Movement of 1919. It was so-called because that was the date when China refused to sign what it considered a humiliating treaty as part of the post First World War settlement at Versailles. The Western powers were seen to be colluding with China's enemy, Japan, to whom they gifted the former German concession of Shandong rather than allow it to revert to China.[37] This provoked demonstrations and the emergence of new political currents, including communism. At the heart of the May Fourth Movement were intellectuals turning to western enlightenment principles of science and rationality in place of, or sometimes in conjunction with, traditional Chinese traditions. A revolution in 1911 had brought an end to the ancient monarchy, and its leader, Sun Yat-sen, was heavily influenced by liberal democracy. However, the Versailles betrayal and Woodrow Wilson's ambiguous role at Versailles—proposing the Fourteen Points for national self-determination but not applying them fairly in practice, especially with respect to Shandong, and standing aloof from the League of Nations—led to disillusionment among some of the intellectuals who turned, instead, to the Russian Revolution model. The Chinese Communist Party was founded in 1922 with less than 250 members. It affiliated to Comintern but the relationship was complex and the parties held each other at arm's length. Chinese communism also had its own complications. Three factors interlinked. The party leadership under Chen Duxiu took an orthodox line of the primacy of the working class in the revolution. However, Comintern in the 1920s, reflecting the principles of NEP within Russia, promoted policies of collaboration between workers and the so-called national bourgeoisie. This last group, consisting of a developing local middle class, were deemed to share, for the next stage of development, the communist goal of throwing off Western imperialism. The national bourgeoisie, to put it briefly, was considered by Comintern analysts to want to supplant the foreign bourgeoisie, to establish themselves in its place. Thus, nationalism and anti-imperialism shared goals in the struggle to free China from Western economic shackles. Comintern ordered the Chinese party to collaborate with the nationalist Kuomintang. Chen even joined its central committee. However, this resulted in disaster.

In 1927, the Kuomintang turned on the communists and, especially in Shanghai and Guangzhou (Canton), engaged in a massacre of thousands of communists. Comintern blamed Chen, though Trotsky argued strongly that the fault lay with Stalin for ordering the cross-party alliance in the first

108   LENIN LIVES?

place. This had the effect of driving the party out of the industrial cities. It led to a major reorientation of the party because the survivors were thrown on the mercy of a maverick member, Mao Zedong, who had been more insistent on incorporating the peasantry into the revolutionary movement. In 1927 he was organizing the peasants of Hunan into a revolutionary force. He had been marginalized by the urban-based leader/founders of the party for his heretical 'populist' views and he also was less enthusiastic about the alliance with the national bourgeoisie. He had clashed with Chen on this point. However, the leadership had to accept Mao's priorities since they were now under his protection in his fiefdom, and he became the most influential of the party's leaders. Comintern expelled Chen in 1929 and he developed ties with the other great party outcast, Trotsky, though it was a coming together of outsiders rather than a meeting of minds and shared ideas. Chen went on to denounce Stalin's dictatorship and promote the importance of democracy and opposition. The authority of Mao was consolidated in the mid-1930s when the Kuomintang tried to completely eliminate the communists. In a controversial episode, Mao and the party fled Hunan in October 1934 and engaged in a dangerous relocation, fighting almost every inch of the way, to the northern province of Yenan, handily placed on the Soviet border should an emergency exit be required. Their epic journey, enshrined in revolutionary mythology as 'The Long March', ended there almost exactly a year after it had begun.

The rise of Chinese communism was, like Vietnam, not so much dependent on reading Lenin's works as following the model of a single, disciplined party and a deeply anti-colonial stance. China, in Mao's case, also went beyond Leninism by incorporating peasants into the revolutionary strategy from the beginning, so much so that the Maoists were seen by many in the party in Moscow as populists in the traditional Russian mode. In both Vietnamese and Chinese cases, nationalism was a much more obvious element than it was in Russia where the idea of internationalism was initially in the forefront. However, while Lenin was ideologically internationalist his practice and attention was almost completely focused on Russia. Even in exile he mixed mainly with Russians and never threw himself into the labour movements of the countries in which he found himself. In one anecdote from around 1903, his wife Krupskaya described Lenin, sitting in a German beer garden with her, admiring a passing parade of German workers. He would not have thought of joining them. Trotsky, by comparison, probably would have done. He participated in local labour struggles in New York and elsewhere. Under Stalin, internationalism was fused into a new form of Soviet patriotism which acknowledged the international revolution but argued that the best service the USSR could do for it was to survive and strengthen itself, to become an anti-capitalist and anti-imperialist fortress. It would provide aid where it could, in the Spanish Civil War, for example, where it was the only actively anti-fascist great power, or provide a model and an inspiration to a world which either knew little or was in denial about the dark side of Stalin's leadership in the 1930s.

It is not possible in the scope of this study to survey all the variants of communism that emerged. However, in many cases we can see variants on the basic themes. In almost all cases communist movements were dominated by an authoritarian, disciplined party structure, ever-vigilant over supposed ideological purity and intolerant of internal diversity. Almost all were organized on a nation-state basis and, as such, often became de facto nationalists, not of the liberal democratic kind vaunting elite figures, imperialists, and military commanders, but a people's nationalism building on the work of the masses—worker and peasant—and undermining the hegemonic bourgeois traditions and culture in their respective countries. In many cases communism thrived where it did not have serious competitors

Fig. 10 Tito (far right) and fellow partisans in the mountains, c.1944.

110   LENIN LIVES?

on the left. This was the case for China and Vietnam, though in Russia, through happenstance rather than calculation, it was thrust into power at the expense of the much larger but less disciplined and centralized Socialist Revolutionaries. Where strong social democratic or other leftist parties existed—Britain, France, Germany, Spain—communism had a harder fight to establish itself.

If we conclude this chapter by looking briefly at other movements we will see the variety of shapes which could be made from these basic ingredients. In Yugoslavia, the third place where communism came to power, it was propelled there by its leading role in the anti-German and anti-fascist resistance which was admired by British officers, including conservatives, notably Fitzroy Maclean, Basil Davidson, and Alan Deakin, who liaised with and even stood alongside Tito during and after the war. Such was Tito's strength that he was able to split off from Moscow and establish Yugoslavia as a leading 'non-aligned' country. China and Vietnam also followed independent lines. Even the fake revolutions of post-war Eastern Europe followed contrasting models. The Catholic Church remained prominent in Polish life. The extent of Soviet-style central planning varied. Collectivization was conducted in Hungary but not in Poland, and so on. However, in all cases the party kept a dictatorial hand on the political world and extensive, though varying, cultural control. All of them wrapped the mantle of people's nationalism around themselves and called themselves people's democracies. Many of them were not ruled by actual communist parties but entities in which the communist and other parties had fused together in a forced marriage, like the East German ruling party which called itself the Socialist Unity Party, or the Polish United Workers' Party, the Hungarian Socialist Workers' Party, and so on. The names were testimony to popular front style origins in early post-war Europe and to the possibility that had the Cold War not taken the shape it did, more genuine multi-party government might have survived longer in those countries. In the, by and large, poorly functioning economies, working people had some priority (though relatively privileged party elites dominated in all of them), and in all of them there was free or almost free education at all levels, including university, and medical services were available. Employment was guaranteed and cheap rent and utilities were the norm. Liberal freedoms and human rights were not. Some of the regimes stood on their own two feet, but Soviet geopolitical control was never far away, though not all of them had permanent Soviet military bases on their territory. However, being artificial creations, they are not particularly authentic examples of Leninist influence. Ideologically they did, of course, promote

LENIN AS ICON AND INSPIRATION: LENINISM AFTER LENIN   111

Marxism-Leninism, but it should also be borne in mind that in Lenin's own homeland his influence was slipping. Khrushchev appears to have been a true believer and his campaign against Stalin took the form of restoring a true Leninism from under the Stalinist distortions. However, by the time Brezhnev had asserted his leadership, Marxism-Leninism was becoming moribund. As a person who visited the USSR many times from 1970 on I would comment, and it was literally the case, that it was the one country I never met a Marxist. The ideology was all-pervasive and universally ignored. As a one-year visiting PhD student at Leningrad University I shared a student hostel room with a Russian postgraduate from Rostov-on-Don who was studying to become a teacher of the official ideology—dialectical materialism. His thesis was on the influence of Hegel on Lenin's philosophy, something quite fashionable in the West at the time thanks to the French Marxist Louis Althusser. 'That sounds interesting', I said. 'No it isn't', he replied and we never mentioned ideology ever again. Other trainee *diamat* teachers in the hostel were the same. It was a cushy, undemanding job no one with ambition and intelligence really wanted to do. At national level, the party drew its legitimacy more from the great achievement of defeating Nazism than from the 1917 revolution. Lenin's image was everywhere. His ideas were nowhere to be seen. In 1982, at almost the same time as Brezhnev himself, the last old-school party ideological chief, Mikhail Suslov, died, and within ten years the apparently mighty party and system were also gone. Despite being more or less independent by the time of Soviet collapse (1991), many communist parties, mostly in western Europe, followed immediately, leaving, at most, uninfluential rump organizations. Trotsky supporters were heartened by the turn of the events, and the hopes of those who felt the terrible crimes of the Stalin era were holding socialism and communism back through association also rose. But to no avail. Triumphant neoliberalism took a grip on the world, more or less unchallenged until the opening of a kind of new cold war on China in 2020–1 and in the course of the Ukraine crisis of 2022 and after.

Before looking at the survival or otherwise of Lenin's influence in those decades there are a number of points to make about other Leninist/communist movements. Each of them has its own history and characteristics and, as we have already seen, 'Leninist' influence is a varying bundle of features which included association with a partly mythical version of the October Revolution in which Bolshevism was swept to power on a tide of working class protest and raised revolutionary consciousness; resolute anti-fascism and/or anti-imperialism; a new kind of people's nationalism from below; and a relatively disciplined and centralized party. Despite adopting many of its core values (freedom, equality, 'democracy'), there was also a rejection of liberalism on the grounds that liberals compromised their values, not least because their central fixation on unlimited property rights contradicted the other core values. These, at least as much as, and probably more than, reading Lenin, tended to be the foundation of communists' own value systems.

The fourth self-generating, and still-surviving, communist revolution occurred in Cuba and is indissolubly linked to the two charismatic figures of Fidel Castro and Ernesto 'Che' Guevara. The Cuban revolution had its anomalies, which included a largely peasant-based path to power, a conflict with the orthodox communist party which was strong within the small Cuban working class, the dependence of the economy on sugar and some tobacco, and the proximity of the United States which, among other things, had turned Havana into an offshore 'playground' of gambling, prostitution, and other activities repressed in the stolidly protestant United States. In 1953, after being captured and put on trial after a failed attempt to spark a revolution, Fidel made an impassioned speech entitled *History Will Absolve Me*, justifying his actions through reference to influences that had inspired

Fig. 11 Fidel Castro and Camilo Cienfuegos enter Havana, 8 January 1959.

LENIN AS ICON AND INSPIRATION: LENINISM AFTER LENIN 113

him. There was no reference to Marx, still less to Lenin. He appealed to traditions which were strong in Latin America, notably the nationalism and anti-imperialism (congruent with anti-Americanism) of José Marti, the iconic Cuban poet and political thinker of the late nineteenth century, and the Catholic theory of tyrannicide and just rebellion elaborated by Juan Mariana in the sixteenth century. Indeed, Castro, in what was by his standards a short speech from the dock which lasted a mere two hours, invoked a host of anti-tyrannical sources. He even included the Cuban Constitution of 1940 which, he said, supports the view 'that resistance to despots is legitimate...and our 1940 Constitution expressly makes it a sacred right, in the second paragraph of Article 40: "It is legitimate to use adequate resistance to protect previously granted individual rights."' He quoted many varied sources including classical Greece, ancient India and China, John of Salisbury, St Thomas Aquinas, Martin Luther, Juan Mariana, John Knox, the English regicides and the 1688 revolutionaries, Milton, Locke, Rousseau, Tom Paine, the American Declaration of Independence, and the French Declaration of the Rights of Man.[38] While not referencing any Marxist-Leninist inspiration might be considered tactical there is no sign anywhere that it had much influence on him before he came to power. Implacable opposition from the United States to his nationalization of US companies in Cuba led to a fierce embargo (most of which is still in place sixty years later), which, in the Cold War binary of the time, led him to turn to the USSR for assistance. This also coincided with him saying, on 2 December 1961, after the failure of the CIA-planned Bay of Pigs invasion to overthrow him, that 'I am a Marxist-Leninist and shall be one until the end of my life'.[39] In a later interview he described himself as 'a socialist, a Marxist, a Leninist'.[40] Many historians agree that Castro was more inspired by the Cuban revolutionary tradition, and Marti rather than Marx and Lenin, and he played up that side to help his relationship with the USSR. Cuban communist ideology had a degree of flexibility, but perhaps the most Leninist feature is the authoritarian one-party state and the nationwide network of Committees for the Defence of the Revolution which reach down into workplaces, villages, and residential blocs, loosely resembling centrally controlled soviets.

Che Guevara was more overtly Marxist-Leninist from his early years but even he, when in power, had a personal line which emphasized achieving economic growth (a Cuban version of productionism) through exhortation and moral incentives rather than material ones. Both factors had Soviet precedent and, in fact, Stalin combined moral and material incentives in his strategy for building socialism. Che had followed an interesting route into

114   LENIN LIVES?

Leninism. He had been brought up in an intellectual, leftist household in Buenos Aires, Argentina, and his father had socialized with veteran exiles from the republican side of the Spanish Civil War. He had also had access to a large family library of several thousand books and he read American, English, and European classical literature and political literature including Marx, Engels, and Lenin, though it was Rudyard Kipling's *If* that he was able to recite by heart. He became an idealistic medical student but the toughening of his idealism into Leninism was unique. It took the form of an 8,000 km journey around Latin America on a worn-out Norton motorcycle with a comrade, Alberto Granado. It began as an idealistic young man's vision of 'seeing the world' and had the praiseworthy goal of ending up at a leper colony in Peru, where he and Alberto spent several weeks providing medical care for the inhabitants. But his journey revealed more than he expected. In his *Motorcycle Diaries*, Che described having his eyes opened to more and more extreme forms of exploitation, largely by American companies. He saw crushing working conditions and impoverishment among copper miners in Chile and excruciating poverty in the many Andean villages through which they passed. He directly experienced the US-backed coup in Guatemala engineered at the behest of the United Fruit Company. By the end of this process he had become convinced of the realities of capitalist exploitation, imperialism, and colonialism and saw the solution in continent-wide proletarian revolution along Leninist lines.

Another intellectual followed a very different revolutionary path which led to one of the most controversial situations in twentieth-century revolutionary history. In post-1945 Indochina a group of bright young boys, some from the village, had worked their way, through sheer ability, to reach the most prestigious lycée (grammar school) in their country, the lycée Sisowath. In a scheme intended to cream off the most intelligent of the younger generation and turn them into adopted French, they went to study at French universities, even though the group in question had engaged in anti-colonial activities in their schools and communities. In Paris they came into contact with French communists. The party (Parti Communiste Français, PCF) was strong and influential around 1950. This was still the era of adulation of Stalin as the global leader of revolutionary struggle and a time when the USSR was basking in the prestige of defeating fascism. Its firm stand against Western imperialism in the Cold War was also attractive to the anti-colonial left.

The young men and their young fiancées and wives found the PCF the most open party to anti-colonial struggle and formed close ties. They adopted a Marxist-Leninist position based on anti-imperialism, the idea of

LENIN AS ICON AND INSPIRATION: LENINISM AFTER LENIN   115

a disciplined party, and the need for armed struggle. These were the hallmarks of many developing struggles for national liberation but this group put it into practice with a demonic ferocity. They joined the Communist Party of Kampuchea (Cambodia) which went through various name changes but became best known as the Khmer Rouge. One of the group wrote a thesis on the Cambodian economy. The basic assumption of the author, Khieu Samphan, was derived from dependency theory, akin to the ideas of Samir Amin who was a student in Paris at the same time. A colony, Khieu argued, would always remain subjected to wealthier and more powerful colonizing powers through the natural functioning of the world market. Khieu came to the fateful conclusion that the only way for a country to create a more balanced and productive national economy was for it to withdraw from the world economy, to go through an intense period of self-sufficiency and major restructuring along co-operative lines, before re-entering the world economy on its own terms. In this iteration it was only socialism which could achieve real national liberation, not just politically but also economically.[41] Khieu Samphan's ideas permeated the movement and illustrated the close match, as in other movements, between Marxism-Leninism and radical nationalism, with many commentators giving precedence to the former over the latter. In Khieu's case key elements of core Leninism, like proletarian hegemony, were absent or marginal and peasants were put in the forefront of revolutionary strategy.

Like Lenin and the *smychka*, Khieu emphasized that his theories could only be put into practice with the consent of the peasants who must be treated with patience and understanding. Catastrophically, when in power, they did exactly the opposite and installed a regime of unprecedented mercilessness and savage coercion. Circumstances led Khieu, along with other members of the group, including Ieng Sary and the leader of the movement, Pol Pot, to taking over Kampuchea after a long and energy-sapping guerrilla war, which had led to the United States withdrawing from the country abruptly as their general position in Indochina collapsed. Not least of the problems for the new regime was the fact that the capital, Phnom Penh, had swollen to some 400,000 inhabitants as the United States had cleared rural areas to make it difficult for guerrillas to operate and refugees had fled to the city. It was fed and supplied by an American air bridge which ended the day they departed, leaving a massive population which could not be provided for. Mass American bombing had destroyed much of the infrastructure which supported fragile economic webs. It created a potential perfect storm for one of the darkest episodes in modern history.

116 LENIN LIVES?

The first phase of the Cambodian revolution saw a cruel and barbarous evacuation of the city. Its population, including patients ejected from hospital wards, was forcibly driven back to the villages where they were expected to fend for themselves or die out of sight. The guerrilla army also exacted revenge on its former oppressors, and the Khmer Rouge government soon chose a policy of massacre and ethnic cleansing against the large Vietnamese and Chinese populations and against Khmers who had supposedly collaborated with the American puppet regime. The outcome was the most extensive set of massacres and genocide apart from the holocaust itself. It is likely almost two million died from a population of around eight million. The Cambodian killing fields were the bitter antithesis of Leninist liberation.

iii) Endgame in Europe—1956–91

In developments that might seem ironic, the prestige of communism in Europe and the broadly Western world began to decline rapidly just as it began to undertake a reckoning with some of its worst failures. Khrushchev's speech of February 1956, criticizing several, but by no means all, of Stalin's crimes began a chain reaction which led to the collapse of European communism. Also ironically, despite the process of dissolution, communism reached its widest influence around 1980. Khrushchev's critique of Stalin was couched in terms of him deviating from 'Leninist norms'. Khrushchev emphasized his attack on the party, and thereby opened up a discourse hitherto limited, pretty much, to followers of Trotsky. There was a 'good Bolshevism' associated with a more democratic Lenin and a 'bad Bolshevism' linked to Stalin. Anti-Stalinist communists spread this discourse. Even Gorbachev had thought this way. Nonetheless, the revelation of the extent of the purges and the innocence of some of the lesser-known victims, plus the probably incorrect attribution to Stalin of the murder of his close associate Kirov, which actually triggered the purges, led to a massive seepage of party members. In particular, its significant attraction to many Western intellectuals weakened, though a number turned to Trotsky for a while.

Between 1945 and 1956 the Soviet Union had, for many, basked in the light of being one of the chief sufferers at the hands of Nazism, with twenty-seven million dead, and also being the chief force ridding the continent of Nazism, with 80 per cent of German and its allied forces being deployed on the Eastern Front even after D-Day. The full story of the outbreak of the Cold War was shrouded in obscurity at the time and, even today, remains a fiercely contested issue. Stalin's expectations of a continuation of the Grand

LENIN AS ICON AND INSPIRATION: LENINISM AFTER LENIN 117

Alliance with the United States and Britain into the post-war world via an active United Nations was met with hostility on the part of the United States. Europe fell into two spheres of influence. An iron curtain appeared separating them. Over the next few years versions of communism, though none had as rigid a command economy as the Soviet Union itself, were constructed in the countries within the Soviet sphere. There were many strains. In most cases, communism had been a very weak force. In some, like Poland, there was a visceral fear and hatred of Russian empire going back nearly two centuries. Most of them deeply resented Russian domination on nationalist grounds. Khrushchev's speech brought many of the pressures to boiling point. At its most extreme, the Soviet Union, which saw its sphere primarily as a defensive barrier against US hostility and a possible German resurgence, was forced to send troops into Hungary to prevent it from slipping away from Soviet control. This blatant intervention added to the decline. From 1956 to 1991, communism/Leninism in Europe, including the USSR itself, went through a fascinating series of attempted renewals as well as a steady decline. Perhaps surprisingly, it was in the USSR itself that the decline was most marked. Khrushchev's appeal to a renewed Leninism did not get an overwhelming response. His successor, Brezhnev, had little interest in socialist ideology and utopian dreams and the focus was on efforts to get the creaking economic planning system to work better. A strange hybrid of nationalism, based on pride in victory in the war, became the active ingredient while the trappings of Leninist utopianism remained in place, but were reduced to an empty ritualistic function exemplified by my ideology-instructor roommate mentioned earlier. A major landmark came in 1959 when the more or less unthinkable happened and China and the USSR split from each other as allies and as ideological twins and turned to polemics against each other. The Soviets were 'revisionists' moving away from pure Leninism (i.e. with a clear Stalinist content), while Moscow reverted, in part, to seeing Mao and his party as rural bandits rather than proletarian communists. Communism had split into two camps. The majority of parties stayed with the USSR. A few Maoist redoubts appeared including North Korea and, improbably, Albania. Yugoslavia had been expelled from the movement by Stalin in 1948 and a number of parties moved to non-aligned status. By the mid-1960s, ideological diversity led to the emergence of ideas of 'national roads to communism' in which the one-size fits all of early Comintern was replaced by multiple centres (polycentrism). In reality, it turned out to be a stage in the disintegration of international Leninism rather than a long-overdue liberating reform, which many at the

118 LENIN LIVES?

time thought it was. Elsewhere, what turned out to be final attempts were made to find a viable form of Leninism.

In most ruling parties decentralizing economic reforms were embarked upon which went furthest in Yugoslavia and Hungary. However, it was in Czechoslovakia in 1968 that the most extensive renewal process attempted to create 'socialism with a human face' by integrating democracy and human rights and greater freedom of expression within the communist shell. Once again the outcome was a reluctant but devastating military intervention by Moscow which shredded what little credibility it had left. However, communism was not yet quite done. In the 1970s, its two inter-war strong points—anti-fascism and anti-colonialism—had their last impact. In his address to the party congress in 1979, Brezhnev was able to boast of further gains, of countries affiliating to the 'Soviet camp' and breaking away from imperial, American, and other control. In the seventies as a whole, southern Africa, notably Angola and Mozambique, had undergone victorious armed national liberation struggles assisted by the USSR and also Cuba which had committed troops to the struggle. Other decolonized nations, like Zimbabwe, also spawned leftist post-colonial governments. The fight for the greatest of African prizes, South Africa, was also stepped up, though it was only successful in 1992, after communism itself collapsed. But it did bring to power the charismatic figure of Nelson Mandela who had himself been deeply influenced by Leninism. In 1973 and 1974 the last two bastions of fascism in Europe—the dictatorships of Salazar in Portugal and Franco in Spain—collapsed and the local communist parties enjoyed a period of success. A form of democratic communism, termed Eurocommunism, began to move further away from the Soviet model and talk about a democratic and even a parliamentary 'road to socialism'. The breaking of the spell of 'October'—that is the 'classic' Soviet model of a supposedly popularly supported, democratic worker-peasant revolution thrusting Lenin into power—was expressed graphically by the Spanish Communist Party leader Santiago Carrillo. 'For many years', he wrote, 'Moscow was our Rome. We spoke of the Great October Socialist Revolution as if it were our Christmas. That was the period of our infancy. Today we have grown up.'[42] Unsurprisingly, Carrillo was refused permission to speak in Moscow at the celebration of the sixtieth anniversary of the October Revolution the following year. The conference at which Carrillo made his dramatic comparison was the 1976 Conference of Communist and Workers Parties of Europe, which included among its declarations the principle of the 'equality and independence of all communist parties and their right to decide their own policies without external interference'.[43]

In the late seventies Eurocommunist parties evolved and were on the brink of power in Spain, France, and Italy, which had had the strongest communist party in western Europe since 1945. In all three cases they had enjoyed the prestige of being the most active resisters to fascism. The advance of communism, especially in Italy and Chile, where Salvador Allende was elected democratically as president in 1970, was seen as a threat by US strategists, the doyen of whom, Henry Kissinger, talking of Allende winning an election and forming a government, told his aides that 'I don't see why we need to stand by and watch a country go Communist due to the irresponsibility of its own people'.[44] Indeed, the 'historic compromise' of an alliance between the Italian Communist Party (PCI) and the Christian Democratic party led by Aldo Moro was being negotiated in 1978 as a way out of Italy's long sequence of weak governments and economic stagnation when a dramatic event had far-reaching consequences. Moro was kidnapped, held in captivity for fifty-five days and then murdered, his body being left in the boot of a car parked halfway between the headquarters of the PCI and the Christian Democrats.[45] The symbolism was clear.

Fig. 12 One of the last photos of Chilean president Salvador Allende, the first of an increasing number of Marxist–Leninists elected to power in a democratic parliamentary system in Latin America, as he gazes skywards at US-backed bombers attacking the Presidential Palace in Santiago to inaugurate a savage coup, 9 November 1973.

120   LENIN LIVES?

The perpetrators did not want the historic compromise. In the turbulent Italian politics of the time, with leftist terrorists and secret pro-fascist cells made of leading judges, military figures, and right-wing politicians, not to mention the perennial mafia and weakness of the Italian state, attribution of responsibility was hard to verify. It was officially blamed on the loose alliance of leftist terrorists, the Red Brigades, but suspicion of the right and even of CIA involvement was widespread. Whoever did it, they succeeded politically beyond their wildest dreams. Not only was the historic compromise compromised forever, the resurgence of communism was weakened.

Along with other factors around 1979, notably the transfer of power in Israel to governments increasingly dependent on religious fundamentalists, the collapse of the American puppet regime of the Shah in Iran leading to the emergence of a Muslim fundamentalist state, and the end of the Keynesian post-war consensus in favour of market fundamentalism in the form of Thatcher and Reagan, the tide had turned. Two communists held portfolios in Mitterand's socialist government in France, but it was a last fanfare. By 1985 Gorbachev had come to power. By 1991 he had abandoned all traditional communist/soviet assumptions—such as the dictatorship of the proletariat, the leading role of the party in society, and, in a much-overlooked but astonishing final conference of the Soviet Communist Party, it abandoned Marxism and Leninism in favour of a blend of the best from all traditions.[46] By then, all the artificial communist states of Eastern Europe had collapsed. In those where Soviet, that is Gorbachev's, influence was strongest the transition was swift and frictionless—for example Czechoslovakia, Hungary, and East Germany. In June 1989, while the world was watching events in Tienanmen Square and Beijing, a remarkable event occurred in Moscow. Poland's first elected non-communist leader, Mazowiecki, was invited to Moscow to be congratulated, where he received Gorbachev's good wishes and was urged to go on with the process of reform in his country. The 'Sinatra doctrine' of 1988—that each country should do things its way—had proven to be genuine. Areas which were least susceptible to Moscow's influence, Romania and, most tragic of all, Yugoslavia, had the most painful and violent transitions. In August 1991 the Soviet Communist Party itself was outlawed. The October Revolution had reached the end of its cycle in its own country. Communist parties in western Europe collapsed or transformed out of Marxism-Leninism. China, Cuba, and Vietnam held the line, but in Europe Leninism appeared to be dead. Has anything survived the wreckage?

LENIN AS ICON AND INSPIRATION: LENINISM AFTER LENIN 121

2. Independent Leninism in Global Thought and Politics

From Fellow Travellers to Liberation Theology

It is an enduring almost paradox of Leninism that, despite dramatically foregrounding the role of the advanced working class, intellectuals, often of middle- and upper-class backgrounds, were at the heart of its transmission. Even in the seminal arguments of 1902–5, the role of intellectuals was highly disputed, Lenin himself adapting the original prescription for a party of 'professional revolutionaries' away from the influence of intellectuals and towards a greater element of workerism. It is likely that his ally of the moment, Alexander Bogdanov, the inspirational advocate of constructing a distinctly proletarian culture, had influenced him in this direction, possibly in the long Alpine walks they took together in 1904. After the October Revolution, intellectuals played a massive role in spreading the ideas of Leninism to the outside world. The key themes of anti-fascism and anti-colonialism were attractive to a wide range of social critics. When it comes to intellectuals, there is no one that can be called 'typical'. Individualism to the point of idiosyncrasy and beyond is the norm. A glance at some influential Leninist intellectuals bears this out.

An important early and enduring focus of non-party Marxism and Leninism was the Institute for Social Research, set up in Frankfurt in 1923. For three decades it became a leading force in radical social analysis, constituting the Frankfurt School. It attracted a galaxy of socially critical, anti-capitalist superstars, from its original inspirer Karl Korsch (though he was never officially affiliated), through Walter Benjamin, Max Horkheimer, Theodor Adorno, and many others down to the present with Jürgen Habermas. While the degree to which the school and its individual members could be called Leninist is very variable, there is no doubt that the influence of the Russian Revolution was a prominent part especially of its early intellectual furniture. Walter Benjamin, for example, lived in Moscow for a number of years in the 1920s and wrote some of his best known works while there. His links to Bolshevism were strengthened by his relationship with Asja Lacis, a Latvian pioneer of political theatre for proletarian children. However, his best-known and most influential works show few if any specifically Leninist strands within a general critical support for the Bolshevik project. Benjamin had a wide range of sources and friendships behind his developing ideas, and they included more overtly Leninist thinkers such as Ernst Bloch and Georg Lukács. The influence of Lenin is

122 LENIN LIVES?

perhaps best seen in Lukács's highly influential work *History and Class Consciousness*, in which a view of the development of class consciousness among proletarians is seen, rather as it is in Lenin, as a vital dimension of the development of proletarian revolution. More explicitly, *Lenin: A Study in the Unity of his Thought*, published shortly after Lenin's death, was an early systematization of Lenin's ideas, one which prioritized the crucial role of the vanguard party in Marxist revolution. For many later Marxist and Leninist intellectuals, it was Lukács as much as Lenin himself who convinced them of the importance of the Leninist view of the party. Lukács was an early recruit to the Hungarian Communist Party and appears, in the revolutionary turmoil of 1919, to have not only condoned terror as a necessary tactic but to have been personally involved in implementing it. Bloch did not become a party member, but was close to the German Communist Party. After the war he became professor of philosophy at Leipzig University, part of the communist-controlled German Democratic Republic which he later abandoned over differences linked to the invasion of Hungary (1956) and the building of the Berlin Wall (1961), living his last years as professor of philosophy at the University of Tübingen in West Germany. His own ideas linked to Marxism and Leninism through having a teleological structure of an ever-improving humanity rising towards a higher mode of life, and also through scientific-utopian and dialectical dimensions similar to Soviet and Stalinist ways of thinking.

In the 1920s, in conformity with the Leninist impulse to 'raise consciousness' and 'win over' the non-Bolshevik population, the Soviet Communist Party developed a category of '*poputchiki*'. The term refers to people who share a journey, a random group who find themselves travelling together to a shared destination. It began to be applied to members of the Soviet intelligentsia who were deemed to be close to, but not officially affiliated with, the party. They were the object of policies aimed to nurture their closeness to the party as opposed to the sanctions, such as expulsion from the Soviet Union and career exclusion, which were applied to intellectuals considered to be inveterate enemies. The concept spread to foreign friends of the revolution. The term 'fellow travellers' became the standard translation of *poputchiki*, a term which, as is the way with politically contentious labels, began to expand its meaning. In this case, particularly in the 1930s, it came to have negative connotations to the point of engaging in what their opponents considered slavish apologetics for, ultimately, Stalinist tyranny. Today's equivalent, 'useful idiot', leaves even less room for dialogue or understanding. However, the term was not only pejorative and, for our purposes, points

LENIN AS ICON AND INSPIRATION: LENINISM AFTER LENIN   123

to a fine line between 'official' and 'independent' Marxist–Leninists. Many intellectuals in western Europe and the United States and other parts of the world became admirers of Stalin and Russian communism. In many cases this was based on the unrelenting struggle conducted by communists against fascism in Germany, in the crucial five years before Hitler seized power, and then in the Spanish Civil War. At national and international level, Moscow was a beacon of resistance to fascism when Britain and the United States (but not France) were prepared to deal. Louis Aragon, Lion Feuchtwanger, Jean-Paul Sartre, Pablo Picasso, Pablo Neruda, Gabriel García Márquez, and Mario Vargas Llosa were deeply influenced by communism/Leninism for a significant part of their lives.[47]

Disgust with government softness towards fascism was an important element in bringing many intellectuals in Britain into, or close to, the communist party. Christopher Caudwell, W. H. Auden, Stephen Spender, John Cornford, Ralph Fox, and many others rallied to the Spanish cause, some of them dying there. Support for communism in Oxford and Cambridge reached an all-time high, and even leading future Labour Party politicians, like Dennis Healey, joined the party for a while. Most spectacularly, a group of young academics and undergraduates, including Kim Philby, Donald Maclean, Guy Burgess, and Anthony Blunt, agreed to spy for the USSR and continued to do so throughout the Second World War and into the early Cold War. A notable exception to this tendency was, of course, George Orwell, who also went to Spain but became very hostile to Moscow's authoritarian interference. However, compared to others in Spain who supported Stalin, directly or indirectly, like Ernest Hemingway, Orwell was a lone voice. It was also the case that empathy with those suffering from the failures of capitalism, such as the poor, the unemployed, those uprooted by the Great Depression, and the persistent racism of American society, led people like John Dos Passos (who later recanted) and Paul Robeson to either become party members or fellow travellers. Of course, sympathy for the USSR also grew during the war and the whole McCarthyite episode in American post-war politics was only possible because many intellectuals did admire the USSR as the rock on which fascism had been shipwrecked. However, as we have frequently encountered, it is hard to say how 'Leninist' any of these positions were. Although his book is largely an acerbic critique of his subjects, one of the great analysts of fellow-travelling, David Caute, attributes the intellectuals' attraction to communism to their understanding of it as an enlightenment project, as the world's most sustained attempt to take hold of society and consciously shape it on rational principles.

124 LENIN LIVES?

They were, Caute believes, so dazzled by the theory that many of them refused to face up to the actual realities and horrors of the Stalin era. Fellow travellers were, Caute argued, 'true sons and daughters of the Enlightenment, of the doctrine of Progress'.[48]

Since 1991, at least in Europe, communist fellow-travelling has scarcely been possible for the simple reason that there are no longer any communist states or major Marxist–Leninist parties to accompany. For many leftists, the demise of state socialism seemed to open up brighter prospects as socialism in general would no longer be held back by association with Soviet malpractices, especially the crimes of Stalin. No longer would left-wing arguments be met with calls to go and live in Russia. These expectations were naive. Right-wing polemics continue to equate socialism with totalitarianism and repression as energetically as ever. While many leftists continue to have a soft spot for Cuba, not unreasonably blaming the vindictive sixty-year blockade by the United States for many of its problems, other surviving communist states, most obviously China, have less magnetism for leftists as they seem to be state capitalist rather than romantically socialist. Even so, Marxist–Leninist ideas have remained influential in minority intellectual circles.

After the reverberations of Khrushchev's revelations and the heavy-handed treatment of Hungary in 1956, Marxism in many of its varieties was shaken to the core. As we have seen, communist states themselves began to take independent lines, seeking national 'roads to communism', a phenomenon known as polycentrism. Elsewhere, outside the official communist movement, unaffiliated Leninist groups delinked from the existing communist states to form an independent 'New Left' in the Western world which looked to the original critic of Stalinism, Leon Trotsky, for ideological inspiration.

At the heart of Trotskyism was the view that, though the revolution was far from faultless in Lenin's day, it was Stalin who had driven it irretrievably off course through a process of bureaucratization. Imperfect though it was, according to Trotsky, Lenin's rule was based on expanding its democratic elements. Stalin replaced them with authoritarian control from the centre, exercised, as we have already mentioned, through party Control Commissions, Worker Peasant Inspectorates, and the ever-more powerful Cheka/GPU/OGPU/NKVD political police. Trotsky and his followers believed it was possible to have a vanguard party and democratic centralism and that, even in a peasant country where party members were few and far between, and, even more crucial, even when the majority of them had little idea of the long-term aims of the party, coercion would be minimal. In fact,

LENIN AS ICON AND INSPIRATION: LENINISM AFTER LENIN 125

in power, Trotsky was as coercive as anyone and was upbraided by Lenin in his political testament for being too obsessed with the administrative side of affairs. Trotsky, no more than Lenin and his followers, could face the fact that the essence of their revolutionary approach of seizing power and then winning over the population was at the heart of this perceived deficiency. Lenin, Trotsky, and Stalin denounced the dead-hand of bureaucrats, but none of them found a workable alternative. Nonetheless, Trotskyism became a lifeboat for Marxist–Leninists to distance themselves from the foundering wreck of the Soviet system and maintain the myth of a purer, more democratic era, and a promising revolution quickly blown off course by internal White enemies, foreign blockades, and exclusion, and by inheriting an economy reduced to medieval levels by war and civil war. All of these things were true but they did not mean Leninism itself could escape all responsibility. The Menshevik Internationalist view, from a similar Marxist foundation to that of the Bolsheviks, put the deformities down to the revolution being 'premature', taking place before the conditions were ripe. Lenin and Trotsky partly agreed with this; Lenin made a big issue of the Russian workers being 'backward', for instance, but argued that the October Revolution would set off a complete collapse of world capitalism. This get-out-of-jail-free card failed and, for the time being, international capitalism shrugged off the challenge and the Soviet revolution had to settle into a period of 'socialism in one country'. Nonetheless, heaping the blame solely on Stalin was a convenient way for Trotskyites and Leninists to evade responsibility.

Although they were a much rarer breed than Moscow fellow travellers, Chinese fellow-travelling attracted a small group of Western intellectuals, especially after 1956. China showed increasing contempt for Khrushchev and his campaign, and Maoism began to attract a few Western admirers. Ironically, this peaked when Maoism was at its worst during the 1959 famine and the Cultural Revolution of 1966–76. Admirers included highly intelligent figures like the French philosopher Jean-Paul Sartre and new-wave filmmakers like Jean-Luc Godard.[49] Although critical, Michelangelo Antonioni co-operated with the Chinese authorities to make his neutral observational documentary *China* during the Cultural Revolution. More deeply embedded, the Dutch filmmakers Joris Ivens and Marceline Loridan produced a twelve-part, thirteen-hour documentary in the same period under the overall title *How Yukong Moved the Mountains*. It was observational and uncritical and implicitly more sympathetic to the Chinese revolutionary cause than Antonioni. During the Cultural Revolution, *Quotations*

126 LENIN LIVES?

from Chairman Mao Tse-tung, better known by its unofficial name, *The Little Red Book*, flooded the West and could be found on the bookshelf of many students and intellectuals. At the time, China was a much more secretive society than the Soviet Union had ever been, and the sympathy for it tended to be for a misunderstood and often wildly incorrect version of what had happened. In the eyes of Western Maoists a popular peasant revolution had overthrown a corrupt elite, established a grass roots people's democracy and self-governing people's courts, had broken the barriers to industrialization and, in the Cultural Revolution, overthrown traditional Confucian ways of thinking. As with other fellow travellers these perceptions were half-truths at best, complete illusions at worst. The realities of terror, mass famine, and mindless violence in the Cultural Revolution were misunderstood, unknown, or glossed over in true fellow-travelling fashion. Intelligent anti-elitists in the West were often themselves from the cream of the cream of the elites they despised, like Sartre, who was the product of the highly elitist French *grandes écoles* which gathered together a few hundred of France's brightest school leavers and gave them a cosseted but rigorous education at a much higher level than the average university. Sartre, Malraux, and numerous others were deeply influenced by the ultra-elitist ideas of Nietzsche and saw themselves as 'Supermen' (*Übermenschen*) not bound by the laws of ordinary people. Despite this, they were highly critical of their own societies and tended to despise the mundaneness and philistine materialism and crassness of their own ruling classes. Abandoning hope for their own societies, they projected their visions onto the remote and dimly known post-revolutionary societies which, it was implied, for all their faults, at least contained the seeds of a better life for humanity. Few of them retained this faith. Malraux, for example, later became Minister of Culture in one of General de Gaulle's governments in France. A handful of intellectuals, like Pablo Picasso, the Chilean novelist Pablo Neruda, and the British historian Eric Hobsbawm were among the few who retained a lifelong allegiance to conventional, Moscow-oriented communism.

The New Left and other anti-Stalinist groups also found inspiration in reinterpreting some of the Marxist and associated thinkers of the revolutionary era, notably Rosa Luxemburg, Walter Benjamin, Karl Korsch, and Victor Serge. In addition to Trotsky, other Russians were also sources of new ideas, including Alexandra Kollontai, Nikolai Bukharin, and Viktor Shklovsky. However, the Marxist–Leninist left was also refreshed by new inspiration derived from the Cuban Revolution, notably the ideas of Fidel Castro and Che Guevara. In the 1960s and 1970s, Latin America was a focus

LENIN AS ICON AND INSPIRATION: LENINISM AFTER LENIN 127

for new revolutionary hopes, as was Africa, where revolutionaries like Amílcar Cabral, Nelson Mandela, Joe Slovo, and Frantz Fanon, plus political activists like Julius Nyerere, Samora Machel, Robert Mugabe, Patrice Lumumba, and many others were associated with anti-colonial revolutions and peoples' liberation movements which raised left-wing hopes. They were often influenced by Leninism, though only a few, notably Mandela, were communist in the traditional sense. It was Che Guevara, martyred for the revolution in Bolivia in 1967, who came to encapsulate the essence of the new anti-colonial liberation movements. In addition to this exciting new injection of ideas and hopes, one forgotten figure of the inter-war period, Antonio Gramsci, came to exert extensive influence.

It was from Gramsci and Che Guevara that a fresh, some would say last, burst of Leninist energy invigorated the left. Their ideas were very different. Gramsci proposed a strategy of intellectual and cultural hegemony while Guevara proposed the proliferation of armed guerrilla cells and armed combat to the extent of starting 'two, three, many Vietnams'.[50] Gramsci's ideas were popularized by the relatively democratic Italian Communist Party (PCI) on its march towards the 'Historic Compromise' which ended tragically with the assassination of the conciliatory Christian Democratic former prime minister, Aldo Moro, mentioned earlier. Gramsci's core notion was that, in a democratic society, the construction of socialism needed to begin in the cultural sphere, in winning the population over to socialist values. To do this the party (as did others) used newspapers, journals, academic freedoms, political festivals (Glastonbury began as a fundraiser for the Campaign for Nuclear Disarmament), and later social media and the web to promote socialism. Many on the right see the rise of 'political correctness', now retreaded as 'wokeness', as a blitzkrieg motivated by Marxist values before which they, the right, stand powerless. Critics of the Gramscian approach on the left dismissed his ideas as a diversion from direct political and economic struggle, an effort by leaders of the PCI to appear to be doing something when power itself was beyond them. Be that as it may, it is interesting to note that this not only ties in with Lenin's end-of-life injunction to conduct 'cultural revolution', but also Gramsci was an admirer of Bogdanov's views on cultural hegemony as a necessary prerequisite (or at least key component) of a successful revolution. Though details remain obscure, Gramsci was part of a small *proletkult* group in Turin in 1920.

Gramsci's views tended to attract mainly west European Marxists. Guevara's guerrilla strategy, the setting up of armed revolutionary *focos*, was mainly followed in Latin America. Guevara thought the Cuban model,

128   LENIN LIVES?

small guerrilla groups descending from the mountains or emerging from forests or the African bush, could spread revolution rapidly from the more lightly guarded peripheries of countries to advance on the urban power centres as they gained strength in a kind of snowball effect. In the 1960s such groups were set up across Latin America. As well as his unsuccessful and fatal effort to realize his model in Bolivia, Guevara also visited Africa and thought a *foco* approach could be applied, for example, in the Congo, where armed revolutionary groups could be set up on the lawless southern shore of Lake Tanganyika to challenge the continent's most tyrannical and bloody post-colonial kleptocracy presided over by the Mobutu family. The philosophy of armed guerrilla war also drew in elements from a version of Maoism, which saw the guerrillas of the People's Liberation Army as the key to revolutionary success in China, and the striking example of the Viet Cong in the Vietnam War, where it seemed peasants on bicycles were out-fighting B-52 bombing campaigns of barbaric severity. This view underestimated the role of the conventional forces of the North Vietnamese Army in the war. Nonetheless, a hybrid form, whereby trained Cuban military units (plus a number of Soviet advisors) joined revolutionary struggles in Angola and Mozambique, succeeded in bringing down colonial rule in Southern Africa and undermined the white supremacist regime in the country of South Africa to such an extent that it too collapsed. The promise of the Southern African revolutions has faded as neither democracy nor prosperity took hold. Instead, dictatorships emerged, from the relatively mild in Angola, via the increasingly repressive in Mozambique, to the neo-Stalinist dictatorship of Robert Mugabe in Zimbabwe. South Africa itself has also been troubled politically and economically.

For our purposes we might note several more points about these developments. Guevarist ideas did attract Europeans. In fact, it was the French socialist Régis Debray who theorized 'Guevarism'. Debray was a typically elitist product of the most elevated grand école, the *École normale supérieure*, where he was taught by arch-Leninist Louis Althusser. Debray's systematization of Guevara's theses, in his book *Revolution in the Revolution* (1967), was very widely read, and translated into all the major western European languages. But it was not only in rural settings that *foco* theory was applied. Urban guerrilla groups emerged in many western countries. In Brazil, the military dictatorship was unsuccessfully challenged by several armed groups. Carlos Marighella was the best-known figure. He gave up conventional politics and turned to urban violence. He was a priority target for the political police and he was shot dead in a police ambush on

LENIN AS ICON AND INSPIRATION: LENINISM AFTER LENIN   129

4 November 1969, less than two years after taking up arms. European urban guerrillas also emerged with a more anarchist than Leninist agenda, but they were also students of Guevarism in many respects. They included the Red Brigades in Italy (believed to be partly infiltrated/controlled by right-wing elements and possibly involved in the Moro affair) and the Baader-Meinhof Group (the Red Army Faction) in West Germany. Perhaps ironically the resumption of terrorism in Ireland after 1968 was associated with a rejuvenated Provisional IRA (Irish Republican Army) which rejected the sclerotic older generation Official IRA, which was more conventionally Marxist–Leninist, in favour of a looser, more romantic combination of nationalism and socialism. Over time, despite its leaders engaging with the ideas of Fanon, Gramsci, and the Vietnamese, the Provisionals were also impressed by the conversion of Nelson Mandela to a successful compromise strategy which brought an end to white rule in South Africa. By and large, apart from the IRA and Basque nationalists in ETA, who also linked nationalism, class struggle, and socialism, such movements were rapidly suppressed. Like the Provisional IRA, ETA abandoned armed struggle and fully dissolved itself in 2018, and some of its leaders even offered a full apology to its victims and declared its violence should never have happened. Rural guerrillas, from the Maoist Naxalites in eastern India (today recovering despite a major repressive government campaign which began in 2009 resulting in some 20,000 members dying, being wounded, or surrendering), to the Shining Path (*Sendero Luminoso*) Maoists in Peru, founded in 1980, or FARC in Colombia, founded in 1964, have lasted much longer and tended to decline as much through their own internal evolution away from violence and towards peaceful political processes, though all three are still active albeit on a much smaller scale than their peak.

An unexpected spin-off, especially from the Latin American liberation movements, has been the involvement of Christians, initially Catholics and later Protestants, in what came to be known as liberation theology. While this often comprised a combination of Marxism and traditional Christian values and Christian social teaching, there was not much Leninist influence, but it does have some implications for our study, not least that orthodox Leninist anti-religious activism may have been counterproductive. Liberation theology was first codified by the Brazilian priest Gustavo Gutiérrez in his seminal work *The Theology of Liberation*.[51] Its precise definition varies among several related movements including black theology and Palestinian liberation theology. Its core, influenced, but not endorsed, by

130 LENIN LIVES?

the Second Vatican Council (11 October 1962–8 December 1965) has been encapsulated in phrases like 'option for the poor'. Christian teaching, it was argued, called for giving preference to the needs of the poor and oppressed over those of the wealthy and powerful. It has been soundly argued that liberation theology originated in Europe rather than Latin America. Gutiérrez himself studied at the radical catholic University of Leuven in Belgium. It also owed a great deal to social initiatives, like the 'worker-priest' movement and the ideas of Georges Bernanos in *The Diary of a Country Priest*, Jacques Maritain, Simone Weil, and others, notably the American radical activist Saul Alinsky and the Catholic activists of the Catholic Worker Movement, especially Dorothy Day and Ammon Hennacy. Despite their diverse ideological-political positions, pioneers like these prepared the ground for full-blown liberation theology.[52] Incidentally, it should be noted that in the 1920s, a group within the Russian Orthodox Church led by Alexander Vvedensky, considered schismatic by the official church, proclaimed a reconciliation between revolutionary and Christian values. It suffered from being seen by many as a simple manipulation by the Soviet authorities rather than being an authentic, spiritually driven movement. As a result it got little traction among believers and was also deeply distrusted by party militants. It was known as the Living Church (*Zhivaia tserkov*) or the Renovationists (*Obnovlentsii*), though the latter embraced a somewhat wider circle.

Liberation theology had many forms which would take us beyond the scope of our current discussion. The domination of military regimes in Latin America pushed many of its followers into taking not only a revolutionary ideological and theological stance, but also a political one of confrontation with the authorities. The influence of Guevarism filtered through, though it was taken up in non-violent and violent forms. Radical Brazilian Catholics set up, in some of the urban slums (*favelas*), what they called 'Base Communities'. They were a kind of civilian, non-violent *foco* in which revolutionary ideas would be discussed and developed and the level of political consciousness of its members would be raised. They would, it was hoped, spread through the community, hopefully shielded from the repressive authorities by their educational and religious mantle. In a linked initiative, the brilliant Brazilian educator, Paulo Freire, set up groups in the slums to teach literacy and raise political consciousness at the same time. At the heart of his methodology was the need to bring the teaching of literacy deep into the experience of the impoverished students. To do this, his method suggested taking words, like the word *favela* itself, which had power and

LENIN AS ICON AND INSPIRATION: LENINISM AFTER LENIN 131

meaning for the students, and build from that. His ideas became very popular among left-wing teachers, and Freire himself, after expulsion from Brazil by the military junta of the time, had a stellar career in UNESCO developing and advising on literacy programmes in poor countries.

While the literacy aspect had conspicuous success, the transition to radical values was more fitful. By contrast, in a few cases, notably that of the Colombian priest Camilo Torres, some followers of liberation theology followed a more violence-based dimension of Guevara's legacy. They reluctantly concluded that the non-violent approach would be insufficient in the face of a ruthless and vicious, violent oppressor, and that it was necessary to take up arms. Sadly, Torres quickly suffered the same fate as Guevara himself. He died in his first military engagement, fighting as part of the National Liberation Army of Colombia (*Ejército de Liberación Nacional*, ELN). Several ELN commanders were priests, and the organization, which brings together largely Cuban inspired Marxism–Leninism with liberation theology, has continued armed resistance down to the present, even after the larger FARC guerrilla movement made the transition to peaceful politics. Some dissident FARC militants switched to the ELN to continue fighting.

During this period from 1964 to the present, dramatic and tragic developments had happened. In 1980, during the civil war in El Salvador, such was the establishment right's fear of liberation theology and Catholic radicalism that two nuns of the Maryknoll order were assassinated and the highest member of the clergy in the country, Archbishop Óscar Romero, was killed by a sniper while he was celebrating mass. Popes John Paul II, Benedict XV, and Francis II all visited Cuba. In 1998, the Castro brothers were present at John Paul IIs papal mass in Havana. In 2015, Castro had a friendly meeting with Pope Francis [see Fig. 13]. There were even suggestions that Fidel's brother and successor Raúl might return to the faith. In his sermon in Havana Pope Francis said 'This caring for others out of love is not about being servile... Service is never ideological, for we do not serve ideas, we serve people'.[53]

The point of these developments, for our present purposes, is to indicate that, with respect to religion and religious policy, Lenin's influence may have been damaging. Liberation theology shows that there are considerable pent-up radical instincts in Christianity which could have been exploited to bring a wider spectrum of reliable revolutionaries into the communist movement. The dialogue and collaboration shown in the history of liberation theology was a long way away from Lenin's sometimes overwrought hatred of religion, shown when he crudely rejected the attempts of his

Fig. 13 Liberation Theology meets Marxism–Leninism. Pope Francis at a meeting with Fidel Castro in Havana, officially described as 'intimate and familial' (19 September 2015). Photograph: Cubadebate/Alex Castro/EPA.

friends and allies Maxim Gorky and Anatoly Lunacharsky to depict socialism as the epitome of human religious development, an endeavour known as God-building (*Bogostroitel'stvo*).[54] Lenin's reaction to an article by Gorky in which he temporarily moved away from his 'God-building' view of socialism verged on the hysterical:

> Whatever are you doing? This is simply terrible, it really is! Yesterday I read your reply in *Rech* to the "howling" over Dostoyevsky, and was preparing to rejoice, but today the liquidators' paper arrives, and *in it there is a paragraph of your article* which was not in *Rech*. This paragraph runs as follows:
>
> 'And "god-seeking" should be *for the time being*' (only for the time being?) 'put aside—it is a useless occupation: it's no use seeking where there is nothing to be found. Unless you sow, you cannot reap. You have no God, you have not *yet*' (yet!) 'created him. Gods are not sought—*they are created*; people do not invent life, they create it.'
>
> So it turns out that you are against 'god-seeking' only 'for the time being'!! It turns out that you are against god-seeking *only* in order to replace it by

LENIN AS ICON AND INSPIRATION: LENINISM AFTER LENIN 133

god-building!! Well, isn't it horrible that such a thing should *appear* in your article? God-seeking differs from god-building or god-creating or god-making, etc., no more than a yellow devil differs from a blue devil. To talk about god-seeking, not in order to declare against *all* devils and gods, against every ideological necrophily (all worship of a divinity is necrophily—be it the cleanest, most ideal, not sought-out but built-up divinity, it's all the same), but to prefer a blue devil to a yellow one is a hundred times worse than not saying anything about it at all.

Really, it is terrible......Why do you do this? It's damnably disappointing.[55]

Here Lenin gives vent to his full-on hatred of all religion in no matter what guise. In practice, party policy before and after the revolution promoted toleration of religious beliefs rather than forceful confrontation of them on the pragmatic grounds that direct persecution would entrench dogmatic attitudes, not eradicate them. The latter task would be accomplished organically, it was assumed, by the greater dissemination of science and reason in society since they were, wrongly, deemed to be incompatible with religious 'prejudices'. Religion would dissolve like a morning mist exposed to the warm rising sun of rationality. However, Lenin lacked the patience necessary and the spirit shown in the letter emerged in the 1920s among leftist elements in the party, and especially in the League of Militant Godless, set up to speed up the demise of religion as part of the broader task of raising consciousness. It was founded in 1925 to drive out religion forcibly and fully embodied the spirit of Lenin's letter to Gorky, but it eventually gravitated back, around 1941, to the more tactful approach embodied in official policy. This also was accompanied by a limited but nonetheless astonishing rapprochement with the church, which became an active supporter of the Soviet war effort. However, it does remind us that Lenin's legacy could have toxic consequences as well as, in many eyes, benevolent ones, an issue to which we will return.

Curiously, two of the most energetic contemporary advocates of the continuing value of Leninism in the present, Louis Althusser and Slavoj Žižek, both link their communism to Christianity. In a typically lordly and somewhat cryptic comment, Althusser claimed in a rare TV interview, for the Italian company RAI, that 'I became communist because I was Catholic. I did not change religion, but I remained profoundly Catholic. I don't go to church...I remained a Catholic, that is, an internationalist universalist. I thought that inside the Communist Party there were more adequate means to realize universal fraternity'. The interview continued:

134 LENIN LIVES?

Renato Parascandolo (Interviewer): What role does Catholic culture have today?

Althusser: Oh...it has a giant role. In my view, today social revolution or a profound social change depends on the alliance between Catholics (I am not saying the church, though the church can also be part of it), the Catholics of the world, all religions of the world, and communists.[56]

Slavoj Žižek describes himself as a 'Christian atheist'. Eschewing all metaphysical elements and embracing a materialist philosophy, Žižek, nonetheless, concludes that Christianity provides the best route into atheism. In the film *The Pervert's Guide to Ideology* he states that because it, uniquely, proclaims the incarnation of God in Christ, which subsumes God into the material universe, Christianity eliminates the necessity for an external guarantee or metaphysical linkage to the deity.[57]

Leninism since the Fall of Soviet Communism: 1991 to the Present

Since the collapse of European communism in 1989–91 the influence of communism has been in what many see as terminal decline. In his homeland Lenin has little influence over contemporary politics. The revolutionary city which was named after him from 1924 to 1991 reverted to its original name of St Peterburg, after the patron saint of its founder Tsar Peter the Great. Most towns, cities, and villages named after Lenin and other prominent political figures of the Soviet era reverted to earlier names. There were hardly any traces of Leninism left in Russian thought, in which there was an unsurprising rush to reconnect with pre-revolutionary ideas, resurrecting the diverse religious, conservative, and liberal ideas suppressed by the communist authorities. It is hard to find anyone in contemporary Russia who would identify as a Leninist. President Putin has heaped enormous quantities of blame on him for the 'disasters', as he sees them, of the revolution and the revolutionary era. In language deeply misunderstood in the West, like so much else of Russian political discourse, he blamed Lenin's errors in lumping territories together by arbitrary administrative decision over the wishes of local inhabitants as one of the tragic causes of the terrible Russo-Ukrainian crisis and war of 2022. The commemoration of the hundredth anniversary of the October Revolution brought no respite. The official line, fully endorsed and expressed unequivocally by Putin, was that

LENIN AS ICON AND INSPIRATION: LENINISM AFTER LENIN   135

Fig. 14 The sculptor, Georgy Frangulyan, stands at the Wall of Grief, Moscow, a memorial to the victims of Soviet-era repression. It was inaugurated by President Putin and the Patriarch Kirill of Moscow in October 2017, around the 100th anniversary of the Bolshevik Revolution.

revolutions are disasters and the Soviet revolution had undermined Russia from its first day. The rout is not, however, complete. The Lenin Mausoleum, containing his embalmed body, remains in Red Square and is still open to pilgrims for twenty hours per week, and the burial sites of leading communists in honoured positions in the grounds of the Kremlin, including that of Stalin, have not as yet been disturbed. While the city of Leningrad changed its name, the county (*oblast'*) which encompasses it is still called Leningrad. The successor to the ruling Communist Party of the Soviet Union, today's Communist Party of the Russian Federation, the largest opposition party in Russia which polls around 20 per cent of the vote, retains an official acknowledgement of Lenin, but its ideology mixes elements of patriotism and Russian Orthodox religion which Lenin would not recognize. Vestigial Marxist and communist parties in Eastern and Western Europe have also tended to absorb a more eclectic range of influences on their Marxist rather than Marxist–Leninist base.

As the world moves into the third decade of the twenty-first century, a decade which, after a long period of globalizing relative stability appears to have turned towards barely controlled volatility and conflict, pushing it ever

136 LENIN LIVES?

closer to the previously almost forgotten nuclear threshold, Leninism seems to have little to bring to the table. The biggest exception to this are the ruling communist parties—most importantly China which, under President Xi Jinping has returned to a more authoritarian and dogmatic communist line, reinforced at the Twentieth Party Congress in October 2022—plus Vietnam and Cuba. Perhaps the most straightforwardly Leninist can be found among widely distributed but usually small Trotskyist groups, though some are locally influential, especially in Brazil and elsewhere in Latin America. However, it is, as we have already seen, sometimes difficult to distinguish distinctively Lenin-derived elements in a tangled ideological skein with which people identify. Such outlooks tend to comprise a cocktail of elements, in varying proportions and combinations, of Marxism, mythical models of October, iconic images of a 'democratic' Lenin, generic forms of anti-capitalism, anti-imperialism, anti-colonialism, and a powerful substructure of left-wing nationalism and national liberation. By and large, the direct influence of Lenin has reached a nadir.

A small but symbolic measure of this was the response to the original call for contributors to an ambitious project, entitled Russia's Great War and Revolution, intended to bring together the most up-to-date scholarship from all over the globe relating to Russia in the years of the Great War, Revolution, and Civil War (1914–22) on the occasion of the rolling centenaries of these immense events. Of over 150 initial offers from frontline scholars from Japan, Russia, Europe, the United States, and elsewhere, none was on Lenin and only two on Bolshevism and the early Soviet state. In the socio-political and ideological sphere there were several offers of items on the tsar and royal family, very many on liberals and the middle classes, none at all on workers or left-wing parties such as the Mensheviks and anarchists, and even the Socialist Revolutionaries—the largest political party in Russia by far in 1917—attracted little attention. To some extent this reflects an opening of the topic, especially in Russia, to allow pursuit of formerly taboo themes, not to mention the generally rightward shift of the Western political spectrum at the expense of all forms of socialism. But to ignore the dominant forces of the revolution in favour of, especially, the very marginal liberals, was very unexpected. Ultimately the editors were able to restore some balance to the series as a whole but the initial response was very surprising.

The worldwide commemoration of the centenary in 2017 also underlined how the band had moved on.[58] It was not only Putin who used it as an occasion to excoriate the Bolsheviks and Lenin. Even exhibitions of the art and

LENIN AS ICON AND INSPIRATION: LENINISM AFTER LENIN   137

culture of the period showed the trend to an admonitory view of the revolution, an example of disaster not triumph. In London, one reviewer vigorously denounced no less august an institution than the Royal Academy for neglecting to point out that the revolution resulted in Stalinism.[59] By contrast, an exhibition of posters and artefacts at the British Library did emphasize the outcome. In Moscow, the Tretyakov Gallery put on an exhibition which largely ignored revolutionary art and presented the paintings of 1917 with the accent on traditional themes of wedding feasts, portraits, and landscapes, with no particular sense of the events of a cataclysmic year apart from some battlescapes.[60]

Much of this would suggest that Lenin's thought and influence had had its day. However, there were some who thought this was the world's loss and Lenin still had lessons needed in the present. For example, among the few books praising Lenin at the time of the centenary of the revolution and 150th anniversary of his birth were supportive items by Tariq Ali and China Miéville.[61] Philip Cunliffe wrote a fascinating 'what if?' alternative history suggesting what the world might have been like had Lenin lived long enough for his principles to take root globally.[62] Not surprisingly, most of those mining Lenin's thought and political practice for inspiration were intellectuals. Leninism had a tradition of attracting intellectuals from its origin, not surprisingly since theory, in particular, is the province of socially engaged intellectuals.

In 1976, during a visit to the USSR with my students, our hosts laid on a seminar in Leningrad on Lenin and the October Revolution. The presentation, by a trusty party old-guardist from Leningrad University, rehearsed the official view of Lenin leading an adoring working class to the victorious overthrow of the Provisional Government. The fiftieth anniversary of the October Revolution had been marked in the Soviet Union by much of the same. The Academy of Sciences put out an official account of the great event[63] and a complete history of Russia and the Soviet Union was published.[64] In some respects the new approach was more realistic than caricatural predecessors. Khrushchev had enlisted history into the anti-Stalin campaign. The new Soviet revision played down Stalin's role in 1917. Documents, notably the minutes of the Bolshevik Central Committee in late 1917, were republished because they showed definitively that the notion that Stalin led the October Revolution as Lenin's equal was not the case. There were serious limitations, however. In 1957, the historian E. N. Burdzhalov published an account of the February Revolution which portrayed the Bolsheviks as divided and uninfluential before Lenin's return in April.

138   LENIN LIVES?

However, it was too much for the party ideological controllers and led to a great debate and academic scandal. He was dismissed from the editorial board of the main historical journal, *Voprosy istorii* (*Problems of History*), and his membership of the Academy of Sciences was not renewed. Remarkably, he retained his party membership and obtained a post at the Moscow Pedagogical Institute (now University, MPGU, *Moskovskii Gosudarstvennyi Pedagogicheskii Universitet*) in 1959, where he was promoted to a chair which he retained until retirement in 1976. In 1967, with a second volume in 1971, he produced a superb account of the February Revolution which barely mentioned the Bolsheviks. This was no more than the truth since they were not a crucial factor in that first phase of the revolution.[65] This opened the way for a number of high quality histories of the revolution to appear. However, the cult of Lenin himself tended to remain in the hagiographic hands of the guardians of orthodoxy.

It was not just Soviet revisionism that emerged as the Cold War evolved. In Western academic circles, more finely shaded representations began to appear in the form of a school of revisionism from the 1970s onwards. The Bolsheviks were shown to have significant support in key areas in 1917 and Lenin was portrayed as a less manipulative, more popular, and more democratic figure than had often been the case earlier.[66] Works on Lenin himself varied from the more 'totalitarian' outlook of Adam Ulam in *Lenin and the Bolsheviks* (1966), to the traditional but more nuanced and multifaceted *Lenin: The Man, The Theorist, The Leader*, edited by Leonard Schapiro and Peter Reddaway (1967), to more acutely revisionist items. Neil Harding revised many encrusted assumptions about Lenin in *Lenin's Political Thought* (1983 and 1985), including arguing convincingly that Lenin's controversial pamphlet *What is to be Done?* was actually within the tradition of orthodox Marxism. In a thoughtful three-volume account of *Lenin: A Political Life* (1985, 1991, 1995), Robert Service allowed more room for a democratic Lenin, though in his later one-volume biography, *Lenin: A Biography* (2001), he took a harsher line. Christopher Read, in *Lenin: A Revolutionary Life* (2005), emphasized, among other things, that it was Lenin's immediate tactics outlined in April rather than his more elaborate theories which brought the Bolsheviks to power, and that in the spring of 1918 he introduced a variety of 'socialism in one country' which served as a model for later Stalinist developments. In 2012, James Ryan's superb account of Lenin's attitude to violence, *Lenin's Terror*, presented a convincing picture of a man prepared to face the necessity of using violence but with reluctance rather than any kind of relish in having to do so.[67]

LENIN AS ICON AND INSPIRATION: LENINISM AFTER LENIN 139

While these examples showed that academic interest continued, especially among British scholars, in wider academia and in the non-academic world interest in Lenin was actually declining. Historians of the Soviet Union were, for whatever reasons, turning to the Stalin era rather than the revolutionary era. Even those still interested in the former period moved away, as we have seen above in connection with the Russia's Great War and Revolution project, from studying the left wing to studying liberals, the right, the tsar and his family, the military, and the war and civil war. In the perestroika era the leadership urged the filling of 'blank pages' in Soviet era history. At first this was understood to mean looking more frankly at the 1930s, but it became clear that Lenin's saintly reputation was also to be challenged. The first archive-based, realistic, even critical, major Russian biography was produced by Dmitri Volkogonov.[68] After 1991, a whole range of sensationalist, lurid, conspiratorial, and fanciful accounts, in accordance with the odd popular-cultural atmosphere of the early post-Soviet years in general, appeared which were of no particular worth. Politically, too, after 1991 Leninism appeared to be imploding like a burst balloon. Communist parties everywhere collapsed, even beyond the Soviet bloc. Remnants of once-powerful parties in Italy, France, and Spain imploded. Smaller Western parties in Great Britain and elsewhere practically disappeared, often taking their newspapers and journals with them. There were exceptions, such as Portugal, where, as late as January 2022, the Portuguese Communist Party was a significant part of a coalition government, but mainly Leninism seemed to be a spent force. It was widely believed by observers in the 1990s that China, too, had abandoned Marxism–Leninism as anything more than a brand name for the regime. Market reforms in Vietnam brought outside specialists to a similar, overhasty, conclusion. Marxism itself had been written off from its earliest days, as indicated, for example, by the unequivocal title of Eugen von Böhm-Bawerk's *Karl Marx and the Close of His System* (1896). Lenin, too, had had many opponents from his earliest days, but the post-1991 conjuncture seemed to be a fatal collapse from within. However, like the villain in a slasher movie, Marxism–Leninism always seemed to rise from the dead. Would it do so again?

Indeed it would! The resuscitating factors were diverse. The capitalist crisis of 2008, in the course of which thirty-five years of neoliberal market deregulation crashed to the ground, was deeply implicated, though it was not the only factor. It unleashed a young generation which had never seen the like before, and began asking questions which helped create a minority but important anti-capitalist movement. Critical thinking, not just Leninist,

140 LENIN LIVES?

had also been stimulated by the large numbers in the Western world and around the globe who were opposed to the rebirth of US liberal imperialism, focused on restoring unipolar American world hegemony, which manifested itself in attacks on Afghanistan, Iraq, and Syria, and, according to many, intervention in Ukraine. Those who were most vocal about government inaction on the pressing issue of climate change became increasingly frustrated and increasingly militant in the form, for example, of Extinction Rebellion. Rising waves of right-wing populism across Europe, including core Brexiteers in the UK, the French National Front, and the German AfD, and the rise in the United States itself of the alt-right, Qanon, Trumpism, and the presidency of Donald Trump, and especially the attempted coup to prolong it, all provoked critical thinking among those alarmed by such developments. Resistance such as Me Too, gender rights, and, especially, Black Lives Matter emerged across the Western world. In Spain and Greece, and Portugal where they had never gone away, a new wave of left-wing parties—Podemos and Syriza, for example—reclaimed leftist positions. Even in the liberal imperialist heartlands, mobilization around Bernie Sanders (United States), Jeremy Corbyn (UK), and Jean-Luc Mélenchon (France) attracted wide support, especially among the young. None of these movements was distinctively Leninist, or even Marxist, but they often contained or stimulated a range of socialist and left-liberal thinking in which Marxism and Leninism jostled for a piece of the action. Many of these phenomena traced to, or through, the 2008 financial crisis.

It was also the case that the absorption of the attention of the United States in the Middle East, its 'war on terror', and 'war on drugs' had led it to divert its gaze and its resources from apparently settled areas. With the weakening of US interest, leftist movements of some significance and a range of left-wing figures—presidents Evo Morales in Bolivia, Hugo Chávez and Nicholás Maduro in Venezuela, Lula in Brazil—together with the less committed but left-leaning politicians associated with the 'pink tide', such as Néstor and Cristina Kirchner in the former neoliberal showcase turned economic basket case of Argentina. Several of these countries formed ties with the United States' bêtes noirs, Cuba, China, and Iran. Marxism rather than Leninism influenced these movements, but the latter was also revived by them and the wider phenomena mentioned in the previous paragraph. Thus the overall picture in the early twenty-first century, while undoubtedly dominated by a resurgence of Western attempts at hegemony peaking in renewed 'cold war' against Russia and China, had also brought a stirring of 'traditional' resistance from the left, as well as new challenges from a variety

LENIN AS ICON AND INSPIRATION: LENINISM AFTER LENIN   141

of fundamentalisms including Muslim and Hindu versions, not least as a response to American-Christian and Jewish fundamentalisms which fuelled the new American right.

Since the time of Marx himself there had been a strong Marxist strand in Western and eventually global culture. Marxist historians, philosophers, economists, literary critics, and political analysts had made a significant mark. After 1991 this had faltered, but in the new era of crisis it began to return. In the forefront was the work of the French socialist economist Thomas Piketty, who produced a widely admired, though obviously contested, interpretation of capitalism's development in his international bestseller *Capital in the Twenty-First Century*. This was followed up by a study, *Capital and Ideology*, underlining the crucial role of slavery in the first stages of accumulation of capital.[69] Though Piketty is not a Marxist, his thought embraces Marxist influences and elements and he has committed to radical socialist causes like Corbyn's Labour Party (though he was disillusioned by its feeble response to Brexit) and the project for a unified left in France. Many other radical voices emerged, including Joseph Stiglitz and Naomi Klein. Few were Leninist but a number of serious, committed Leninist works emerged. Three blockbusters dominated the field, books which called for Lenin to be 'reconsidered', 'rediscovered', and 'reloaded'. Lively and more open Marxist–Leninist journals like *Jacobin* and the perennial *New Left Review* and *Monthly Review*, and publishers such as Verso, Haymarket, and Pluto, had a new lease of life and an expanding readership. Has a case been made to show that Lenin continues to be relevant?

The first of the three dreadnoughts to engage in battle was Lars Lih's *Lenin Rediscovered*, which appeared in 2005.[70] At one level the commitment of 887 pages to an interpretation of Lenin's *What is to be Done?*, including the text of Lenin's pamphlet which occupies 165 pages, indicates that, for Lih at least, Lenin's ideas were still worth studying. Like much of Lih's engaging work on Lenin, the author claimed to be presenting a fresh interpretation of Lenin's key concepts, which Lih frequently linked to overlooked influence from Karl Kautsky. Around 1900 Kautsky was acknowledged by the whole social democratic movement as the nearest thing to an heir to Marx and Engels. Later he became an arch-fiend in Bolshevik demonology but, in 1902, he was the touchstone of orthodoxy. Lih aimed to put the cold-war-distorted record straight to show that Lenin had not become the Marxist heretic he was often presented to be. The volume was a major step in Lih's campaign to, in his words, retrieve 'the historical Lenin',[71] by which he meant hack away the layers of Stalinist, totalitarian, and, though less

142 LENIN LIVES?

energetically, Trotskyist myths, misunderstandings, and malicious misinterpretations which encrusted the image of Lenin. Lih's aim was to set the record straight on what Lenin had said and done and how it fitted into its immediate context rather than being paraded as a founding text of Bolshevik totalitarianism. As Lih put it:

> *What Is to Be Done?* became enshrined in the textbooks as the founding document of Bolshevism. In the words of one of the most prominent American experts on Soviet Russia, 'the argument and the flavour of *What Is to Be Done?* have remained imbedded in the values and beliefs of the Soviet system. They are evident in the pronouncements of Khrushchev as they were in those of Stalin and Lenin.'[72]

This was unfortunate in Lih's view because

> [t]here could hardly have been a worse choice. WITBD was written to score off some very specific opponents and to advocate some very specific policies that were relevant only for a fleeting moment. It certainly was not written with the intention of making Lenin's basic beliefs clear to readers decades later.[73]

As Lih points out, Lenin did not refer to it after 1907, at which time Lenin said it belonged to 'a specific and by now long-past period in the development of our party'.[74] One might also understand its topicality by going no further than its subtitle, *Burning Questions of our Movement*.

Some of his key points had been previously remarked on by Neil Harding some twenty years earlier.[75] This applied to Lih's main proposition, notably that Lenin's vision of the party was initially seen as being perfectly orthodox and was welcomed by the senior figures in the party like Plekhanov, who, for the moment, saw Lenin as a rising star of the movement. It was only when Lenin started to kick over its structures and use manipulation and deceit as normal weapons in the struggle to control the leadership and direction of the party, including disrespect of Plekhanov, that many among the Russian social democratic leaders began to see a more malign aspect to his approach. Lih's main concern was to add to the scholarship on Lenin rather than to issue any rallying calls for his continuing relevance. This was implicit in Lih's enterprise but was not proclaimed in any great detail or with any great ceremony. 'We will', Lih assures us, 'literally *rediscover* a Lenin who is close to the complete opposite of the Lenin of the textbooks.'[76]

LENIN AS ICON AND INSPIRATION: LENINISM AFTER LENIN 143

In this sense Lih was presenting a less authoritarian and more democratic Lenin who, he implies, might serve as a better revolutionary role model than the totalitarian version.

From our point of view of assessing Lenin's relevance today, Lih's interpretation is somewhat paradoxical. It creates a more user-friendly view of Lenin's ideas on the party, devoid of Stalinist and anti-communist accretions, but does so in part by showing that Lenin himself did not think it had much relevance outside its immediate context. Something of a Pyrrhic victory from the point of view of a Leninist.

Another dreadnought to enter the combat zone was *Reconstructing Lenin: An Intellectual Biography* by the eminent Hungarian historian Tamás Krausz, published in 2015, which weighs in at a relatively modest 522 pages. Why has Krausz offered us this 'reconstruction' of Lenin's ideas? We have to wait until the final sentence of the book for the fundamental claim. Lenin's topicality, we are told, arises from his transformation of 'his own historical experiences into a set of theoretical concepts' which 'destroy any justifications for bourgeois society' and, despite contradictions, provide 'tools for those who still think of the possibilities of another, more humane world'.[77] Where Lih's aspirations to suggest the relevance of Lenin's ideas remained understated, Krausz takes a step further forward. He is offering a compendium of Lenin's policies, leaving it to the reader to select what is relevant. The contents of his box of treats is fairly conventional. He is uncritical of Lenin's early career and principles of party construction and also promotes the ideas of *The April Theses* and *The State and Revolution*. He distances himself from the violence of Lenin's early dictatorship without forming any causative link between it and Lenin's conception of revolution. By and large his account is as academically oriented as Lih's, and Krausz does not, himself, suggest where the key ideas—of a centralized party, soviets, state capitalism, and so on—might be deployed today in a new world of global interdependence and climate challenge. Nonetheless, there is no doubt that Krausz intended his book to be a praxis, an act, an intervention, in the current of history, not just an analysis of a forgotten time. There is no way of knowing who, if anyone, is planning to take anything up, though Krausz himself certainly believes Leninism is a powerful tool for those who want to 'go beyond capitalism'.[78] The Lenin that emerges from Krausz's depiction is predominantly old left, apart from the critique of Lenin's violence rather than a blanket justification for it. Krausz does not have anything new to say about Lenin's anti-religious fanaticism and understates his tendency to splitism and ideological purity which, in many respects, undercuts Krausz's

144   LENIN LIVES?

desire to present a more sympathetic dialogic and convivial Lenin. Similarly, he presents a plausibly anti-authoritarian interpretation of *The State and Revolution* without pointing to the vast gap between this aspect of Lenin's theory and his actual practice, in which soviets and popular channels of representation were rapidly taken under party and state control. In a sense, we are being invited to do as Lenin says, not as he does. In any case, it is clear that Krausz believes not only in Lenin's relevance, but that his ideas are vitally important, though we are not given details of exactly how we are expected to apply them.

A third battle-cruiser also sallied forth in the struggle in the form of the 2007 volume *Lenin Reloaded: Towards a Politics of Truth*, a compilation of essays edited by Sebastian Budgen, Stathis Kouvelakis, and Slavoj Žižek.[79] As the names of the distinguished editors suggest, this vessel was crewed, to a total of seventeen, by eminent flag-officers of Lenin's new flotilla of defenders. The title indicates that we were invited to consider precisely the question of Lenin's relevance. They clearly advocated that he should be reloaded into the contemporary armoury of ideas and, implicitly, practices. While the collection is diverse, in many respects it does belong in a series associated with Žižek devoted to analysing the world through a perspective derived from the ideas of the great neo-Freudian psychoanalyst Jacques Lacan. A number of contributors also give considerable weight to the fact that Lenin's first intellectual and political reaction to the outbreak of war in August 1914 was to disappear into the libraries of Zürich for three months and embark on an intensive study of Hegel. As the authors rightly say, the effect of this episode on Lenin's thought has been neglected by earlier commentators and biographers, with the exception of my Leningrad roommate mentioned earlier. Clearly this book was aimed at a highly sophisticated and philosophically inclined readership, not average workers or trade union and party activists. It is bursting with ideas and analyses linked to Lenin's theory and praxis. The emphasis on Lenin's renewed Hegelianism translates into the suggestion of a renewed absorption of the dialectical method into Lenin's thinking, that is one based on the view that even an apparently static entity can contain potentially dynamic elements in the ever-changing, ever-interacting course of events, of history, rather than a uniform, linear, dogmatic progression. To prove the point, Kevin Anderson quotes Lenin saying 'Hegel analyses concepts that are dead and shows that there is movement in them'.[80] About half of the book is devoted to this theme of dialectical dynamism. According to Stathis Kouvelakis, as a leading example, it explains Lenin's proclamation in September 1914 that the imperialist war should be

LENIN AS ICON AND INSPIRATION: LENINISM AFTER LENIN   145

transformed into a European civil war and, in dispute with his fellow author Kevin Anderson, Lenin's rejection of a 'third way' between idealism and materialism. The problem with this new approach is that the phenomena referred to have been the subject of analysis from their first utterance. When Kouvelakis assures us that Lenin's readiness to go from the bourgeois-democratic revolution to the proletarian revolution is part of his new thinking and is not linked to the theory of stages (i.e. that there was a sequence from feudal to bourgeois to communist society), and 'was in no way an organic development or a linear radicalisation, a passage from the "minimum programme" to the "maximum programme"', we might object on several grounds.[81] For instance, this resembles Trotsky's theory of permanent revolution, which emerged around 1905. Also, others had a similar outlook while Lenin himself used 'linear' terminology. The crucial *April Theses* of 1917 set out from the 'theory of stages'. Consequently, we might wonder exactly what new insight Kouvelakis is bringing to the table. The essays on this theme are fascinating but it is hard to see how they change much in the interpretation of Lenin's career.

The other half of the book expands on what we have already seen as key to Lenin, his views on war and empire, and a section on politics looking at his views on the party, soviets, and so on. There are many great insights which stimulate new thinking. Alain Badiou makes a point we have been engaged with, that 'pure' Leninism was traditionally seen through a Stalinist prism and that now is the time to 'retrieve' him from later accretions including Maoism.[82] Althusser tells us, startlingly, that reality is too complicated to be captured by theory, but Lenin shows us how to alternate between theory and practice; but, one might think, so do many people. Similarly, Alex Callinicos rightly claims that Lenin differs from softer leftists by being ready to use harsh methods to get the job done, but once again we could say this is not unique to Lenin and, for one, Stalin comes to mind.[83] Althusser pinpoints three issues which make Lenin relevant today—his 'strategic analysis of capitalism', even though he 'is not the greatest Marxist economic thinker'; his insistence on the centrality of politics' which shows that 'it is in the structures of the state that all the contradictions of class society are concentrated and fused'; and consequently the third point, the necessity of political organization with a centralized strategy. These three requirements make a political party essential rather than looser 'movements' like the anti-Vietnam war protests (today we might refer to Extinction Rebellion or the Stop the War Coalition as equivalents).[84] Fredric Jameson concludes a rather opaque disquisition with a rather obvious conclusion: 'The true meaning of Lenin is

146 LENIN LIVES?

the perpetual injunction to keep the revolution alive.'[85] In a kind of antithesis to Althusser, Terry Eagleton presents a lively view of Lenin and postmodernism which concludes with the words that 'whatever his failings, Lenin stands as a perpetual [that word again—CR] reminder that only those who enjoy the benefits of modernity can afford to be scornful about it.'[86]

There are many strong points of analysis in this collection and it is no accident that, remembering what we have already seen, many of them relate to imperialism. In a fine analysis, Domenico Losurdo traces the way capitalist imperialism embodied white supremacy in dividing its own citizens from the 'barbarians' being colonized, aiming not only at De Tocqueville, for whom First Nations were irrelevant to 'American' democracy, but also J. S. Mill, who justified 'tyranny' in ruling 'barbarians' provided it was guiding them towards higher democratic forms of government.[87] He also reminds us of its universal tendency to exploit weakly drawn borders and exploit ethnic and tribal tensions to its own ends. Georges Labica argues that capitalist globalism is no more than a fig leaf for imperialism,[88] and that true globalism 'is still something to be won'.[89] Antonio Negri argues that imperialism continues to establish its hegemony over intellect,[90] that Lenin left his project half accomplished in that he captured power but failed to abolish the state,[91] that 'our Winter Palace' that needs to be stormed is 'the White House which, it must be admitted is somewhat difficult to attack', and that 'though its summit is in the United States the Empire is not American—it is rather the Empire of collective capital'.[92] Lars Lih gives an airing to arguments developed in and from his 'rediscovery' of Lenin, plus a fine analysis of 'consciousness' as a key aspect of Lenin's thought leading him to compare Lenin to a 'revivalist missionary'.[93]

Undoubtedly, *Reloaded* is a formidable enterprise with many positive aspects, but the extent to which it proves a case for Lenin's contemporary relevance is not self-evident. The problem we have encountered so often, how do we untangle the specifically 'Leninist' from a tangled skein of Marxism, the image of the October Revolution, Lenin's synthesis of other thinkers, and so on, makes assessment difficult. Some of the points claiming Leninist inspiration, like the 'centrality of politics' (Althusser), 'keeping the revolution alive' (Jameson), or defining the nature of imperialism with its hypocritical 'civilising mission' and tendency to divide and rule through exploiting local divisions, plus the dialectical dynamism stressed by several contributors, *can* all be derived from Lenin but do not *necessarily* have to be so derived as many others have said similar things. Breaking with a 'dogmatic' approach to Lenin and replacing it with a flexible, dialectical

LENIN AS ICON AND INSPIRATION: LENINISM AFTER LENIN 147

understanding has been a stock-in-trade of the New Left for over fifty years.[94] Contemporary revival of Marxism (from which one can derive many of the above propositions) is dismissed as a deficient 'academic fashion' which denies 'politics proper' which can only be revived by a *return to Lenin*.[95] The collection at least mentions 'Lenin's failings', but like many defenders of Lenin, does not specify them or engage with them, so there is little about the intolerance; excessive violence; a combination of dogmatism and lack of a clear vision leading him to make major errors, especially in dealing with peasants and rural society; the suppression of free soviets and the popular movement symbolized by Kronstadt; and his failure to establish a solid succession, to name but a few.[96] Key questions, like Lenin's own assertion that his ideas for the party in *What is to be Done?* were only relevant to the Russian situation, as, indeed, were many other of his analyses, tactics, and strategies, would relativize Lenin rather than, as the contributors occasionally say and frequently imply, seeing him having universal significance.[97] 'Relevance' might well include later followers learning from these issues. There are inconsistencies between the authors. Notably Anderson's surprising comment that Lenin's view of the vanguard party, an aspect put in first place on the agenda by many who say Lenin has relevance, was, in fact, 'a concept that cannot be found in Marx', an observation made by many, but startlingly continuing, 'but which has burdened us for too long with a poor model of revolutionary organisation'.[98] This clashes with several other authors as does his criticism of Lenin over the one-party state and the philosophical crudity of *Materialism and Empiriocriticism*, a work praised by Michael-Matsas and other contributors.[99] Such differences are a sign of healthy debate for sure and do not in themselves detract from the force of the volume. *Reloaded*, however, does not fully make a case for returning to Lenin specifically. It has some very significant contributions to scholarship on Lenin, but that is very different in that one might add weight to any thinker without claiming they were a vitally necessary component of a contemporary political and revolutionary strategy.

Similar considerations apply to many other enterprises claiming to be, at least in part, influenced by Leninism. Radical socialist publishers like Haymarket and Pluto have impressive line-ups of first-rate analysis including social, political, environmental, historical, gender, economic, philosophical, and literary themes. Stimulating journals like *Jacobin*, *New Left Review*, and *Historical Materialism* are also impressive. Similar publishers and journals occur in many other language areas. There is a vast subcurrent of radical socialist publishing and discussion, but precisely what Lenin, any more than

148   LENIN LIVES?

Trotsky, Rosa Luxemburg, Bukharin, Karl Korsch, Bakunin, Kropotkin, Gramsci, and many others brings to the party is not easy to distinguish.

Let us conclude our enquiry by checking one more barometer of Leninist influence, the 2017 commemoration of the hundredth anniversary of the Russian Revolution. Overall, the centennial was muted and often took surprising national colorations.[100] However, we can look at a number of aspects reflecting our theme. A number of participants focused on Lenin. These largely comprised a few Leninist intellectuals and official comments from communist and radical socialist governments. One left-field survey was conducted by Elena Campbell, from the Henry Jackson Institute, of one of the handful of public statues of Lenin scattered across the United States, in unlikely venues such as Las Vegas and Atlantic City, to focus on the relatively small numbers in the United States who still looked to Lenin for inspiration. She organized an evening watch on the statue in her home town of Seattle on the anniversaries of the October Revolution (October 25 and November 7 according to the Old Style Russian and current New Style calendars) to see who turned up, since the statue had, at various times, attracted demonstrations and reactions from the citizens of the city. It was often dressed seasonally, in Halloween costume or adorned with Valentine's Day symbols. On Lenin's birthday bunches of flowers sometimes appeared. Others spilled red paint on it and around it to point to the suffering and terror associated with Lenin. The outcome on the anniversary—an empty space with only a couple of people passing by, including, on 25 October, a young couple from a farming background in Minnesota who thought Lenin could inspire future positive transformation and, on 7 November, a recently arrived student from the Middle East curious to know more about a figure concealed from view in his home country.[101]

With respect to publications connected to the anniversary, one major French research engine returned the following number of items published in 2017 under the keywords '1917'—forty-eight books; 'Russian Revolution'—eight-seven books; 'Lenin'—forty-two books; and 'Russia'—fourteen books.[102] This gives no support to Lenin's relevance since we don't know what proportion of the books associated with Lenin referred to that, but it does show sizeable interest. More specifically, a number of items praised Lenin for his role in 1917 and his continuing relevance. Two of the most influential and widely read books sympathetic to 1917 and October in particular were published in London by the novelist China Miéville and the radical writer Tariq Ali. Miéville praised the popular energy and Ali argued for the centrality of Lenin: 'Without Lenin there would have been no socialist revolution in 1917. Of that we can be certain.'[103] In fact, Tariq Ali's statement was incorrect. Soviet Second Congress delegates were mandated to declare soviet power without any influence from Lenin, though it would have been more accurate to say that the October Revolution we know would not have taken the shape it did without Lenin, which is a quite different concept. However, Tariq Ali was an outlier, and relatively few other publications followed the line of celebrating 1917 as opposed to simply remembering it and focusing the elements remembered through a contemporary prism.

Different countries adapted the occasion to contemporary purposes.[104] In a sense that is what radical socialist and communist governments around the world did also, and a number of them claimed continuing relevance for Lenin. In China the official tendency was to defend the October Revolution and its consequences by showing, among other things, that, 'the fundamental principles of the October revolution are eternal', which is clearly an implied endorsement of Lenin's continuing relevance.[105] A similar line was taken in Cuba. José Ramón Machado Ventura, second-in-command to Raúl Castro, told his audience at a commemorative rally that:

Fig. 15 Communists in Kerala, south India, celebrate the election of 21-year-old student Arya Rajendran as mayor of the 2.5 million population capital city on 28 December 2021 (from Monthly Review).

150 LENIN LIVES?

> Nowadays there exists a tendency to minimize the importance of the Revolution which led to the founding of the world's first socialist state and opened the path to hope and a new social regime which would prove that a world free of exploiters and the exploited was possible. The principles of equality, solidarity, internationalism, social justice, the people's right to self-determination, independence, and sovereignty, were the basis of the October Revolution and will also continue to be the basis of ours.[106]

Clearly there were places where Lenin was revered. One might surmise that the Marxist-inspired governments had a tendency to glorify Lenin rather than specifically follow him, but there remain a few active revolutionary movements, like the Indian Naxalites and small groups in Nepal and elsewhere in South Asia, that do. In Kerala, a democratically elected communist government has held a share of power since 2016 and for half of the thirty-five years prior to that [see Fig. 15]. Should we, also, pay more attention to Lenin? Does he still present us with an important legacy?

Conclusion

Does Lenin live? Clearly, he made a big impact on the twentieth century, inspiring many of the most determined anti-fascists and anti-colonialists. For all its horrors, the twentieth century was characterized by hope and the expectation of progress. However, is there anything in Lenin and Leninism that speaks to our pessimistic, dystopian world of environmental limitations and catastrophes; a nuclear threat seen more acutely in the light of the Ukrainian crisis; the exposed fragility of a capitalist globalization, which is interpreted by Leninists and others as little more than a rebranded imperialism linked to a desperate attempt by the United States to assert unilateral hegemony in an increasingly multipolar world; the development of obscene material inequalities. All contrast with the imperative for global governance to provide an answer and maybe even survival in the face of these challenges. For many of the people in our study, Lenin still has something to add to the discussion. For others, clinging to Leninism is an obstacle and his remaining influence is more malignant than benign. Without doubt, some of the most penetrating analyses of our predicament by, to name only a few, Paulo Freire, Mike Davis, David Harvey, Naomi Klein, Thomas Piketty, and even Pope Francis, have been Marxist-influenced even though they are not all canonical Marxists. However, more dogmatically self-defined Marxist–Leninists gathered around citadels of Trotskyism, and more committed journals like *Jacobin* and *Historical Materialism*, and publishers like Haymarket and Pluto, have also produced much acute and stimulating criticism, though it is not easy to find specifically Leninist elements. Some hardliners promote a classical Leninist party model—which, ironically, did not exist in Lenin's time and certainly was not exemplified by the Bolshevik Party before 1917, and, arguably, was only realized in a crude form by Stalin—plus a sometimes simplistic workerism over which Lenin himself actually blew hot and cold.

In a completely unscientific way I have, since embarking on the present task, pestered friends, colleagues, acquaintances, mainly from academia but also some from beyond, to say if they thought Lenin had any relevance

Lenin Lives?. Christopher Read, Oxford University Press. © Christopher Read 2024.
DOI: 10.1093/oso/9780198866084.003.0004

152   LENIN LIVES?

today. There were some twenty substantial written responses from people to whom I sent a summary of my initial ideas. Interestingly, no two pointed to the same features. Occasionally, there was overlap in what they thought but always with different emphases for different reasons. Responses revolved around one of three axes. Some said Lenin's ideas and praxis still had relevance. Some said he no longer wielded significant influence, and some, who surprised me most but proved to have a point, said his influence was still felt but it had a negative impact. There were also interesting contradictions. Some thought my depiction of Lenin's view of the party-worker relationship as Confucian was illuminating because it focused on its tutelary underpinnings, while a Chinese specialist who had some sympathy with Leninism thought it was bizarre given that Confucianism was very conservative. There were many interesting points but the great diversity was surprising. Where I had expected a number of respondents might have pointed to Lenin's conception of a revolutionary vanguard party as definitive, none did. Here are some of the points made.

For one respondent the adoption of NEP was something that still resonated. The point was that in NEP Lenin had harnessed the vast creative, active force of the middle class to the revolutionary endeavour, a phenomenon being successfully repeated in China today:

> Lenin is best recalled for his NEP. That was when he applied the truth of Marx's remark in *The Communist Manifesto* that: "The bourgeoisie, historically, has played a most revolutionary part." And it goes on doing so, does it not, as Deng Xiaoping understood, and now Xi Jinping in his turn.[1]

Another insightful comment compared the terrible odds Lenin faced in his time and to the overwhelming domination of right-wing forces today:

> Lenin was a political leader who took on and tried to defeat what he saw as the major cause of the terrible problems the world faced during his lifetime. The enemy was global capitalism and we face a similar crisis today. We have to deal with oppression, exploitation, injustice, misery, and grave economic and environmental threats. What is interesting about Lenin is the way he tried to confront and defeat the same, or very similar, threats and bring the world from this grossly unequal condition to a society based on freedom, liberty, and social justice. His life and work is a record of the grave and multiple problems he faced, how he

CONCLUSION   153

analysed them and sought solutions. He was highly intelligent, quite determined, and a ruthless realist.[2]

In other words, his struggle is potentially inspirational even though his solutions and methods were not always so admirable.

Responding to my suggestion that Lenin, unlike 'softer' radicals, prepared for the eventuality that ruling classes would not relinquish property and privilege without a struggle, another respondent asked:

> Is it historically the case that removing injustice inevitably involves violence and a ruling group will otherwise always maintain their grasp on their privileges with ruthless efficiency? That frame of thought clouded perspectives on two of the biggest issues of our time, the ending of Soviet authoritarianism and apartheid in South Africa. Mandela eventually mandated armed struggle by the ANC but primarily against specific targets and these actions were not the major factor in apartheid's collapse. I do think some situations are highly likely to involve clear social confrontation rather than just evolutionary development...[but] power structures are quite often undermined from within and more often than not those behind them do not display the ruthless efficiency Lenin attributed to them.

The respondent continued:

> Also, is the goal of ending injustice in itself unimpeachably democratic without regard to the means used to achieve it? The democratic centralism Lenin advocated is sensible enough for a political party and is widely applied, but its democracy depends very much on whether it operates in a plural system or not. The Bolshevik innovation was not democratic centralism so much as the one-party state. What was innovatory about revolution from above was not the concept itself but the claim it could be democratic, though Blanqui anticipated Lenin here. Lenin's overriding priority was surely revolution, not democracy, and if he thought, as he did, that social revolution through a party of professional revolutionaries was automatically democratic, he also thought many things that give one pause. To stand for a world proletarian (working class) revolution which...would destroy capitalism and imperialism and usher in a perfect society suggests a basic   millenarianism built in with his tactical and

154 LENIN LIVES?

strategic genius. I can't help thinking his politics were a regression from the political experience of the nineteenth century, notably the expansion of parliamentary systems, to the French Revolution, which was torn apart by failure to reconcile party-political organization with pluralism. Of course, as you stress, Russian circumstances were radically different. In the Third World, conditions were in some ways closer and Lenin showed his acumen by turning to it—a master stroke.[3]

My plan to include reference to Lenin's insensitivity to religion and the need to take the beneficiaries, the workers, along with himself in the revolutionary process rather than force them into it evoked another interesting response:

I'm with Gramsci on the importance of the 'war of position'—of the need to win over the masses (or a significant proportion of them) before trying to seize state power from the ruling class. In a parliamentary democracy, where elements of the left are likely to participate in the exercise of state power *before* there is any decisive showdown with the existing economic elites, the possibility of winning over the masses this side of the revolution may be rather less bleak than your sketch might imply. I'm with you on religion: both in recognizing that many believers reject clerical hierarchy and alignment with the ruling classes, and that there is no necessary contradiction between religious belief and scientific enquiry.[4]

Several of these points were supported by a more fragmented reply which included the following: 'Consciousness vs spontaneity in his idea of the Party—proletariat can only reach consciousness through the Party—is not really democratic—Party substitutes for Proletariat.' Nonetheless, my respondent continued, Lenin could be very astute on the forces at play in the current moment, being 'especially astute and articulate' on agrarian and other problems as represented in 'his 1917 writings on this' which 'maybe represent his best merging of ideas and political practice', which is not what is most frequently mentioned about Lenin today. But also, the response continued, there is a tendency to overlook the more repressive aspects. In particular, top-down bureaucratism existed from early 1918, not only after the Tenth Party Congress in March 1921. By then, the 'fate of factory committees, trade unions, Soviets, creation of *Rabkrin* (The Worker-Peasant Inspectorate), and party Control Commissions' were evidence of the 'triumph of a bureaucratic principle which Lenin held to obsessively (even while always speaking the language of anti-bureaucracy).'[5]

CONCLUSION 155

A former member of a Trotskyist party responded like this:

I don't see a future for Bolshevik-style politics. My Marxism was always more Victor Serge than Trotsky—and it was when Tony Cliff turned the International Socialists into a Leninist party that I departed its ranks. That said, the tragedy of our situation today seems to be that there is no shortage of powerful ideas on the left about how to create a better future for humanity, yet making them organizationally effective—i.e. making them a forceful rather than merely symbolic political challenge to the status quo—proves exceptionally hard (Corbyn, Podemos, Chavez).[6]

Another socialist, who continued to admire Lenin, found a curious hesitation in my plans and posed the awkward and very pertinent question: 'It also seems to me that if, as you suggest, Lenin's practice was simply a reflection of (now vanished) conditions, and his ideas were not very good, then the judgement should overall be a negative one. And yet you don't want to jettison him...why not?'[7]

Some respondents argued that a weakening of Leninist influence would be a good thing for the global left. This sometimes took the form of thinking that the end of European Communism opened up paths to a more democratic form of socialism. Personally I welcomed it for that reason, as did others, and have been surprised that even now, over thirty years on, its ghost is still called to the banquet to discredit a left that had nothing to do with it. This was put more subtly by a respondent. 'In the event I was surprised how depressed I was by the collapse of state socialism in 1989/91, but not surprised it brought no renewal of socialist politics. Intellectually, I despised the [Soviet] system; emotionally, however, it signified the possibility of an alternative to capitalism.' Others argued that, for example, Lenin had cast a shadow over a large part of the left by diminishing the importance of the rule of law, by reducing it to nothing more than the rules of the rulers, which in many cases it is, without establishing it as a core principle for a modern society, one to which governments themselves should be subject. Similarly Lenin had coarsened the related ideas of liberalism and democracy. The Marxist tradition clearly challenged liberal individualism but only to establish its own superior, in its view, definition of the interdependence of individual freedom with the freedom of all. Rather like Marx's view of religion which was coarsened by Lenin, the concepts of human rights, liberalism, and democracy were also mocked.[8]

Fig. 16 From history to heritage—Marx, Lenin, and Stalin impersonators by the Kremlin Wall.

On a recent visit to Russia I was able to elicit a few interesting responses to the question of Lenin's relevance. His status is still slightly ambiguous. A few statues remain standing, including a large one in October Square in Moscow, and his remains are still on display in his mausoleum, though the area is as frequented by impersonators and selfie seekers as devotees [see Fig. 16]. The county around the renamed former capital St Petersburg is still called Leningrad. On the other hand, President Putin has roundly and frequently denounced Lenin, Stalin, and the whole communist project. Very few Russians I talked to had any time for Lenin. An Academician historian emphasized Lenin's ruthlessness and cruelty. However, as in other cases, the ghost could not be completely silenced. Talking to a small group of students, one spoke up for Lenin, and there was consensus that he had an increasing number of admirers among students as a 'person who got things done'. This may be a version of the view that he remains inspirational because he fought for his cause and won when the odds were against him—rampaging international imperialism, powerful capitalist states with, in most cases, only weakly organized socialist opposition movements—mirror today's neoliberal capitalist dominance.

Of course Lenin and Leninism had attracted many critics. Liberals, conservatives, nationalists, and fascists profoundly disagreed with the whole

CONCLUSION   157

socialist tradition. Interestingly, some opponents nonetheless adopted some Leninist features. The bitter enemies of the Chinese Communist Party, Chiang Kai-shek and the Kuomintang, adopted a vanguard party model and a one-party state. Nazism, the complete antithesis of Leninism, also adopted the one-party state, just as Stalin may have been influenced towards mass violent purges of his political rivals by Hitler's attack on the 'left' of his party in the Night of the Long Knives (30 June–2 July 1934). Many critics of Lenin had, at times, been personally close to him; Martov and Bogdanov, for example, and their associate Maxim Gorky. Gorky set up a newspaper in 1917 which was highly critical of Lenin and the Bolsheviks for risking the cultural acquisitions of Russia, obtained through the brilliance of its intelligentsia, in a desperate gamble on uneducated workers and uncultured peasants whom Gorky considered to be near barbaric. In 1909, a celebrated critique of the whole leftist and materialist revolutionary tradition was the intellectual event of the year in Tsarist Russia. Several of the contributors to the critique were former Marxists, and one of them, Peter Struve, who became a tsarist imperialist, was taken up as a counterweight to the left by Richard Pipes, a Harvard historian who himself became a national security advisor to President Ronald Reagan. Some, like the cosmopolitan revolutionary Victor Serge, who found what he called 'a revolution dying' when he arrived in Petrograd in 1919, remained loyal to the October Revolution and to Trotsky, while others on the left, mainly anarchists, were among the first to denounce Bolshevism on leftist revolutionary grounds, accusing it of suppressing basic freedoms and repressing working people. Many powerful critiques were to follow. In 1920, Bertrand Russell's highly perceptive *Practice and Theory of Communism* expressed deep scepticism about the revolution and many critics were evolving within Soviet Russia. In the 1930s, Serge denounced Stalin to a largely uninterested West which did not want to hear ill of a potential anti-Nazi force. André Gide repented his fellow-travelling in his *Retour de l'URSS* (*Return from the USSR*) following a visit in 1934, as did a group of former Stalinists who switched sides in the cold war and published a powerful collection entitled, evocatively, *The God that Failed*. George Orwell's *Homage to Catalonia* and later items like *Animal Farm* and *1984* established an anti-Stalinist and non-communist tradition on the British left which was continued by Aneurin Bevan, Tony Benn, and Jeremy Corbyn to name the most prominent. Right-wing anti-communism became a cement of Western cold war ideology and seems, in a curious way, to have morphed into virulent Russophobia since the collapse of the Soviet Union.

158   LENIN LIVES?

However, our focus is not on a full-spectrum analysis of Lenin and Leninism but a narrower one on why he was influential and whether he still retains any influence, for good or ill. However, a new and unexpected challenge has arisen from deep within the Leninist camp itself. Eric Blanc has challenged the *Historical Materialist* and Trotskyist community, plus all other surviving Leninists, to abandon the, as he sees it, excessive influence of Lenin.[9] His book, *Revolutionary Social Democracy: Working-Class Politics Across the Russian Empire*, in the author's words, 'marshals extensive new primary data from across the Russian Empire to challenge longstanding myths about the Russian Revolution—and to challenge unhelpful Leninist (aka "revolutionary socialist") political strategies based on these myths.'[10] Blanc, not unlike Lih, puts revolutionary fire back into the interpretation of Kautsky and the Second International and proposes that there is no Bolshevik 'exceptionalism', that is, Lenin's thought is not especially distinctive from that of other democratic socialists of the time:

> All too many Marxists have overgeneralised lessons from a Russian labour movement whose dynamics were determined in large part by autocratic conditions. Simplistic accounts of the Second International have played an important role in pushing generations of radicals to view the presumed innovations of the Bolsheviks as necessary components of effective socialist strategy in all countries.
>
> Since democratic socialism has been overshadowed for most of the past hundred years by Leninism and Social Democracy, retrieving the lost tradition of revolutionary social democracy is particularly pertinent. This book has underscored the surprising relevance of aspects of imperial Russia's political history for socialists working in legal, parliamentary conditions. Many of the goals and dilemmas of class formation confronted by socialists over a century ago remain with us today.[11]

In many ways, if it were sustainable, Blanc's critique of Lenin and Leninism would be the most corrosive. However, he largely focuses on the revolutionary process and, less surprisingly, for someone trying to play up the importance of provincial and non-Russian perspectives, his reinterpretation demands a detailed examination which would take us beyond our current brief. But it does constitute an original challenge to the domination of the Lenin myth. Curiously, as far as the Bolsheviks are concerned, Blanc shares his outlook with the current dominant mainstream school of Russian historiography which pays little attention to Lenin and the Bolsheviks, except

CONCLUSION 159

as manipulators and destroyers of the 'true' conservative and liberal-democratic revolution. Unlike Blanc and almost every other non-Russian school of interpretation, it is largely dismissive of worker and peasant forces which are seen as archaic and backward-looking remnants trying to turn the clock back. Royalists, nationalists, including White generals, and liberals are seen as the active forces in the revolution.[12]

To return to the awkward question I was asked—should we jettison Lenin? What can we say about him and his relevance to the problems of the twenty-first century? Why should we expect him to have influence? Our attention is drawn to him in the first place, not because of the power of his ideas, but because he was the figurehead and leader of the biggest rebellion against capitalism the world had seen at the time, and because that challenge dominated the twentieth century and, via its transfer to China, continues to do so. There is no doubt that the historical Lenin had an enormous influence on the development of the world since 1917. For better or worse, capitalism in Europe and beyond was facing its second major challenge, if one counts the brief but fiery flame of the Paris Commune (1871) as the first. The first lasted seventy-one days, the second nearly seventy-five years. Most likely, had Lenin remained a theorist only, his name and writings would be known only to a few specialists, a Bakunin or a Rosa Luxemburg, rather than a Hegel or a Marx. And yet he is seen by some as a great thinker and, in particular, as a 'philosopher king' who put his great thoughts into practice.

So it would seem reasonable to expect Lenin to continue to be, in part at least, a role model in the modern world and, indeed, the few active left-wing revolutionary groups in the non-European world do, in many cases, acknowledge him as inspiration and guide. However, contemporary Western radical groups, especially those who prioritize climate change, have little time for Lenin. Like Marx, Lenin's expectations were for a teleological process of endless progress and rising living standards driven by unlimited industrial production and technological advance. Today's 'pessimism' on that score is very different. With those considerations in mind, can we summarize Lenin's legacy and importance.

First and most obviously, Lenin lived and made a great mark on history, but that is divided between the historical Lenin and the mythical (pro and anti) Lenin. Let's start here. Lenin's theory is praised by admirers and excoriated by 'cold warriors' and their descendants for bringing about the October Revolution. However, the historical Lenin was not propelled into power by his theories or calculated strategies. The Bolsheviks were marginal until two

160   LENIN LIVES?

or three months before October and came to power because of the failures of their opponents, the crassness of the far right, and the willingness of the Bolsheviks to stand with a mass movement they fundamentally disagreed with. The masses wanted Peace, Bread, Land, and Soviet Power; Lenin knew a new revolution would bring civil war, collective farming, economic disruption, and Bolshevik power. October was a mass revolution but the Bolsheviks conducted a coup to stand at the head of it. Lenin's main programmatic texts which are believed to have been behind his tactics—*What is to be Done?* and *State and Revolution*—had little or no bearing on the October Revolution or its early development. The Bolshevik party in 1917 was not a well-oiled and disciplined machine, it was an ill-organized shambles. This is neither surprising nor reprehensible. In the chaos of 1917 and in the light of a membership increasing from something like 10,000 in February 1917 to some 250,000 by the end of the year, the organization was likely to be rough and ready. It was not a primed, disciplined, ideologically sound instrument. Arguably, it was only in Stalin's day that it took on this form, albeit in an increasingly lifeless and caricatural fashion. The key to Lenin's success lies in the much more modest *April Theses*. One provision stands out in connection with coming to power—'No support for the Provisional Government'. While Lenin proposed this for other reasons, it turned out to be the ace of trumps. As other parties on the left lost credibility by compromising with the centre and the right, the Bolsheviks remained the only large party which was untarnished. Small wonder the mass movement for soviet power and so on turned to them. Concealing his deeper aims, Lenin put the Bolsheviks at the head of this movement. At the crucial moment, to be a 'Bolshevik'—whether new party member, newspaper reader, or voter—meant supporting Peace, Bread, Land, and Soviet Power. World revolution, socialist transformation of humanity, and the emergence of communist society were unknown to almost all of them. The consequence of this is that while the seizure of power was relatively simple—it was not incorrectly said that they did not seize power but found it lying in the street and picked it up—holding it and using it were much more challenging. A full account of this is beyond our scope here.

Two more aspects of the historical Lenin. The theoretical canon which most people associate with him, the two items mentioned above and *Imperialism: the Highest Stage of Capitalism*, were contributions to ongoing Russian debates and were not framed as global models. We have already discussed this with relation to *What is to be Done?*. While *Imperialism* is a text that stands scrutiny outside of its immediate context, it was also

CONCLUSION 161

addressed to the key dilemma facing Russian Marxists, namely, how can one envisage a Marxist, that is a post-capitalist, revolution in a barely capitalist society. *Imperialism* was intended to provide the answer. Capitalist imperialism is a worldwide system and it can be challenged at any of its levels. As we have seen, this became a crucial consideration in, unexpectedly, turning Leninism around from being a supposed challenge to the capitalist metropolises and instead spreading like wildfire after 1919 into the imperial and colonial periphery where it had its greatest successes. This was achieved by shrewd decisions and contingency rather than theoretical foresight. Secondly, some of his key works are not in the canon and are much less well-known, even to the point of being overlooked by specialists. Indeed, the vanguard nature of the party is more explicit in *One Step Forwards, Two Steps Back* rather than *What is to be Done?*, and the uncharismatically titled *Immediate Tasks of the Soviet Government* of April 1918 unlocks an essential phase in Lenin's view of the transition to socialism. It also outlines many of the parameters of 'socialism in one country' and is the scheme which party militants tended to equate with 'communism', to prefer to NEP, and which Stalin reverted to in his transition policies from 1928–9 onwards. Many Leninists pay little attention to writings like this, which are close to what was implemented, while they draw extensive conclusions from *What is to be Done?*—notably about a disciplined, conspiratorial, vanguard party, which are scarcely in it or intended primarily for autocratic conditions like those of Russia at the time it was written—and *State and Revolution*, which is almost the antithesis of Soviet reality as it evolved not only under Stalin but also under Lenin. In other words, even the Lenin that lived, after 1924, often had a tenuous connection to the historical Lenin. Consequently, one might argue that even 'Leninists' have been admiring an incomplete and inaccurate version of Lenin derived distantly from official Soviet views.

Arguably, given that the first chief sculptor of Leninism was Stalin, the tenuousness between the historical and the mythical grew. Until 1956, Leninism was chiefly the Stalinist variant. Up to that point the Trotskyite position was marginal and heretical. However, Trotskyism also bought into play a number of the key myths, such as October as a proletarian revolution led by Lenin, Trotsky, and the Bolsheviks, and the crucial question of international revolution, among others. If anything, Trotsky tilted towards even greater authoritarianism and coercion than Stalin. It was Trotsky who had his detachment literally decimated when they wavered in battle, and it was Trotsky who energetically promoted militarization of labour over the

162   LENIN LIVES?

independence of trade unions. He was also an energetic supporter of the suppression of the Kronstadt uprising. None of these was a promising indicator of future policy. In reality, Leninism pivoted, in 1919–21, with Trotsky's full approval, towards the colonies, and its greatest influence came in the anti-colonial struggles of the twentieth century. In the developed world it became more influential as a bedrock in the fight against fascism as much as it was a bulwark of proletarian revolution. Today, the problems facing humanity are very different in some essentials—climate change, globalization, post-industrialization—which can only be solved by global co-operation. However, in other respects there is continuity—capitalist imperialism drives on though sometimes in new, hip guises of high-tech and social media saturation. Human rights throw up increasingly thorny issues of gender identity and abortion. Democracy remains lopsided towards wealth and a persistent ruling class. The state sprawls ever more widely across society, especially in its cultural and hegemonic class influence. Neoliberal proponents of the supposedly 'small' state nonetheless promote its cultural, judicial, and military power as much as, even more than, anyone else. The 'neoliberal' Pentagon, as an extreme example, has a budget of $1.64 trillion, larger than that of many countries.[13] A re-energized Marxism has arisen to address these questions, but does Leninism help? Lenin did point to the near inevitability, albeit undesirability, of violence in engaging in struggle and, although some Leninists we have looked at dispute its relevance, the supposedly Leninist model of a vanguard party is still deemed to be necessary, though, in fact, most left-wing parties of significance are committed to democratic and/or parliamentary roads to power. In all these respects, specifically Leninist models seem outdated, though possibly aspects of 'Leninist' analysis remain. *Imperialism* might be an exception though it is highly dependent on Marx, Hilferding, Hobson, Bogdanov, and Bukharin, rather than being purely a creation of Lenin.

But still that hesitation to completely jettison Lenin remains. Perhaps a recent celebration of Lenin's 150th birthday helps to explain this. A publication by an eclectic selection of admirers of Lenin from around the world, many of whom were linked through a nexus in Kyrgyzstan, introduced an element often missing from Leninist discourse—humour, sociability, and inclusiveness. The editors were the 'politburo', the contributors the 'central committee'. Even though the editor deprecates the efforts, saying the resultant volume still leans towards the male, colonialist gaze, it makes a creditable effort at diversity, reaching not only Central Asia, but also South Africa, India, and China. In this respect it contrasts with the First World

CONCLUSION 163

academicism of the reloadings, reconsiderings, and reconstructions, valuable though they are. In fact, the volume overlaps with them in including items by Badiou, Žižek, Kevin Anderson, Ron Suny and others who often repeat and underline points made in the earlier books. The tone of this one, however, is very different. It contains poems, essays, memories, and photos, the main photographer himself musing on the significance of Soviet-made Zenit cameras to budding photographers with a limited budget around the world in the 1970s and 1980s. The contributors are presented with and selected according to two criteria—'critical solidarity with Lenin', and 'writing with joy'. (ii-iii) The editor regrets being unable to pay contributors—'all you need is love' was the rule—and says this, sadly, meant some invitees would not attend, leading the editor to rue 'the recent going-out-of-fashion of forced labour'.[14] Where else is there a contributor to a highly insightful book about Lenin, who searched for him 'in Bishkek...flanked by the beautiful snow-capped Ala-Too mountains, listening to Belle and Sebastian'?[15] There are contributions on culture, theatre, witchcraft, gender, LGBT issues, and coronavirus, as well as commentaries from a refreshing variety of global perspectives. If Leninism can still inspire such affection and insight how can it be fully jettisoned?

Let us leave the last word to one of the contributors to *Lenin Reloaded*, Jean-Jacques Lecercle, who reminds us that Lenin perhaps still deserves to live, not least because 'he, after all, gave world capitalism the worst fright it ever had!'[16] That, in itself, is quite a legacy, for good or ill.

Endnotes

Introduction

1. For a deeply insightful, thoughtful, and stimulating account of the complexities of Lenin's view of violence, see James Ryan, *Lenin's Terror: The Ideological Origins of Early Soviet State Violence* (2012).
2. V. I. Lenin, *Selected Works*, i (1968), 189.
3. Lenin, Selected Works, 189–90.
4. Lenin, *Selected Works*, 196.
5. A term coined by the Roman poet Juvenal who concluded the masses could be led away from revolt by being bought off by satisfying their most basic needs and creating distractions and entertainments.
6. From a Marxist perspective nationalism, racism, and, controversially, gender have been used most recently to interrupt the formation of class identity and of common human identity, the end-point of class struggle being the overcoming of divisions and the gathering together of all humanity, so that, as Marx and Engels said in *A Contribution to the Critique of Political Economy* in 1859, 'the prehistory of human society ends'. 'Divide and rule' has been characteristic of polities from classical Greece and the Roman empire via Machiavelli to modern imperialisms, dictatorships, and parliamentary democracies. Historically, consciously weakening opposition by playing on clashes within it between, for example, ethnic groups, or deliberately widening social and religious divisions, have been key tactics to implement divide and rule.
7. Marx, K. 'Introduction to A Contribution to the critique of Hegel's Philosophy of Right' *Deutsch-Französische Jahrbücher*, February 1844, Paris. https://en.wikipedia.org/wiki/Opium_of_the_people#cite_note-:3-5.

Part One

1. Quoted in Valentinov, N. *The Early Years of Lenin* University of Michigan Press, Ann Arbor 1969, p. 135.
2. For a discussion of Plekhanov's foundational ideas, see Samuel Baron, *Plekhanov: The Founder of Russian Marxism* (1963), and Christopher Read, 'George Plekhanov, *Socialism and Political Struggle* (1883)', in Rachel Hammersley, ed., *Revolutionary Moments: Reading Revolutionary Texts* (2015), 125–32.

166 ENDNOTES

3. Nadezhda Krupskaya, *Reminiscences of Lenin* (International Publishers: New York, 1967). https://www.marxists.org/archive/krupskaya/works/rol/rol07.htm.
4. These aspects of Lenin's life are covered in many of the biographies, for example, Christopher Read, *Lenin: A Revolutionary Life* (2005), ch. 2.
5. Lenin, V. I. *What Is to Be Done?* Part II A https://www.marxists.org/archive/lenin/works/1901/witbd/ii.htm
6. Marx, K. and Engels, F. *The Communist Manifesto* Chapter 4. https://www.marxists.org/archive/marx/works/1848/communist-manifesto/ch04.htm
7. Lenin, V. I. 'The April Theses'. https://www.marxists.org/archive/lenin/works/1917/apr/04.htm
8. Alexandra Kollontai, *The Workers' Opposition*, https://www.marxists.org/archive/kollonta/1921/workers-opposition/ch03.htm.
9. For a fuller account of these complex developments see Christopher Read, *Religion, Revolution and the Russian Intelligentsia: The Vekhi Debate and Its Intellectual Background* (1979), esp. ch. 2. On party schools, see Christopher Read, *Culture and Power in the Russian Revolution; the Intelligentsia and the Transformation from Tsarism to Communism* (1991), 115–18. Some aspects will be considered in the next chapter.
10. Sergei Nechaev, *Catechism of a Revolutionary* (Chernetsky: Geneva, 1869), https://www.marxists.org/subject/anarchism/nechayev/catechism.htm.
11. Angelica Balabanoff, *Impressions of Lenin* (1970), 15.
12. Yekaterina Sinelschikova, 'Why Did Vladimir Lenin Adopt the Name "Lenin"?', *Russia Beyond* (9 October 2020), https://www.rbth.com/history/332831-vladimir-lenin-nickname.
13. Maxim Gorky, *Nicolai Lenin the Man* (1924), https://www.marxists.org/archive/gorky-maxim/1924/lenin-the_man.html.
14. Robert Service, *Lenin: A Biography* (2000), 158.
15. Quoted in Read, Christopher. *Lenin: A Revolutionary Life* Routledge, London and New York, 2005 p. 101. The originals can be found in Lenin, V.I. *Collected Works* Progress Publishers, Moscow (1960–70) v.37 p. 451 and 372, respectively.
16. Krupskaya, Nadezhda. *Memories of Lenin* London 1970 p. 65 quoted in Read (2005) p. 46. https://www.marxists.org/archive/krupskaya/works/rol/rol04.htm
17. Read, *Lenin*, 43–8, 101.
18. Read, *Lenin*, 104.
19. Lenin, V. I. *Collected Works* v.43 p. 432.
20. Krupskaya (1970) quoted in Read (2005) p. 135. https://www.marxists.org/archive/krupskaya/works/rol/rol20.htm
21. Lenin, V. I. 'Preface to the French and German Edition' *Imperialism, The Highest Stage of Capitalism. A Popular Outline* Petrograd (1917). https://www.marxists.org/archive/lenin/works/1916/imp-hsc/pref02.htm
22. Curiously, in a very similar case, when Trotsky was detained by the British in Canada as he tried to return from New York by sea, it was a request for his

ENDNOTES 167

release by Provisional Government Foreign Minister Paul Miliukov which allowed him to proceed. Miliukov's request was partly motivated by having to implement the government's principles of political freedom, including release of all political prisoners, and partly from pressure from the Petrograd Soviet and elsewhere on the left on which the government was dependent for its survival.

23. Semion Lyandres, 'The Bolsheviks' "German Gold" Revisited: An Inquiry into the 1917 Accusations', *Carl Beck Papers in Russian and East European Studies*, 1106 (Feb. 1995).

24. All quotations in this paragraph are from: Lenin V. I. 'Lecture on the 1905 Revolution' given on 9/22 January 1917. First published in *Pravda* 18 22 January 1925. https://www.marxists.org/archive/lenin/works/1917/jan/09.htm

25. This phrase is widely attributed to former British prime minister Harold Macmillan, but there is no confirmatory source.

26. Lenin, V. I. 'The April Theses'. https://www.marxists.org/archive/lenin/works/1917/apr/04.htm

27. All quotations in this paragraph are from https://www.marxists.org/archive/lenin/works/1917/apr/04.htm

28. See, for example, Robert Tombs, *The Paris Commune 1871* (1999).

29. Both quotations here are from the 'April Theses': https://www.marxists.org/archive/lenin/works/1917/apr/04.htm

30. Karl Marx, 'General Rules of the International Working Men's Association', *The Bee-Hive Newspaper* (12 Nov. 1864), and *Address and Provisional Rules of the Working Men's International Association*...(London, Nov. 1864), 1, https://www.marxists.org/history/international/iwma/documents/1864/rules.htm.

31. V. I. Lenin, *The State and Revolution*, ch. 3 (1918).

32. All quotes in this paragraph come from the third chapter of Lenin, V. I. *The State and Revolution* Zhizn' i znanie, Moscow (1918). https://www.marxists.org/archive/lenin/works/1917/staterev/ch03.htm#s5

33. Ibid. https://www.marxists.org/archive/lenin/works/1917/staterev/ch03.htm#s5

34. V. I. Lenin, 'The Immediate Tasks of the Soviet Government', *Pravda* and *Izvestiia* (28 Apr. 1918), https://www.marxists.org/archive/lenin/works/1918/mar/28.htm

35. Lenin, *State,* ch. 5. All three quotes come from the same page. Incidentally, this is one of the only references to soviets in the entire work, though Lenin implies he would have more to say in what remain the unwritten sections of the work.

36. Marx used the term 'armed people' in *The Civil War in France*, whence it was picked up by Engels and passed on to Lenin.

37. Current politics around the world suggests this might have been an overoptimistic assumption!

38. Lenin, *State,* ch. 6.

39. Lenin, *State,* ch. 4, part 2.

168 ENDNOTES

40. Lenin, *State*, ch. 5 for all quotes in this section unless otherwise stated.
41. Lenin, V. I. 'The April Theses'. https://www.marxists.org/archive/lenin/works/1917/apr/04.htm
42. From Chapter 3 of Lenin, V. I. *The State and Revolution* Zhizn' i znanie, Moscow (1918) https://www.marxists.org/archive/lenin/works/1917/staterev/ch03.htm#s5
43. There is a multitude of accounts of Lenin's campaign for an insurrection and the unfolding of the events in Petrograd on the fateful days from 24 to 29 October. The most complete is the magisterial Alexander Rabinowitch, *The Bolsheviks Come to Power: The Revolution of 1917 in Petrograd* (1976). Others include Christopher Read, *From Tsar to Soviets: The Russian People and Their Revolution 1917–21* (1996), 169–76, and Christopher Read, *War and Revolution in Russia 1914–22* (2013), ch. 5, 95–117.
44. The tiny group of Menshevik Internationalists largely shared Lenin's vision of a future socialist society but believed it had to be built on a democratic consensus. They detected dictatorial and authoritarian tendencies within Bolshevism and did not trust Lenin to share power. The journal *Untimely Thoughts*, edited and funded by Gorky, was their mouthpiece. For an excellent selection of extracts, see M. Gorky, *Untimely Thoughts: Essays on Revolution, Culture and the Bolsheviks 1917–1918*, ed. and tr. H. Ermolaev (rev. edn, 1995).
45. Lenin, V. I. 'To the Citizens of Russia' published in *Rabochii i soldat'* 25 October 1917. https://www.marxists.org/archive/lenin/works/1917/oct/25.htm
46. From the Postscript to: Lenin, V. I. *The State and Revolution* Zhizn' i znanie, Moscow (1918) https://www.marxists.org/archive/lenin/works/1917/staterev/postscpt.htm
47. V. I. Lenin, 'One of the Fundamental Questions of the Revolution', *Between the Two Revolutions* (Moscow: Progress Publishers, 1972), 379, https://www.marxists.org/archive/lenin/works/1917/sep/27.htm.
48. Trotsky, L. *A History of the Russian Revolution* ch.47 vol.3 Izdatel'stvo Granit, Berlin (1930) https://www.marxists.org/archive/trotsky/1930/hrr/ch47.htm (translation modified)
49. *The Bolsheviks and the October Revolution: Minutes of the Central Committee of the Russian Social-Democratic Labour Party (Bolsheviks), August 1917–February 1918*, tr. A. Bone (London, 1974), 136–40.
50. Lenin, 'Immediate Tasks'.
51. Lenin V. I. 'The Immediate Tasks of the Soviet Government' *Pravda* 83 and *Izvestiia* 85 28 April 1918 https://www.marxists.org/archive/lenin/works/1918/mar/x03.htm
52. Lenin, 'Immediate Tasks'.
53. Lenin, 'Immediate Tasks'.
54. Lenin, 'Immediate Tasks'.
55. For example, in September 1914 Lenin wrote that the German 'bourgeoisie will together with the Junkers, exert every effort to support the tsarist

monarchy against a revolution in Russia'. V. I. Lenin, 'The War and Russian Social-Democracy' (1914), https://www.marxists.org/archive/lenin/works/1914/sep/28.htm.

56. Lenin, 'Immediate Tasks'.

57. Lenin, 'Immediate Tasks'.

58. Lenin, 'Immediate Tasks'.

59. Lenin, 'Immediate Tasks'.

60. V. I. Lenin, ' "Left-Wing" Childishness' (Apr. 1918), *Collected Works* (4th English edn, 1972), xxvii, 323–34, https://www.marxists.org/archive/lenin/works/1918/may/09.htm.

61. A. Markevich and M. Harrison, 'Russia's Home Front: The Economy', in C. Read, P. Waldron, and A. Lindenmeyr, eds, *Russia's Home Front in War and Revolution: Book 3: National Disintegration*, Russia's Great War and Revolution series (2018), 23–44. An earlier version appeared as 'Great War, Civil War, and Recovery: Russia's National Income, 1913 to 1928', *Journal of Economic History*, 71/3 (2011), 672–703.

62. 'Ninth Party Congress, On the Question of the Trade Unions and Their Organization. Resolution. April 1, 1920', *Seventeen Moments in Soviet History*, https://soviethistory.msu.edu/1921-2/militarization-of-labor/militarization-of-labor-texts/the-party-and-the-trade-unions/.

63. Marx, K. 'The Class Struggles in France' Ch.2. https://www.marxists.org/archive/marx/works/1850/class-struggles-france/ch02.htm

64. V. I. Lenin, 'Economics and Politics in the Era of the Dictatorship of the Proletariat', *Pravda*, 250 (7 Nov. 1919), repr. in *Collected Works* (4th English edn, 1965), xxx, 107–17, also at http://marx2mao.com/Lenin/EPDP19.html.

65. Quoted in, among many examples, Riasanovsky, N. V. *A History of Russia* (sixth ed.). (Oxford: Oxford University Press 2000), p. 414.

66. I. Getzler, *Kronstadt*, showed that Trotsky's propagandistic assertion that these were not the heroes of 1917 but unsophisticated peasant replacements under the influence of White remnants was not true.

67. All quotations in this paragraph taken from |V. I. Lenin, 'Letter to the Congress' (22 Dec. 1922–5 Jan. 1923), https://www.marxists.org/archive/lenin/works/1922/dec/testamnt/congress.htm.

68. See, for example, the later chapters of Read, *Lenin,* for a fuller account.

69. V. I. Lenin, 'On Co-operation' (1923), https://www.marxists.org/archive/lenin/works/1923/jan/06.htm.

70. Lenin, 'On Co-operation'.

71. Lenin, 'On Co-operation'.

72. Lenin 'On Cooperation'.

73. V. I. Lenin, 'Our Revolution' (1923), https://www.marxists.org/archive/lenin/works/1923/jan/16.htm.

74. Lenin, 'On Co-operation'.

170 ENDNOTES

75. Lenin, V. I. 'Better Fewer, But Better' *Pravda* 49 4 March 1923 https://www.marxists.org/archive/lenin/works/1923/mar/02.htm.

76. Christopher Read, 'Values, Substitutes and Institutions: The Cultural Dimension of the Bolshevik Dictatorship', in V. Brovkin, ed., *The Bolsheviks in Russian Society: The Revolution and the Civil Wars* (1997), 298–318.

Part Two

1. At different times four different years from 1890 to 1895 have been quoted as his birth year.

2. J. V. Stalin, 'On the Death of Lenin. A Speech Delivered at the Second All-Union Congress of Soviets', *Pravda* (30 Jan. 1924).

3. Stalin, J 'Introduction' *Foundations of Leninism* Moscow 1924: https://www.marxists.org/reference/archive/stalin/works/1924/foundations-leninism/introduction.htm

4. Stalin, J 'Introduction' *Foundations of Leninism* Moscow 1924: https://www.marxists.org/reference/archive/stalin/works/1924/foundations-leninism/introduction.htm

5. J. V. Stalin, *The Foundations of Leninism* (1924) [Russ. orig., *Osnovyi Leninizma*], https://www.marxists.org/reference/archive/stalin/works/1924/foundations-leninism/introduction.htm.

6. Stalin, *Foundations*, ch. 1, https://www.marxists.org/reference/archive/stalin/works/1924/foundations-leninism/ch01.htm.

7. Ibid. Chapter 1: https://www.marxists.org/reference/archive/stalin/works/1924/foundations-leninism/ch01.htm

8. Ibid.

9. Ibid.

10. Stalin, *Foundations*, ch. 3, https://www.marxists.org/reference/archive/stalin/works/1924/foundations-leninism/ch03.htm.

11. In his recent exhaustive account of Stalin's life, Stephen Kotkin accuses Stalin of basing his account on work by a Soviet journalist named Filipp Ksenofontov. Stephen Kotkin, *Stalin: Paradoxes of Power, 1878–1928* (2015), ch. 12 passim. The jury is out on the issue, but it is not disputed that Stalin drafted the work.

12. Ibid. Chapter 4: https://www.marxists.org/reference/archive/stalin/works/1924/foundations-leninism/ch04.htm

13. Ibid. Chapter 5: https://www.marxists.org/reference/archive/stalin/works/1924/foundations-leninism/ch05.htm

14. Ibid. Chapter 6: https://www.marxists.org/reference/archive/stalin/works/1924/foundations-leninism/ch06.htm

15. Trotsky, L 'The Enforced Nature of this Work and its Aim'. *The Permanent Revolution* Chapter One: https://www.marxists.org/archive/trotsky/1931/tpr/pr01.htm

ENDNOTES 171

16. Stalin, J *Problems of Leninism* Moscow 1924: http://www.marx2mao.com/Stalin/FL24.html

17. For an insightful, comprehensive, accessible account of Soviet political ideology from the revolution to perestroika and collapse, see the excellent Mark Sandle, *A Short History of Soviet Socialism* (Routledge, 1998).

18. Karl Marx, 'General Rules of the International Working Men's Association', *The Bee-Hive Newspaper* (12 Nov. 1864), and *Address and Provisional Rules of the Working Men's International Association*...(London, Nov. 1864), https://www.marxists.org/history/international/iwma/documents/1864/rules.htm.

19. K. Marx, *Capital* (1867), i, ch. 32, https://www.marxists.org/archive/marx/works/1867-c1/ch32.htm.

20. Marx, *Capital*.

21. The minutes of the Second Party Congress are available at https://www.marxists.org/history/international/social-democracy/rsdlp/1903/index.htm.

22. Programme of the Russian Communist Party, Adopted at Eighth Party Congress 22 March 1919. https://www.marxists.org/history/ussr/government/1919/03/22.htm

23. Bukharin, N.I and Preobrazhensky, E.A. *ABC of Communism* Gosizdat: Petrograd 1920. https://www.marxists.org/archive/bukharin/works/1920/abc/intro.htm#004

24. Lenin, V. I. 'Terms of Admission into the Communist International' 1920: https://www.marxists.org/archive/lenin/works/1920/jul/x01.htm

25. 'Conditions of Admission into the Third Communist International July 1920' *The Second Congress of the Communist International, Verbatim Report* (Communist International: Petrograd 1921). https://www.marxists.org/archive/lenin/works/1920/jul/x01.htm. Only nineteen conditions drafted by Lenin are included here. There is a full list on Wikipedia, https://en.wikipedia.org/wiki/Twenty-one_Conditions, accessed February 2022.

26. Franz Borkenau, *World Communism: A History of the Communist International* (1962), 26.

27. Borkenau, World Communism, 42.

28. Borkenau, *World Communism*, 43.

29. Borkenau, *World Communism*, 44.

30. V. I. Lenin, 'Integrated Economic Plan', *Pravda*, 39 (22 Feb. 1921), repr. in Collected Works (Moscow: Progress Publishers, 1965), xxxii, 145, https://www.marxists.org/archive/lenin/works/cw/volume29.htm.

31. Ho Chi Minh, 'The Path Which Led Me to Leninism', in Bernard Fall, ed., *Ho Chi Minh on Revolution: Selected Writings 1920–66* (1967), 23 [Russ. orig. in *Voprosy vostoka (Problems of the East)* (Moscow, 1960)].

32. Ho Chi Minh, 'Annamese Women and French Domination', in Fall, *Ho Chi Minh*, 29–30 [orig. in *Le Paris* (1 Aug. 1922)].

33. Ho, 'The Path', 23–4.

172 ENDNOTES

34. Charles Fenn, *Ho Chi Minh: A Biographical Introduction* (1973), 39, quoting Paul Mus, *Vietnam: Sociologie d'une Guerre* (1952).

35. Fenn, *Ho Chi Minh*, 40; quoting Mus, Vietnam.

36. Fenn, *Ho Chi Minh*, 40; quoting *Histoire du Président Ho* (1949), 33.

37. Concessions were areas of Chinese territory in which the laws and administration of the concession-holding country took precedence over the Chinese equivalents. The main European imperialist powers, including France, Germany, and Britain, negotiated concessions in different Chinese cities and regions.

38. Fidel Castro, 'History will Absolve Me' [speech] (16 Oct. 1954), https://www.marxists.org/history/cuba/archive/castro/1953/10/16.htm.

39. Fidel Castro Speaks on Marxism-Leninism, 2 December 1961. (Full text): http://www.walterlippmann.com/fc-12-02-1961.html

40. Castro, Fidel, *My Life: A Spoken Autobiography* New York 2009, p. 157.

41. For a translation of the crux of Khieu's thesis with an unnamed editor's introduction, see Khieu Samphan, *Underdevelopment in Cambodia, Indochina Chronicle,* 51–2 (Sept.–Nov. 1976), https://archive.org/details/IndochinaChronicle51-52Sept.-Nov.1976/page/n1/mode/2up?view=theater.

42. Santiago Carrillo, speech at the 'Conferencia de Partidos Comunistas y Obreros de Europa', *Mundo Obrero* (June 1977).

43. For the text of the agreed but unsigned document from this meeting, see*For Peace, Security, Cooperation, and Social Progress in Europe. On the Results of the Conference of the Communist and Workers' Parties of Europe, Berlin, June 29–30, 1976* (1976). The quotation is from the Preface of the Document. A vivid account of the divisions and the weakening of traditional Marxism–Leninism within the communist movement itself, revealed especially in the conference speeches, can be found in James P. McGregor, 'The 1976 European Communist Parties Conference', *Studies in Comparative Communism*, 11/4 (Winter 1978), 339–60.

44. National Security Archive, '"Allende Wins"; Chile Marks 50th Anniversary of Salvador Allende's Election. Declassified Records Capture U.S. Reaction to First Free Election of a Socialist Leader. September 4, 1970, Historic Vote Prompted Nixon/Kissinger Regime Change Effort' (4 Sep. 2020), https://nsarchive.gwu.edu/briefing-book/chile/2020-09-04/allende-wins.

45. Mark Sandle, 'The Final Word: The Draft Party Programme of July/August 1991', *Europe-Asia Studies,* 48/7 (Nov. 1996), 1131–50.

46. Mark Sandle, 'The Final Word: The Draft Party Programme of July/August 1991', *Europe-Asia Studies* 48/7 (Nov. 1996), 1143–44.

47. David Caute, *The Fellow Travellers: A Postscript to the Enlightenment* (1973 and 1977) contains informative but hostile portraits of many of them.

48. Caute, *Fellow Travellers*, 3 and ch. 7, where the issue is discussed at length.

49. See the excellent essay by Pauline Kael, 'La Chinoise: A Minority Movie—Review by Pauline Kael', *New Yorker* (6 Apr. 1968), https://scrapsfromtheloft.com/movies/la-chinoise-review-pauline-kael/.

ENDNOTES 173

50. Guevara, Ernesto Che, 'Create Two, Three, Many Vietnams – That is the Watchword' *Tricontinental Magazine 2 Special Supplement* 16 April 1967, pp. 3–24. https://s3-eu-west-1.amazonaws.com/s3-euw1-ap-pe-ws4-cws-documents.ri-prod/9781138824287/ch10/4._Ernesto_Che_Guevara,_Create_Two,_Three,_Many_Vietnams,_1967.pdf

51. Gustavo Gutiérrez, *A Theology of Liberation: History, Politics, and Salvation* (1973).

52. See Gerd-Rainer Horn, *Western European Liberation Theology, the First Wave (1924–1959)* (2008); Gerd-Rainer Horn, *The Spirit of Vatican II: Western European Left Catholicism in the Long Sixties, 1959–1980* (2019); and Gerd-Rainer Horn, *The Moment of Liberation: Western Europe (1943–1948)* (2020).

53. Stephanie Kirchgaessner and Jonathan Watts, 'Pope Meets Fidel Castro in "Intimate and Familial" Encounter', *The Guardian* (20 Sep. 2015), https://www.theguardian.com/world/2015/sep/20/pope-francis-meets-with-fidel-castro-cuba-visit.

54. There is an account of this moment in Christopher Read, *Religion, Revolution and the Russian Intelligentsia: The* Vekhi *Debate and Its Intellectual Background* (1979), 77–94.

55. V. I. Lenin, letter to Maxim Gorky, sent from Cracow to Capri (13 or 14 Nov. 1913), published in *Pravda*, 51 (2 Mar. 1924), https://www.marxists.org/archive/lenin/works/1913/nov/00mg.htm.

56. Interview on RAI TV, April 1980. Transcribed in Louis Althusser, 'The Crisis of Marxism: An interview with Louis Althusser', *New Left Review* (11 July 2017), https://www.versobooks.com/blogs/3312-the-crisis-of-marxism-an-interview-with-louis-althusser.

57. There is an increasing body of work on the connections between Marxism and Christianity. Horn's work has already been referenced above. There is also the work of Charles Taylor, notably *A Secular Age* (1998); numerous studies by Roland Boer, such as *Red Theology: On the Christian Communist Tradition* (2019), and *Criticism of Heaven: The Author's Cut* (2012), https://rolandtheodoreboer.files.wordpress.com/2021/11/2012-criticism-of-heaven-authors-cut-cclm.pdf; and many others.

58. Emphases in original. For comment on this and on current historiography of the revolution, see Christopher Read, 'Ten Months That No Longer Shake the World', *Revolutionary Russia*, 34/1 (2021), 91–137.

59. Jonathan Jones, 'We Cannot Celebrate Russian Revolutionary Art – It Is Brutal Propaganda', *The Guardian* (1 Feb. 2017), https://www.theguardian.com/artanddesign/jonathanjonesblog/2017/feb/01/revolutionary-russian-art-brutal-propaganda-royal-academy.

60. Zhanna Vasil'eva, 'Нечто в багровых тонах Выставка "Некто 1917" открылась в Новой Третьяковке' [Something in Crimson Tones: 'Someone—1917' Opens at the New Tretiakov], *Rossiiskaia gazeta RG.ru* (2 Oct. 2017), https://rg.ru/2017/10/02/vystavka-nekto-1917-otkrylas-v-novoj-tretiakovke.

174 ENDNOTES

html. The item includes a few images of included items which give the flavour of the exhibition (photos by Sergei Kuksin). There is a superb exhibition catalogue: *Nekto 1917* (Moskva: Tret'iakovskaia galereia, 2017).

61. China Miéville, *October: The Story of the Russian Revolution* (2017). Tariq Ali, *The Dilemmas of Lenin: Terrorism, War, Empire, Love, Revolution* (2017).

62. Philip Cunliffe, *Lenin Lives!: Reimagining the Russian Revolution 1917–2017* (2017).

63. Istoriia velikoi oktiabr'skoi sotsialisticheskoi revolyutsii [A History of the Great October Socialist Revolution] (1967).

64. *Istoriia SSSR s Drevneishikh Vremen' Do nashikh Dnei*, 11 vols (1966–7).

65. There is a succinct, informative, and insightful account of Burdzhalov's life and views at Donald J. Raleigh, 'News of the Profession: Eduard Nikolaevich Burdzhalov (1906–1985)', *Slavic Review*, 45/3 (Autumn 1986), 599–604,https://www.jstor.org/stable/2499106. E. N. Burdzhalov, Вторая русская революция: Восстание в Петрограде (1967), Eng. trans. by Donald J. Raleigh, *Russia's Second Revolution: The February 1917 Uprising in Petrograd* (1987). Вторая русская революция: Москва. Фронт. Периферия (*Russia's Second Revolution. Moscow. The Front. The Periphery.*) (1971).

66. See numerous works by Alexander Rabinowitch, Stephen Smith, William Rosenberg, Sheila Fitzpatrick, and many others in the 1970s and 1980s and beyond in some cases.

67. Adam Ulam, *Lenin and the Bolsheviks* (1966); L. Schapiro and P. Reddaway, *Lenin: The Man, the Theorist and the Leader* (1967); N. Harding, *Lenin's Political Thought*, 2 vols (1983 and 1987); Robert Service, *Lenin: A Political Life*, 3 vols (1985, 1991, 1995); Robert Service, *Lenin: A Biography* (2001); Christopher Read, *Lenin: A Revolutionary Life* (2005); and James Ryan, *Lenin's Terror: The Ideological Origins of Early Soviet State Violence* (2012).

68. Dmitri Volkogonov, *Lenin: Life and Legacy* (1995). Strictly speaking, the first major biography in Russia was written by the dissident Marxist and Leninist Roy Medvedev, but his access to sources was much more limited than Volkogonov's. Nonetheless, it remains a great work and a monument on Soviet-era historiography.

69. Major items in English by Thomas Piketty include: *Capital in the Twenty-First Century* (2014); *Chronicles: On Our Troubled Times* (2016); *Capital and Ideology* (2020); and *Time for Socialism: Dispatches from a World on Fire, 2016–2021* (2021).

70. Lars T. Lih, *Lenin Rediscovered: 'What Is To Be Done?' In Context* (2005; repr. 2008).

71. Lih, Lars (2003). 'How a Founding Document was Founded, or One Hundred Years of Lenin's *What is to be Done?*', *Kritika*, 4(1): 49.

72. Quote from A. Ulam and S. Beer, eds, *Patterns of Government: The Major Political Systems of Europe* (2nd edn, 1962), 615.

ENDNOTES 175

73. Lih, *Lenin Rediscovered*, 4–5.
74. Lih, *Lenin Rediscovered*, epigraph, 7.
75. Harding, *Political Thought*, i.
76. Lih, Lars, *Lenin Rediscovered: 'What is To Be Done?' in Context* Leiden and Boston: Brill (2006) p. 5.
77. Tamás Krausz, *Reconstructing Lenin: An Intellectual Biography* (2015), 370.
78. Krausz, *Reconstructing Lenin*, 369.
79. Sebastian Budgen, Stathis Kouvelakis, and Slavoj Žižek, eds, *Lenin Reloaded: Toward a Politics of Truth* (2007).
80. Budgen, Kouvelakis, Žižek, *Lenin Reloaded*, 126. Lenin quote from V. I. Lenin, *Collected Works*, xxxviii, 114.
81. Budgen, Kouvelakis, Žižek, *Lenin Reloaded*, 195.
82. Budgen, Kouvelakis, Žižek, *Lenin Reloaded*, 12–13.
83. Budgen, Kouvelakis, Žižek, *Lenin Reloaded*, 18–23.
84. Budgen, Kouvelakis, Žižek, *Lenin Reloaded*, 36–8.
85. Budgen, Kouvelakis, Žižek, *Lenin Reloaded*, 68.
86. Budgen, Kouvelakis, Žižek, *Lenin Reloaded*, 58.
87. Budgen, Kouvelakis, Žižek, *Lenin Reloaded*, 240–1.
88. Budgen, Kouvelakis, Žižek, *Lenin Reloaded*, 231.
89. Budgen, Kouvelakis, Žižek, *Lenin Reloaded*, 235.
90. Budgen, Kouvelakis, Žižek, *Lenin Reloaded*, 300.
91. Budgen, Kouvelakis, Žižek, *Lenin Reloaded*, 298.
92. Budgen, Kouvelakis, Žižek, *Lenin Reloaded*, 303.
93. Budgen, Kouvelakis, Žižek, *Lenin Reloaded*, 283–6.
94. Budgen, Kouvelakis, Žižek, *Lenin Reloaded*, Introduction, 3.
95. Budgen, Kouvelakis, Žižek, *Lenin Reloaded*, Introduction, 2–3. Emphasis in original.
96. Budgen, Kouvelakis, Žižek, *Lenin Reloaded*, 58, Eagleton, 58.
97. e.g. Budgen, Kouvelakis, Žižek, *Lenin Reloaded*, Introduction, 3.
98. Budgen, Kouvelakis, Žižek, *Lenin Reloaded*, 120–1.
99. Budgen, Kouvelakis, Žižek, *Lenin Reloaded*, 112.
100. See Read, 'Ten Months'.
101. Read, 'Ten Months', 103, and Gennadii Bordiugov, ed., *Revoliutsiia-100: Rekonstruktsiia iubileia* (2017), 769–70.
102. Read, 'Ten Months', 102, and Bordiugov, *Revoliutsiia-100*, 796.
103. Miéville, *October*; Ali, *Dilemmas of Lenin*, quotation from Introduction, 1.
104. There are many examples in Read, 'Ten Months'.
105. Bordiugov, *Revoliutsiia-100*, 640.
106. https://www.telesurtv.net/english/news/Latin-America-Celebrates-the-Russian-Revolution-20171107-0021.html

176 ENDNOTES

Conclusion

1. Personal message from Fred Reid, Honorary Professor, University of Warwick.
2. Personal message from my former colleague and dear friend Dr Robin Clifton, who sadly died on 4 December 2022.
3. Personal message from Emeritus Professor Robin Okey, University of Warwick.
4. Personal message from Emeritus Professor James Hinton, University of Warwick.
5. Personal message from Professor Dan Orlovsky, Southern Methodist University, Dallas.
6. Personal message from a source who preferred to remain unnamed.
7. Personal message from Professor Lee Jones, Queen Mary University London.
8. Personal message from Emeritus Professor Robert Service.
9. Eric Blanc, *Revolutionary Social Democracy: Working-Class Politics Across the Russian Empire (1882–1917)* (2021).
10. Eric Blanc, 'Can Leninists Explain the Russian Revolution?', *Historical Materialism* (7 Jan. 2022), https://www.historicalmaterialism.org/blog/can-leninists-explain-rr.
11. Blanc, *Revolutionary Social Democracy*, 407.
12. For a powerful and well-informed critique, see Michael Ellman, 'Boris Mironov's New Interpretation of the Russian Revolution', a review of Boris Mironov, *Rossiiskaia modernizatsiia i revoliutsiia* (2019), in *Revolutionary Russia*, 35/1 (May 2022). On Buldakov and others, see Christopher Read, 'Ten Months That No Longer Shake the World', *Revolutionary Russia*, 34/1 (2021), 114–17.
13. In the words of the official USAspending.gov profile of the Department of Defense—'How much funding is available to this agency? $1.64 Trillion in budgetary resources: 14.3% of the FY 2022 U.S. federal budget'. See https://www.usaspending.gov/agency/department-of-defense?fy=2022. If it were itself a country it would be fourteenth in the world, just ahead of Spain and Mexico, see https://ceoworld.biz/2022/03/31/economy-rankings-largest-countries-by-gdp-2022/.
14. Hjalmar Jorge Joffre-Eichhorn, Patrick Anderson, and Johann Salazar, eds, *Lenin 150 (Samizdat)* (Aug. 2020; rev. 2nd edn, 2021), ii–iii.
15. Joffre-Eichhorn, Anderson, and Salazar, *Lenin 150*, 259.
16. Sebastian Budgen, Stathis Kouvelakis, and Slavoj Žižek, eds, *Lenin Reloaded: Toward a Politics of Truth* (2007), 270.

Bibliography

Note that Lenin's complete works and the writings of many radicals, socialists, and communists are freely available on the very extensive Marxists Internet Archive (marxists.org).

Ali, Tariq, *The Dilemmas of Lenin: Terrorism, War, Empire, Love, Revolution* (London: Verso, 2017).

Althusser, Louis, 'The Crisis of Marxism: An Interview with Louis Althusser', *New Left Review* (11 July 2017), https://www.versobooks.com/blogs/3312 -the-crisis-of-marxism-an-interview-with-louis-althusser.

Balabanoff, Angelica, *Impressions of Lenin* (Ann Arbor: University of Michigan Press, 1970).

Baron, Samuel, *Plekhanov: The Founder of Russian Marxism* (London: Routledge and Kegan Paul, 1963).

Besançon, Alain, *Les Origines Intellectuelles du Léninisme* (Paris: Calmann-Levy, 1977).

Blanc, Eric, *Revolutionary Social Democracy: Working-Class Politics Across the Russian Empire (1882–1917)* (Leiden: Brill, 2021).

Blanc, Eric, 'Can Leninists Explain the Russian Revolution?', *Historical Materialism* (7 Jan. 2022), https://www.historicalmaterialism.org/blog/can-leninists-explain-rr.

Boer, Roland, *Critique of Heaven: On Marxism and Theology* (Chicago: Haymarket Books, 2009).

Boer, Roland, *Criticism of Heaven and Earth*, 5 vols (Chicago: Haymarket Books, 2009–20). [Series includes the two volumes below.]

Boer, Roland, *Criticism of Heaven: The Author's Cut* (Leiden: Brill, 2012). https://rolandtheodoreboer.files.wordpress.com/2021/11/2012-criticism-of-heaven-authors-cut-cclm.pdf.

Boer, Roland, *Red Theology: On the Christian Communist Tradition* (Leiden: Brill, 2019).

Bordiugov, Gennadii, ed., *Revoliutsiia-100: Rekonstruktsiia iubileia* (Moscow: AIRO-XXI, 2017).

Borkenau, Franz, *World Communism: A History of the Communist International* (London: Faber and Faber, 1938; repr. Ann Arbor: University of Michigan Press, 1962).

178 BIBLIOGRAPHY

Braunthal, Julius, *History of the International: 1914–1943*, ii (London: Thompson Nelson and Sons, 1967).

Brown, Archie, *The Rise and Fall of Communism* (London: Bodley Head, 2009).

Budgen, Sebastian, Kouvelakis, Stathis, and Žižek, Slavoj, eds, *Lenin Reloaded: Toward a Politics of Truth* (Durham, NC: Duke University Press, 2007).

Burdzhalov, E. N., Вторая русская революция: Восстание в Петрограде (Nauka: Moscow 1967), Eng. trans. by Donald J. Raleigh, *Russia's Second Revolution: The February 1917 Uprising in Petrograd* (Bloomington: Indiana University Press, 1987).

Burdzhalov, E.N. Вторая русская революция: Москва. Фронт. Периферия (Russia's Second Revolution. Moscow. The Front. The Periphery.) (Nauka: Moscow 1971).

Carrillo, Santiago, speech at the Conferencia de Partidos Comunistas y Obreros de Europa, *Mundo Obrero* (June 1977).

Castro, Fidel, 'History will Absolve Me' [speech] (16 Oct. 1954), https://www.marxists.org/history/cuba/archive/castro/1953/10/16.htm.

Caute, David, *The Left in Europe since 1789* (London: Weidenfeld and Nicolson, 1966).

Caute, David, *The Fellow Travellers: A Postscript to the Enlightenment* (London: Weidenfeld and Nicolson, 1973, and London: Quartet Books, 1977).

Claudin, Fernando, *The Communist Movement from Comintern to Cominform* (Harmondsworth: Penguin, 1975).

Claudin-Urondo, Carmen, *Lenin and Cultural Revolution* (Hassocks: Harvester Press and Atlantic Highlands, NJ: Humanities Press, 1977).

Crossman, Richard, ed., *The God that Failed* (New York: Harper, 1949).

Cunliffe, Philip, *Lenin Lives!: Reimagining the Russian Revolution 1917–2017* (London: Zero Books, 2017).

'Department of Defense: Agency Profile', *USASpending.gov*, https://www.usaspending.gov/agency/department-of-defense?fy=2022.

Desai, Meghnad, ed., *Lenin's Economic Writings* (London: Lawrence and Wishart, 1989).

Dimitropoulou, Alexandra, 'Economy Rankings: Largest Country by GDP, 2022', CEOWorld Magazine (31 Mar. 2022), https://ceoworld.biz/2022/03/31/economy-rankings-largest-countries-by-gdp-2022.

Ellman, Michael, 'Boris Mironov's New Interpretation of the Russian Revolution', review of Boris Mironov, *Rossiiskaia modernizatsiia i revoliutsiia* (St. Petersburg: Dmitrii Bulanin, 2019), in *Revolutionary Russia*, 35/1 (May 2022).

BIBLIOGRAPHY   179

Fall, Bernard, ed., *Ho Chi Minh on Revolution: Selected Writings 1920–66* (New York: Frederick A. Praeger, 1967).

Fenn, Charles, *Ho Chi Minh: A Biographical Introduction* (London: Studio Vista, 1973).

For Peace, Security, Cooperation, and Social Progress in Europe. On the Results of the Conference of the Communist and Workers' Parties of Europe, Berlin, June 29–30, 1976 (Moscow: Novosti Press, 1976).

Getzler, I., *Kronstadt* (Cambridge: Cambridge UP, 1983).

Gide, André, *Retour de l'URSS* (Paris: Gallimard, 1936).

Golwitzer, Helmut, *The Christian Faith and the Marxist Criticism of Religion* (New York: Charles Scribner's Sons, 1970).

Gorky, Maxim, *Nicolai Lenin the Man* (London: Daily Herald Press, 1924) [online facsimile], https://www.marxists.org/archive/gorky-maxim/1924/lenin-the_man.html.

Gorky, M., *Untimely Thoughts: Essays on Revolution, Culture and the Bolsheviks 1917–1918*, ed. and trans. H. Ermolaev (rev. edn, New Haven and London: Yale University Press, 1995).

Gramsci, Antonio, *Prison Letters, New Edinburgh Review*, 2 vols (Edinburgh University Student Publications/Arts Council, Edinburgh: Edinburgh, 1974).

Gramsci, Antonio, *Selections from the Prison Notebooks of Antonio Gramsci* (New York: International Publishers, 1992).

Gutiérrez, Gustavo, *A Theology of Liberation: History, Politics, and Salvation* (Maryknoll: Orbis, 1973).

Harding, N., *Lenin's Political Thought*, 2 vols (London: Macmillan, 1983 and 1987).

Histoire du Président Ho (Hanoi: Foreign Languages Press, 1949).

Ho Chi Minh, 'Annamese Women and French Domination', in Bernard Fall, ed., *Ho Chi Minh on Revolution: Selected Writings 1920–66* (New York: Frederick A. Praeger, 1967, 29–30) [Fr. orig. in *Le Paris* (1 Aug. 1922)].

Ho Chi Minh, 'The Path Which Led Me to Leninism', in Bernard Fall, ed., *Ho Chi Minh on Revolution: Selected Writings 1920–66* (New York: Frederick A. Praeger, 1967, 23–25) [Russ. orig. in *Voprosy vostoka* [*Problems of the East*] (Moscow, 1960)].

Horn, Gerd-Rainer, *Western European Liberation Theology, the First Wave (1924–1959)* (Oxford: Oxford University Press, 2008).

Horn, Gerd-Rainer, *The Spirit of Vatican II: Western European Left Catholicism in the Long Sixties, 1959–1980* (Oxford: Oxford University Press, 2019).

180 BIBLIOGRAPHY

Horn, Gerd-Rainer, *The Moment of Liberation: Western Europe (1943–1948)* (Oxford: Oxford University Press, 2020).

Istoriia SSSR s Drevneishikh Vremen' Do nashikh Dnei, [A History of the USSR from the Earliest Timers to the Present] 11 vols (Moskva: Akademiia nauk SSSR, Institut istorii, 1966–7).

Istoriia velikoi oktiabr'skoi sotsialisticheskoi revolyutsii [A History of the Great October Socialist Revolution] P. N. Sobolev, Y. G. Gimpelson, G. A. Trukan, Eds (Moskva: Izdatel'stvo 'Nauka', 1967).

Joffre-Eichhorn, Hjalmar Jorge; Anderson, Patrick; and Salazar, Johann, eds, *Lenin 150 (Samizdat)* (Hamburg: Kick-Ass Books, Aug. 2020; rev. 2nd edn, Quebec: Daraja Press, 2021).

Joll, James, *Gramsci* (Glasgow: Fontana/Collins, 1977).

Jones, Jonathan, 'We Cannot Celebrate Russian Revolutionary Art—It is Brutal Propaganda', *The Guardian* (1 Feb. 2017), https://www.theguardian.com/artanddesign/jonathanjonesblog/2017/feb/01/revolutionary-russian-art-brutal-propaganda-royal-academy.

Kael, Pauline, 'La Chinoise: A Minority Movie—Review by Pauline Kael', *New Yorker* (6 Apr. 1968), https://scrapsfromtheloft.com/movies/la-chinoise-review-pauline-kael/.

Khieu Samphan, *Underdevelopment in Cambodia, Indochina Chronicle*, 51–2 (Sep.–Nov. 1976), https://archive.org/details/IndochinaChronicle51-52Sept.-Nov.1976/page/n1/mode/2up?view=theater.

Kirchgaessner, Stephanie and Watts, Jonathan, 'Pope Meets Fidel Castro in "Intimate and Familial" Encounter', *The Guardian* (20 Sep. 2015), https://www.theguardian.com/world/2015/sep/20/pope-francis-meets-with-fidel-castro-cuba-visit.

Kollontai, Alexandra, *The Workers' Opposition* [online facsimile], https://www.marxists.org/archive/kollonta/1921/workers-opposition/ch03.htm.

Kotkin, Stephen, *Stalin: Paradoxes of Power, 1878–1928* (Harmondsworth and New York: Penguin, 2015).

Krausz, Tamás, *Reconstructing Lenin: An Intellectual Biography* (New York: Monthly Review Press, 2015).

Krupskaya, Nadezhda, *Reminiscences of Lenin* (International Publishers: New York, 1967), https://www.marxists.org/archive/krupskaya/works/rol/rol07.htm.

Krupskaya, Nadezhda, *Memories of Lenin* (London: Panther/Lawrence and Wishart, 1970).

Lefebvre, Henri, *La Pensée de Lénine* (Paris: Bordas, 1957).

Lenin, V. I., *Collected Works* (English edition) 45 vols. Progress Publishers: Moscow, 1960–1970.

BIBLIOGRAPHY 181

Lenin, V. I., letter to Maxim Gorky, sent from Cracow to Capri (13 or 14 Nov. 1913), published in *Pravda*, 51 (2 Mar. 1924), https://www.marxists.org/archive/lenin/works/1913/nov/00mg.htm.

Lenin, V. I., 'The War and Russian Social Democracy' (1914), https://www.marxists.org/archive/lenin/works/1914/sep/28.htm.

Lenin, V. I., *The State and Revolution* https://www.marxists.org/archive/lenin/works/1917/staterev/

Lenin, V. I., '"Left-Wing" Childishness' (Apr. 1918), *Collected Works* (4th Eng. edn, Moscow: Progress Publishers, 1972), xxvii, 323–34, https://www.marxists.org/archive/lenin/works/1918/may/09.htm.

Lenin, V. I., 'The Immediate Tasks of the Soviet Government', *Pravda* and *Izvestiia* (28 Apr. 1918), 83–85. https://www.marxists.org/archive/lenin/works/1918/mar/28.htm.

Lenin, V. I., 'Economics and Politics in the Era of the Dictatorship of the Proletariat', *Pravda*, 250 (7 Nov. 1919), repr. in *Collected Works* (4th Eng. edn, Moscow: Progress Publishers, 1965), xxx, 107–17, http://marx2mao.com/Lenin/EPDP19.html.

Lenin, V. I., *Imperialism, The Highest Stage of Capitalism. A Popular Outline* Petrograd (1917). https://www.marxists.org/archive/lenin/works/1916/imp-hsc/index.htm

Lenin, V. I., 'Integrated Economic Plan', *Pravda*, 39 (22 Feb. 1921), repr. in *Collected Works* (Moscow: Progress Publishers, 1965), xxxii, https://www.marxists.org/archive/lenin/works/cw/volume32.htm.

Lenin, V. I., 'Letter to the Congress' (22 Dec. 1922–5 Jan. 1923), https://www.marxists.org/archive/lenin/works/1922/dec/testamnt/congress.htm.

Lenin, V. I., 'On Co-operation' (1923), *Pravda* 115–116, 26–27 May. https://www.marxists.org/archive/lenin/works/1923/jan/06.htm.

Lenin, V. I., 'Our Revolution', (1923). *Pravda* 117, 30 May. https://www.marxists.org/archive/lenin/works/1923/jan/16.htm.

Lenin, V. I., *Philosophical Notebooks,* repr. in *Collected Works* (4th Eng. edn, London: Lawrence and Wishart and Moscow: Foreign languages Publishing House, 1963), xxxviii.

Lenin, V. I., *On Literature and Art* (Moscow: Progress Publishers, 1967).

Lenin, V. I., *Selected Works*, 3 vols (Moscow: Progress Publishers, 1968).

Lenin, V. I., 'One of the Fundamental Questions of the Revolution', *Between the Two Revolutions* (Moscow: Progress Publishers, 1972), https://www.marxists.org/archive/lenin/works/1917/sep/27.htm.

Lih, Lars T., *Lenin Rediscovered: 'What Is To Be Done?' In Context* (Leiden: Brill, 2005; repr. Chicago: Haymarket Books, 2008).

182 BIBLIOGRAPHY

Lih, Lars, *Lenin* (London: Reaktion Books, 2011).

Lukacs, György, *History and Class Consciousness: Studies in Marxist Dialectics* (Cambridge, MA: MIT Press, 1971).

Lyandres, Semion, 'The Bolsheviks' "German Gold" Revisited: An Inquiry into the 1917 Accusations', *Carl Beck Papers in Russian and East European Studies*, 1106 (Feb. 1995).

Mao Tse Tung, *Selected Works*, 4 vols (Peking: Foreign Languages Press, 1961–5).

Markevich, A. and Harrison, M., 'Russia's Home Front: The Economy' in C. Read, P. Waldron, and A. Lindenmeyr, eds, *Russia's Home Front in War and Revolution: Book 3: National Disintegration*, Russia's Great War and Revolution series (Bloomington, Indiana: Slavica, 2018), 23–44.

Marx, Karl, 'General Rules of The International Workingmen's Association', *The Bee-Hive Newspaper* (12 Nov. 1864), and *Address and Provisional Rules of the Working Men's International Association...*(London, Nov. 1864), https://www.marxists.org/history/international/iwma/documents/1864/rules.htm.

Marx, Karl, *Capital* (1867) (Swan Sonnenschein, Lowrey, & Co.: London 1887). https://www.marxists.org/archive/marx/works/1867-c1/index.htm.

Marx, Karl and Engels, Friedrich, *The Communist Manifesto* (Workers' Educational Association: London 1848) https://www.marxists.org/archive/marx/works/1848/communist-manifesto/

McGregor, James P., 'The 1976 European Communist Parties Conference', *Studies in Comparative Communism*, 11/4 (Winter 1978), 339–60.

Miéville, China, *October: The Story of the Russian Revolution* (London and New York: Verso, 2017).

Mus, Paul, *Vietnam: Sociologie d'une Guerre* (Paris: Editions du Seuil, 1952).

Nechaev, Sergei, *Catechism of a Revolutionary* (Chernetsky: Geneva, 1869), https://www.marxists.org/subject/anarchism/nechayev/catechism.htm.

National Security Archive, ' "Allende Wins"; Chile Marks 50th Anniversary of Salvador Allende's Election. Declassified Records Capture U.S. Reaction to First Free Election of a Socialist Leader. September 4, 1970, Historic Vote Prompted Nixon/Kissinger Regime Change Effort' (Washington DC: National Security Archive, 4 Sept. 2020), https://nsarchive.gwu.edu/briefing-book/chile/2020-09-04/allende-wins.

Nekto 1917 [exhibition catalogue] (Moskva: Tret'iakovskaia galereia, 2017).

'Ninth Party Congress, On the Question of the Trade Unions and their Organization. Resolution. April 1, 1920', *Seventeen Moments in Soviet History*, https://soviethistory.msu.edu/1921-2/militarization-of-labor/militarization-of-labor-texts/the-party-and-the-trade-unions/.

BIBLIOGRAPHY   183

Orwell, George, *Animal Farm: A Fairy Story* (London: Secker and Warburg, 1945).

Orwell, George, *1984* (London: Secker and Warburg, 1949).

Piketty, Thomas, *Capital in the Twenty-First Century* (Cambridge, MA: Belknap Press, 2014).

Piketty, Thomas, *Chronicles: On Our Troubled Times* (London and New York: Viking, 2016).

Piketty, Thomas, *Capital and Ideology* (Cambridge, MA: Harvard University Press, 2020).

Piketty, Thomas, *Time for Socialism: Dispatches from a World on Fire, 2016-2021* (New Haven and London: Yale University Press, 2021).

Programme of the Russian Communist Party (1919). https://www.marxists.org/history/ussr/government/1919/03/22.htm

Rabinowitch, Alexander, *The Bolsheviks Come to Power: The Revolution of 1917 in Petrograd* (New York: W. W. Norton and Company, 1976).

Raleigh, Donald J., 'News of the Profession: Eduard Nikolaevich Burdzhalov (1906–1985)', *Slavic Review,* 45/3 (Autumn 1986), 599–604, https://www.jstor.org/stable/2499106.

Read, Christopher, *Religion, Revolution and the Russian Intelligentsia: The* Vekhi *Debate and Its Intellectual Background* (London: Macmillan, and New York: St Martin's Press, 1979).

Read, Christopher, *Culture and Power in the Russian Revolution; The Intelligentsia and the Transition from Tsarism to Communism* (London: Macmillan, and New York: St Martin's Press, 1991).

Read, Christopher *From Tsar to Soviets: The Russian People and Their Revolution 1917–21* (London and New York: UCL and Oxford University Press, 1996).

Read, Christopher, 'Values, Substitutes and Institutions: The Cultural Dimension of the Bolshevik Dictatorship' in V. Brovkin, ed., *The Bolsheviks in Russian Society: The Revolution and The Civil Wars* (New Haven and London: Yale University Press, 1997), 298–318.

Read, Christopher, *Lenin: A Revolutionary Life* (London and New York: Routledge, 2005).

Read, Christopher, *War and Revolution in Russia 1914–22* (Basingstoke and New York: Palgrave, 2014).

Read, Christopher, 'George Plekhanov, *Socialism and Political Struggle* (1883)', in Rachel Hammersley, ed., *Revolutionary Moments: Reading Revolutionary Texts* (London: Bloomsbury, 2015), 125–32.

Read, Christopher, 'Ten Months that No Longer Shake the World', *Revolutionary Russia,* 34/1 (2021), 91–137.

184 BIBLIOGRAPHY

Russell, Bertrand, *The Practice and Theory of Communism* (London: George, Allen and Unwin, 1920).

Ryan, James, *Lenin's Terror: The Ideological Origins of Early Soviet State Violence* (London: Routledge, 2012).

Sandle, Mark, 'The Final Word: The Draft Party Programme of July/August 1991', *Europe-Asia Studies*, 48/7 (Nov. 1996), 1131–50.

Sandle, Mark, *A Short History of Soviet Socialism* (London and New York: Routledge, 1998).

Schapiro, L. and Reddaway, P., *Lenin: The Man, the Theorist and the Leader* (London: Pall Mall, 1967).

Serge, Victor, *The Case of Comrade Tulyaev*, trans. Willard R. Trask (New York: New York Review of Books Classics, 1967).

Serge, Victor, *Naissance de Notre Force* (Paris, Rieder, 1931); trans. Richard Greeman as *Birth of our Power* (New York: Doubleday, 1967).

Service, Robert, *Lenin: A Political Life*, 3 vols (London: Palgrave Macmillan, 1985, 1991, 1995).

Service, Robert, *Lenin: A Biography* (London and New York: Macmillan, 2000).

Service, Robert, *Lenin: A Biography* (London: Macmillan, 2001).

Service, Robert, *Comrades. Communism: A World History* (London: Macmillan, 2007).

Sinelschikova, Yekaterina, 'Why Did Vladimir Lenin Adopt the Name "Lenin"?', *Russia Beyond* (9 October 2020), https://www.rbth.com/history/332831-vladimir-lenin-nickname.

Stalin, J. V., 'On the Death of Lenin. A Speech Delivered at the Second All-Union Congress of Soviets', *Pravda* 23 (30 Jan. 1924).

Stalin, J. V., *The Foundations of Leninism* (1924) [Russ. orig., *Osnovyi Leninizma*], https://www.marxists.org/reference/archive/stalin/works/1924/foundations-leninism/introduction.htm.

Taylor, Charles, *A Secular Age* (Cambridge, MA: Belnap Press, 1998).

The Bolsheviks and the October Revolution: Minutes of the Central Committee of the Russian Social-Democratic Labour Party (Bolsheviks), August 1917–February 1918, trans. A. Bone (London: Pluto Press, 1974).

Tombs, Robert, *The Paris Commune 1871* (London: Routledge, 1999).

Tumarkin, Nina, *Lenin Lives! The Lenin Cult in Soviet Russia* (Cambridge, MA and London: Harvard University Press, 1989).

Ulam, Adam, *Lenin and the Bolsheviks* (New York: Vintage, 1966).

Ulam, A. and Beer, S., eds, *Patterns of Government: The Major Political Systems of Europe* (2nd edn, New York: Random House, 1962).

Vasil'eva, Zhanna, 'Нечто в багровых тонах Выставка "Некто 1917" открылась в Новой Третьяковке' [Something in Crimson Tones: 'Someone—1917' Opens at the New Tretiakov], *Rossiiskaia gazeta RG.ru* (2 Oct. 2017), https://rg.ru/2017/10/02/vystavka-nekto-1917-otkrylas-v-novoj-tretiakovke.html.

Volkogonov, Dmitri, *Lenin: Life and Legacy* (London and New York: Harper Collins, 1995).

Weber, Gerda and Weber, Hermann, *Lenin: Life and Works* (London and Basingstoke: Macmillan, 1980).

Williams, Gwyn, 'Proletarian Forms: Antonio Gramsci, the Turin Movement and the origins of Italian Communism' in Antonio Gramsci, *Prison Letters, New Edinburgh Review*, 2 vols (Edinburgh University Student Publications/ Arts Council, Edinburgh: Edinburgh, 1974).

Wolfe, Bertram, *Strange Communists I Have Known* (London: George, Allen and Unwin, 1966).

Index

For the benefit of digital users, indexed terms that span two pages (e.g., 52–53) may, on occasion, appear on only one of those pages.

Africa, Southern, revolutions 127–28
African Marxist revolutionaries 126–7
Albania 116–18
Althusser, Louis 110–11, 133–4
Angola 118
Armand, Inessa 28–9
armed requisitioning 70–2
  peasants resist 71–2

Baku Congress (Congress of Peoples of
  the East) 94, 103
Bakunin, M.A. 6–7, 25–7, 32, 42–3, 47, 57–8,
  148, 159
Bakuninism *see* Bakunin
Beethoven, Ludwig van 29
Benjamin, Walter 121–2
Bernstein, Eduard 18–19, 35–6
Blanc, Eric 158
  Revolutionary Social Democracy:
    Working-Class Politics Across the
    Russian Empire 158–9
Bogdanov A.A. 5–6, 25–7, 121
  inspires Gramsci 127
Bolsheviks *see* Communist Party
Borkenau, Franz, on professional
  revolutionaries and party 92–3
Brezhnev, Leonid 110–11, 116–18
Bukharin, N. 5–6, 77, 79
Bund 22–3
Burdzhalov, E.N. 137–8

Cambodian Revolution 114–16
Carillo, Santiago 118
Castro, Fidel 112–13, 126–7
  'History Will Absolve Me' 112–13
Catholic radicals 129–30
Chen Duxiu 107–8
Chernyshevsky, Nikolai 12–13
  What is to be Done? Tales of the New
    People 12–13, 28

China 120
  Tienanmen demonstration (1989) 120
Chinese revolution 107–9
  fellow travellers 125–6
climate summits 7–8
Cold War, begins 116–18
Comintern (Third Communist
  International) 94
  antifascism 95–7
  Conditions for Admission 91–2
  diversity of membership 97–8, 101
  failure in China (1927) 101
  First Congress 94–7
  formation of Communist Parties around
    the globe 97
  link to internal Soviet policy
    changes 101–3
  Second Congress 97–8
  splits opposition to Nazism 101–2
Communist Party (Chinese) 78–9, 101
  Chinese revolution 107–9
  massacre of members in
    Shanghai 101, 107–8
Communist Party (Russian and Soviet)
  and Mensheviks 24–5
  as better Mensheviks 54
  Central Committee 51–3
  Congresses of 3; Second Party
    Congress 21–3; Tenth Party
    Congress 3, 72
  Defining Bolshevism 56–7
  funding of (1905–14) 29–30
  influence in 2020s 134–5
  leading role/vanguardism 4
  outlawed in Russia (1991) 120
  party programme 1919 87
Conference of Communist and Workers'
  Parties of Europe 118
Confucianism 15, 44–5, 72–3, 105,
  125–6, 151–2

188 INDEX

Congress of Soviets, First All-Russian 41–2;
    Second All-Russian 56–7
Cuba 118
Cuban Revolution 112–14

Destalinization 116–18, 124

Economists (Political group) 23–4
Engels, Friedrich, *Condition of the Working
    Class in England* 16–17
Eurocommunism 118–20
    Italy 119–20
    Portugal 118
    Spain 118
    evolutionary socialism 18–19

fascism, as reaction to communism 98–9
Fellow travellers 122–4
Frankfurt School (Institute for Social
    Research) 121–2
Freire, Paulo 130–1
Fundamentalisms 120

Germany, East 110–11
Gorbachev, Mikhail 120
    Sinatra doctrine 120
Gorky, Maxim 20–1, 25–30, 54–5, 67–8,
    131–3, 156–7
    peasants 67–8
Gramsci, Antonio 4–5, 127, 154
Guevara, Ernesto 'Che' 113–14
    Motorcycle Diaries 113–14, 126–7
    visits Africa 127–8
Guterriez, Gustavo *The Theology of
    Liberation* 129–30

Hilferding, Rudolf 35, 43, 48
Ho Chi Minh 78, 98, 103–6
Hobson, J.A. 35
Hungary 110–11, 118, 124

imperialism 5–6, 103–16
intellectuals 78–9, 121, 125–6, 137
    antifascist 122–4
    British 123–4
    revisionist Russian Marxists
        126–7
    role of in party 121
iron curtain 116–18
Iskra (The Spark) 20–1

Italy 119–20
    assassination of Aldo Moro 119–20, 127
    historic compromise 119–20, 127

July Days 41–2, 50

Kahlo, Frida 78–9
Kamenev, Lev. 59–60
Kamphuchea: *see* Cambodian Revolution
Kautsky, Karl 35–6
Kerala 78–9, 149–50
Kerensky, Alexander Fyodorovich 50–1
    Kornilov affair 50–1
Khieu Sampan 114–15
Khmer Rouge 114–16
Khrushchev, Nikita 110–11
    destalinization 110–11, 116, 124
Kombedy (committees of poor peasants) 70–1
Korea, North 116–18
Kornilov affair *see* Kornilov
Kornilov, Lavrenty 50–1
Krausz, Tamás 143–4
    *Reconstructing Lenin: An Intellectual
        Biography* 143–4
Kronstadt rebellion (1921) 73
    demands return to principles of 1917 73
Krupskaya, Nadezhda 15
    accompanies Lenin to western
        Europe 18, 77
    in Siberia with Lenin 17–18
Kuomintang (Guomindang) 107–8

Lenin, V.I.
    adoption of NEP 72
    adopts pseudonym 'N. Lenin' 18–19
    'April Theses' 24–5, 39–50, 69–70, 72–3
    arrest (1897) 17–18
    arrives in Petrograd 1917 38–9
    attempts to limit
        bureaucratisation 72–3, 76–7
    bicycle accident (Paris) 13–14
        (Geneva) 16
    bureaucratism of 154
    childhood and family 10–14
    commemorations of centenary of his
        birth 136–7, 148–50
    conflicting models of Leninism 86–7
    contemporary Russian historiography
        of 158–9
    criticized by President Putin 134–5

declining academic interest in since
1991 136, 139
decrees on Peace and Land 55–6, 70
execution of his brother 11–12
exile in Siberia (1897–1899) 17–18
expectations for revolution in early
1917 37–8
food requisitioning squads 70–1
friendship, enmity, reconciliation 28–9
from Zürich to the Finland Station 36–7
heads first Soviet government 59–60
'Immediate Tasks of the Soviet
Government' 60–7, 160–1
contains elements of 'socialism in one
country' 160–1
*Imperialism: the Highest Stage of
Capitalism* 5–6
writes 35–6
not intended to be global model 160–1
in Krakow 30–2
Inessa Armand and 28–9
influence of in Russia today 134–5, 156
internationalism 108–9
journalism 20–1
July Days 42
Kienthal and Zimmerwald Peace
conferences 35
leaves Finland (1907) 27
leaves Poland for Switzerland (1914) 30–2
leaves Russia (1899) 18
life in emigration 30–2
love of mountains 34–5
love of nature 16, 29
Materialism and Empiriocriticism 25–7
meets Plekhanov, Lafargue and Liebknecht
for the first time 17–18
Moscow armed uprising 27
moves to second plan for transition 61–7
music 29
October Revolution 51–3
'On cooperation' and cultural
revolution 74–6
party funding 29–30
'Party Organisation and Party
Literature' 25–7
peasants 67–70
political testament 73–4
reads Marxist classics for first time 16–17
religion 6–7, 25–7
returns to Finland July 1917 42

returns to Switzerland (1914) 34–5
revolution from above 3–4
revolution of 1905 25–7
revolutionary consciousness 4–5,
44–5, 154
revolutionary transition 44–50
Socialism and Religion' 25–7
spa holiday in Tschudiwiese 34–5
split in second International 33
splits the party (1903) 22–3
State and Revolution 42–50, 72–3
writes *State and Revolution* 1917 42–3
statues of in USA 148
stress and illnesses 16, 30–2
strokes and declining health 73–4
the party and 'professional
revolutionaries' 2–3, 21–3
theory of revolution 57–9
third stroke and death 77
funeral 79
travels from 1895–1917 15
u-turns 25, 65–7, 70
role in party 25
views on religion 131–3
violence and the process of
revolution 1–2, 29–30, 36
western historiography of 138
What Is To Be Done 21–3, 44–5
world revolution 3–4
writes *The Development of Capitalism in
Russia* 17–18
writing style 20–1
Leninism 57–8, 79–80
Baku Congress of People's of the East 94
concept of the party 88–94, 151
at Second Party Congress 90
cell structure 91–2
centralisation (democratic
centralism) 91–2
characteristics of a member 93–4
Comintern definition 90
conflicting models of Leninism 86–7
Lenin and party c.1900 89–90
Marx and worker self-emancipation
89–90
one-party state 55–6, 59–62, 65–7, 73,
112–13, 146–7, 153–4, 156–7
purges 91–2
vanguard institutions 91
contemporary support for 147–8, 150

190   INDEX

Leninism (*cont.*)
  core values 111–12
  decline of support for since 1991 134–9
  foundations of 80–5
  harmful influence of on democratic
    left 155
  imperialism 103–16
  influence of on Kuomintang 156–7
  influence of on Nazism 156–7; as
    heritage 156
  national liberation 105, 127–8
  nationalism 105
  relevance of summarized 159–63
  revival of support for since 2000 139–47
    in Latin America 140–1
  Stalin's definition of 83–5
    dictatorship of the proletariat 80, 84
    imperialism 83–4
    internationalism 80, 82
    strategy and tactics 85
    style in work 85
    the national question 85
    the party 80, 85, 159–60
    the peasant question 84–5
  Stalinism as Leninism 106–7
  struggle against fascism 95–103
    antifascism as chief recruiter for
      111–12, 122–4
  world revolution 94–121
    Comintern founded 94
Lenin 150 162–3
Liberation theology 129–31
Lih, Lars 141–2
  Lenin Rediscovered 141–3
Living church 129–30
Lukács, Georg 121–2
  History and Class Consciousness 121–2
  *Lenin: A Study in the Unity of his
    Thought* 121–2
Luxemburg, Rosa 98, 126–7, 147–8, 159

MacDonald, Ramsay 33
Mandela, Nelson 118, 153
Mao Zedong 101, 105–8
Maoism 116–18
Martov, Iulii 20–3, 54–5
Marx, Karl 4–5
  Communist Manifesto 16–17, 152
  Das Kapital (Capital) 16–17
  peasants 67–8

revolutionary transition 44–5
worker self-emancipation 89–90
Marxism 4–5
  in post Stalin Russia 110–11
Mensheviks 23–5, 53–4
  Menshevik Internationalists 124–5
Mozambique 118

narodism see populism
narodnichestvo see populism
national roads to communism
  (polycentrism) 116–18
Nechaev, Sergei 28–9
  Catechism of a Revolutionary 28–9
New Economic Policy (NEP) 45, 72, 152
New Left 124
Novaia zhizn' 20–1

October Revolution 51–3

Paris Commune 42–3, 59–60
party schools (Capri, Bologna,
  Longjumeau) 25–7
PCF (Parti Communiste Français) 103–4,
  114–15, 120
peasant revolution 67–70
peasant revolution 5–6, 103–16
Petrograd Soviet 51
  Kornilov affair 51
Piketty, Thomas 141
  Capital and Ideology 141
  Capital in the Twenty-First Century 141
Plekhanov, Georgii 13–15, 20–1
  defencism in 1914 33
  peasants 67–8
  Socialism and Political Struggle 21–2
Pol Pot 115
Poland 110–11, 116–18, 120
Pope Francis II 131
populism 13–14
Pravda 20–1
productionism 4–5, 64–5, 76
Provisional Government, overthrown 53–4
Putin, Vladimir, blames Lenin and
  Bolsheviks 134–5

religion 6–7
revolution of 1905 18–19, 25–7
Russo-Japanese war 18–19
Russo-Polish War (1920) 95–7

INDEX 191

Second International
  defencists and internationalists
    emerge 33–4
  denounces imperialism 32
  splits over first World War 32–3
Serge, Victor 155–7
socialism with a human face 118
Socialist Revolutionary Party
  3–4, 53–4
  decree on land 70
South Africa 118, 153
Spanish Civil War 98–100
Stalin, J.V. 20–1, 45, 51–3, 79
  as high priest of Lenin cult 80–6; vows at
    Lenin's funeral 80–2
  conflicting models of Leninism
    86–7
  dogmatizes Leninism 87
  Foundations of Leninism 81–5, criticism
    of 85–6, definition of Leninism in,
    see 'Leninism'
  Problems of Leninism 85–6
  socialism in one country 94
  Stalinism as Leninism 106–7, 161–2
Sukhanov, N.N. 54–5
Suslov, Mikhail 110–11

Tito, Josip Broz 78–9, 109
Tkachev, P. 57

Trotsky, Lev 24–5, 27, 51–3, 61–2, 79, 124–5
  assassination of 102–3
  authoritarianism of 161–2
  criticise bureaucratisation of USSR 102–3
  crushes Kronstadt 73
  permanent revolution theory 24–5
  supports USSR against Nazism 102–3
Trotskyism 101–3, 106–7, 124–5, 161–2

Ukraine 7–8
  war in (2022-) 9
Ulyanov, Alexander (Sasha) 11–13
Ulyanova, Olga death 16
urban terrorism 128–9
useful idiot 122–3

Viet Nam 78, 155

Workers' Opposition 72–3

Yugoslav revolution 110–11, 116–18

Zimbabwe 118
Zinoviev, Grigorii 51–3, 59–60
Žižek, Slavoj 134
  Lenin Reloaded: Towards a Politics of Truth
    (with Sebastian Budgen and Stathis
    Kouvelakis) 144–7, 163
  The Pervert's Guide to Ideology (film) 134